The Saturday Morning Gardener

A Guide to
Once-a-Week
Maintenance

Revised Edition

Donald Wyman

COLLIER BOOKS

A Division of Macmillan Publishing Co., Inc.
NEW YORK
COLLIER MACMILLAN PUBLISHERS
LONDON

Macmillan Publishing Co., Inc.
866 Third Avenue, New York, N. Y. 10022
Collier-Macmillan Canada Ltd.

Library of Congress Cataloging in Publication Data

Wyman, Donald, 1903–
    The Saturday morning gardener.

    1. Gardening.   I. Title.
SB453.W9   1974   635.9   73-11833
ISBN 0-02-632100-9
ISBN 0-02-063950-3 (pbk.)

The Saturday Morning Gardener is also published in a hard-
cover edition by Macmillan Publishing Co., Inc.

Revised Edition

First Collier Books Edition 1974
Second Printing 1974
Printed in the United States of America

Preface

The objective in this book is to point out to the busy gardener the many shortcuts he can take to make a beautiful garden with a minimum amount of effort. The book is divided into four main parts: Planning a Garden; Shortcuts and Aids in Maintenance; Low Maintenance Plant Lists; A–Z Listing of Low Maintenance Plants.

Proper planning saves costly errors later. Shortcuts and aids in maintenance reduce garden effort and expense. Most important of all is the proper selection of low maintenance plants—just the right ones for just the right place. There are over 900 in the following pages from which to choose.

The lists of low maintenance plants (see Chapters 3 and 4) include only those plants which we found to be generally insect- and disease-free. All others have been excluded. The low maintenance garden is not the place for plants which are known in advance to require special attention. The gardener with plenty of time can experiment to his heart's content, but some of us simply do not have that kind of time and want to reduce our garden work to a minimum. This book offers succinct information for doing just that. It should be used as a guide to once-a-week maintenance.

The lists of low maintenance plants for special purposes are designed to give pertinent information at a glance—the name of the plant, height, hardiness zone, and in some cases, color of flower, time of flower, and color of fruit; whether it is an evergreen, a tree, a shrub or perennial. If one wants a ground cover, merely turn to pages 127–133 and there they are. If one's garden has a shady spot, pages 158–166 list all low maintenance plants withstanding shade conditions. If one wants to find a little more information about these plants, the alphabetical descriptions (pages 197–359) will give it, but, for those in a hurry, most pertinent facts will be in the lists.

For more detailed information the gardener can consult *Wyman's Gardening Encyclopedia,* published by Macmillan Publishing Co., Inc., but the most important facts needed to make plant selections quickly will all be easily found in the following pages.

Acknowledgments

I am most indebted to my wife Florence Dorward Wyman, who not only read and reread the original manuscript and typed it several times but who also grew most of the bulbs, perennials, and smaller shrubs in her low maintenance garden, keeping notes on their performance through the years. The information on "dual purpose" plants was a result of her efforts and interest over a long period. Thanks are also due my daughter, Barbara Wyman Skiff, who typed the manuscript for this revised edition.

Constance B. Schrader, Senior Editor at Macmillan Publishing Co., Inc., made many excellent suggestions for the revised manuscript, all of which have been gratefully accepted and worked into the text.

Robert G. Williams, Superintendent of the Arnold Arboretum, made the excellent drawings. Grateful thanks should also be given to the staff members of the Arnold

Arboretum, who through the years have materially aided us in our knowledge of these plants, most of which have been grown in the Arnold Arboretum in Boston, Massachusetts.

Contents

Introduction

The "simple art" of caring for one's garden today has become a baffling and complex task, requiring a knowledge of pests, "controls," the many new varieties of plants, and their many special requirements. Compare the simplicity of gardening in early colonial times, when the homeowner was not bothered with a multitude of insects and diseases. His lawn was a patch of grass to be hand-scythed occasionally, or left as pasture for his cows, goats, or sheep. He kept the plants that were there, or he dug some from the woods nearby. Only as life brought more leisure, did the colonists begin to landscape their grounds, enlarge their gardens, and gradually bring in rare plants from the woods and import others from abroad.

Since those early times, literally hundreds of destructive insects and diseases have appeared. At the same time, many plants that require constant attention have gained acceptance because they are unusual—or just plain cantankerous, a challenge to the gardener's skill just to keep them alive. With the gradual accumulation of this kind of plant and the dramatic increase in insect pests and diseases, garden chores have increased tremendously, for they must be performed regularly if the plants are to be kept in good condition.

All this means that supplying garden accessories is truly big business today. The home gardener can ride in comfort as he cuts his lawn, fertilize it at the same time that he turns on his hose, and aerate the soil by punching holes in it with a mechanized roller. If weeds appear, there is a plethora of chemicals to kill them; if soils dry out too quickly, there are a dozen different mulches available. All too often, the homeowner invests in far more equipment and material than is necessary.

Which brings me to the point that there are two kinds of gardener. One is willing to spend large amounts of time and money to have beautiful plantings. He thinks nothing of hiring gardeners or spending a large proportion of his own spare time to see that pruning, weeding, grass cutting, and spraying are all done perfectly and on time, with the best of materials and equipment.

The second kind includes those who admire a pleasant garden, but through lack of time, money, physical strength, or because of the competition of other interests or responsibilities, cannot allow gardening to absorb too much of their spare time and money. It is to this group of gardeners that this book is primarily addressed—those who are continually on the lookout for new labor-saving devices, truly low maintenance plants, and the many shortcuts that will make garden upkeep easier.

There is a strong case to be made today for planting the smaller shrubs and the smaller trees—in terms of lower cost and reduced maintenance. Many of the new houses being built nowadays are only about fifteen to twenty-five feet high. Tall-growing shrubs—like the Common Lilac—that can reach the third story of an old-fashioned house, if used near a small home, will need constant pruning to be kept to a proportioned height. Not only that, but the Common Lilac, if allowed to go unpruned, can grow as wide as it is tall—twenty feet at least—sending out lateral suckers that must be restrained by pruning almost every year. If the modern homeowner must have a lilac and no other shrub will do, plant a lilac by all means, but make a mental commitment at planting time to prune the shrub regularly to keep it within proper bounds. For the person who is willing to take a substitute for the lilac, there are many other plants that will mature at lower heights and will not need repeated pruning to be kept in scale.

In the same way, planting smaller trees may be far more practical today. At one time a home planting was not complete without a stately elm overshadowing the house. Elms grow over a hundred feet high, and in recent years many a property owner has found to his sorrow what it costs to remove one of these giants once it becomes diseased and starts to die. Smaller trees—trees that grow only twenty-five or thirty-five feet tall—are frequently just as serviceable and attractive. They will give beauty and shade, they will grow above the roof of the small house, and still not be so costly to remove if it should become necessary to do so. Nor will they be so expensive to prune and spray.

Ground covers are another important asset for the low maintenance garden. Their extensive use can provide a weed-free and attractive underplanting for shrubs and trees.

In summary, smaller shrubs, lower trees, and

ground covers are the all-important low maintenance plants to be used about the small home grounds. Not all are easily found in every nursery catalogue for many nurserymen have not yet recognized the demand for some of these plants. But all are being grown somewhere in this country, and most are available. If local nurseries fail to provide some of these plants, sources can be recommended by state agricultural colleges, horticultural societies, and the various arboretums and botanical gardens.

1

Planning a Garden

Every garden should be beautiful as well as utilitarian. The smaller the area, the more important it is to make a careful choice. Keep in mind always *how long* each plant has beauty and interest. The shrub or tree that is attractive for only a week or two while in bloom, but which has no good autumn color or interesting fruits, should be discarded. Choose instead ones that have outstanding flowers in the spring, good form all year round, bright-colored fruits in summer, and a vivid autumn beauty. There are such plants and they deserve prime consideration in any garden plan. If they can be chosen from among those plants that require minimum care, you can establish a garden that is both beautiful and easy to care for.

The most important way to save labor later on is to plan the garden intelligently from the first. The first thing to do, then, is to make an overall plan. If you start with a completely empty space, you are free to create your garden from scratch. If you inherit a garden which already has plantings, make an inventory of them and keep only the ones that you like. Be ruthless about discarding those that do not fit in with your final design.

Whether you start with an empty garden, or with existing trees and shrubs, once the house is in place and the drives and walks have been located, a number of other factors will influence your choice of plantings and where you will need to put them.

PERSONAL NEEDS

In the first place, how is the garden to be used? For entertaining, some area should be set aside near the house—preferably a terrace or patio—suitably shielded by evergreens and hedges to insure year-round privacy. For smaller homes, the "outdoor living room" is often merely a small patio, or a corner of the house where shade, and possibly a pool or fountain, help provide a peaceful, relaxing atmosphere. Modern homes tend to be discarding the old-fashioned, built-in outdoor fireplaces; the small, portable charcoal grills make fire building and cooking far simpler.

For the larger gardens, space may be needed for a game area: a badminton court (44' x 20'), a tennis court (78' x 36'), a basketball backboard, or space for some other game requires careful planning. If a swimming pool is going to be installed, its location should be decided on even before the trees are placed, since the source of water supply and drainage are essential factors in its location. If there are small children in a family, their needs should certainly be considered. A secluded area, near enough to the house to be able to check on easily, in shade, and where possibly a sandbox could be located, would be a very desirable asset.

Two service areas may be needed: a laundry yard, suitably hidden by a fence or hedge, or some arrangement for a collapsible laundry wheel or permanent hooks for connecting lines; and an area for a dog run, again suitably screened and fenced, or some arrangement for an exercise line included.

Will you plan to have a vegetable garden, and how large will it be? When we moved into a new house while our children were still very young, we wanted a vegetable garden, but planned it so that it was large enough to be made into a tennis court when our children were older.

Do you plan to grow annuals, perennials, and bulbs in large quantities, or are there to be just a few here and there around the foundation planting. Will you plan to have regular flower borders—if so, they should be planned to take advantage of full sun, away from trees whose roots compete for water and nourishment.

These are all personal needs that should be thought out and carefully planned before deciding on your final garden design, a design that should include provision for future needs as well as current ones.

TREES

Once recreational and service needs have been decided on, placing the trees should be next on the agenda. First, decide what the trees are to contribute to the planting scheme. Some will certainly be chosen to shade certain parts of the house or terrace or play area. If it's shade that's needed, where is it to fall, and how tall and how wide must a tree or trees be to give the proper amount of shade on the proper place at the

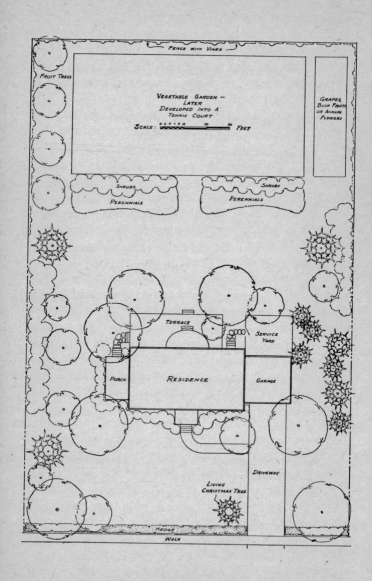

A good garden plan.

proper time? This is important to plan for, for once a tree is well on its way to mature growth, it is both expensive and difficult to move.

Trees are also used to give an interesting background to a house when viewed from the main road, or even to frame the house, as in a picture.

To some people, such considerations may be more important even than providing shade to parts of the house or garden. Again, some trees are used to screen off objectionable views, and still others are chosen merely for beauty of flower, fruit, or autumn color. It is extremely important, in the new planting, that tree placement be given very careful consideration, for trees should be planted as soon as possible, and much thought should go into the selection of just the right species for the right places.

The expected spread of the tree branches is another important factor in placing trees properly. Small trees, for instance, like the crab apples, dogwoods, Japanese Maples and magnolias will eventually have a spread of 20 feet. Medium-sized trees like the Canoe Birch, Katsura-tree, lindens, and Sorrel-tree may have a spread of 30 to 35 feet. Large trees like the beech, Ginkgo, Sweet-gum, Honey-locust, maples, cedars, pines, hemlocks, etc., may have spreads of 40 feet or more. When planning where to place a tree near a house, these factors must be kept in mind. The branches of a tree planted too near the house may eventually touch it or rub it and have to be removed, spoiling the shape of the tree.

One other point might be kept in mind which can save on early maintenance. Usually a tree 7 to 8 feet tall at planting time will grow faster the first few years than a 12 to 14 foot tree. Additional money can be spent on providing the small tree with the best possible soil and growth conditions, so that sometimes it may pay to buy smaller trees at the start. If, however, large trees must be moved in to give immediate shade or beauty, one must be prepared for additional expense and maintenance in providing perfect growing conditions for these larger trees to grow quickly and normally. It can be done.

Trees are also used for their conspicuous flowers (dogwoods, magnolias, and crab apples) and for their beauty of form and habits of growth. The Flowering Dogwood and many conifers have a horizontal branching habit; some of the maples and fastigiate English Oak are columnar in habit; while one of the European beeches is pendulous in habit. There are trees for utilitarian purposes as well as for beauty of flower, form, and foliage, and one should decide in advance just why a tree is wanted, where the best spot for it is, and what tree will serve the desired purpose best.

Finally, before planting trees, one should make certain they are not placed where their roots will feed ravenously in flower gardens. Elms, beeches, and maples are notorious for having hundreds of feeding roots very close to the surface of the soil. It is usually impossible for shrubs or flowers to grow underneath them, especially if their branches sweep the ground. To remove the lower branches of such trees, thus allowing light to reach the ground in an attempt to grow other plants underneath them, really defeats the purpose for which they were planted in the first place. Nor should they be placed near water pipes, drain pipes, or cesspools where their roots might eventually enter such pipes and clog them, causing serious maintenance problems later.

Hence, in planning the garden thought should be given to placing the trees where they best will serve their functions in the landscape plan, but will not compete for water and soil nourishment with other desired plantings or clog water and drain pipes.

THE LIVING CHRISTMAS TREE

Those who like to string colored lights on a tree at Christmas will want to choose a special spot in their garden for a living Christmas tree. Placing a specimen evergreen somewhere near the front of the house is always a good idea; it acts as a screen every day of the year and its beauty and symmetry of outline add materially to any well-planned landscape planting.

The ideal Christmas tree is a narrow-leaved evergreen that is pyramidal in habit, with stiff branches borne in whorls and with spaces between the whorls so that lights can be hung and properly displayed near the trunk of the tree as well as at the tips of the branches. Some trees, like the stiff-growing firs and spruces, are excellent as Christmas trees—their sturdy branches can be heavily strung with wires and lights without noticeable bending. Other types, like the graceful hemlocks and the White Pine, have branches that are too easily bent to display lights to good advantage. A dense-growing tree like an arborvitae is not a desirable one on which to string lights, for when the job is done, they are all on the outside of the plant. The same is true of some of the pines like the Red and Yellow Pines whose branches grow too coarsely to permit lights to be hung near the central trunk.

It might be pointed out here that certain types of trees which are popular as *cut* Christmas trees in different parts of the country (Balsam Fir in the East, Douglas-fir on the northwest Pacific Coast, White Fir in the Rocky Mountain area, and so on) may not be suitable for planting in your garden. This is particularly true of the Balsam Fir; this tree, native over a wide area in the mountainous, cooler, and more humid parts of the northern United States, does not grow well under any other conditions. It is popular as a cut tree at Christmas because it is available and inexpensive, but it should practically never be chosen for ornamental planting outside its native habitat.

The tree species that might be selected for planting (near the house and not too far from an electrical outlet) for Christmas-tree purposes are the following:

Abies species	Firs
Cedrus species	Cedars
Juniperus scopulorum	Western Red-cedar
Juniperus virginiana	Red-cedar
Libocedrus decurrens	California Incense-cedar
Picea species	Spruces
Pseudotsuga menziesii	Douglas-fir

THE DWARF-SHRUB PERENNIAL GARDEN

One of the most fascinating activities in growing plants is to experiment with new types or to place old, recognized species in new environments to see how they prosper. Without this activity, many plant growers would lose interest entirely. This section, then, is not for the young and enthusiastic gardener who wants to try anything and everything for himself. This is, of course, the best way to learn the facts of gardening, and most of us go through this stage. It takes time, money, and labor, and brings many disappointments, but it also brings interest and knowledge. The things that one learns this way seem so new and important that one tends to believe it is the first time such discoveries have been made. More power to those who approach gardening with this attitude!

There are gardeners, however, who have gone beyond this stage. They still want to plant, and they have discovered many interesting facts about growing plants, but they are anxious now to learn shortcuts so that they will still have a colorful garden in continuous bloom, but without so much hard work. It is for such gardeners that the following notes may prove of value.

My wife and I found, for instance, that some specific pests for certain plants were so predominant in our garden, or under our soil conditions, or in our area that we continually lost the plants. Take delphiniums, for instance; we tried to grow many beautiful hybrids, but with only mediocre success. Eventually, they were broken off by summer windstorms or by the root borer that seems to be vicious under our local conditions. As a result, we have resigned ourselves to the situation and do not plant delphiniums anymore.

We used to take great delight in growing new Sweet Williams from seed each year so that the following year we would have blooming plants. It paid off while we did the work, but with increasing demands on our time we had to eliminate them also.

Then there were the annuals: there is nothing so good for summer color as annuals, and years ago we planted large numbers of these every spring. It was fun to grow them, first germinating them in tin cans, after having sterilized the soil in the pressure cooker. Then we planted them in flats and grew them in the electric hotbed, which incidentally is an extremely important garden asset. In later years we merely sowed the seed and let someone else take care of the seedlings in a greenhouse, but we did the actual planting in the garden.

At first weeds were a necessary adjunct of growing annuals, and we welcomed the time we spent battling them in the fresh air of spring and summer. But one year we left the garden unattended for six weeks, and on our return, could hardly find the annuals for the weeds. After that, and with other more important things demanding our attention, garden weeding had so many drawbacks that we began to reduce the number of annuals. We planted more of the tried and true perennials, merely to take up space in the garden, since we did not want to turn the land back into lawn. However, we did not give up the annuals altogether, but relegated them to a cutting garden by themselves, where they were planted in rows and cultivated by machine—a much easier method of raising annuals, at least for us.

This left the garden uninteresting in summer, and especially so in the fall and winter. It was then that we started to plant a few dwarf shrubs in the perennial borders to take up the space left vacant by the declining number of plants. This proved to be an ideal way to bring interest back into our garden. The types of shrubs used were all very dwarf, of several different forms. Some were deciduous and flowered; some were evergreen. Each one had some special ornamental characteristic as far as form was concerned, and, being woody plants, once they were in place, no further care was needed. The real interest came late in the fall after the tall perennials had been scythed to the ground. Formerly, when this was done, the garden was left flat and uninteresting until the bulbs bloomed in early May. But with the dwarf shrubs we had interesting forms and shapes in the garden that came into their own each fall. With winter snows there were still all sorts of odd-shaped mounds about the beds, and as the snow melted at various times between new storms the plants became visible. This lent form and considerable interest to our garden throughout the entire year. Then, with the profuse bloom of the early bulbs and the vigorous growth of the perennials, these dwarf shrubs became less and less conspicuous until the fall clean-up brought them out in the open once again.

This happy combination of bulbs, perennials, and dwarf woody plants makes for an interesting garden that is attractive every season of the year. It affords a low planting—just as low as the perennials used will grow—that can be placed where such borders or formal gardens have most value in the landscape plan and it allows you to eliminate as many annuals as you like. For those who want annuals, the space can be obtained by using fewer perennials, but the dwarf shrubs are always there to give the garden year-around interest.

One thing this combination does not do: it does not eliminate weeds. Unfortunately, they still find their way into such a planting. Though no weed killers can be used in such close quarters, mulching materials can be applied to excellent advantage. With the proper kind and amount of mulch around these perennials and shrubs, a major part of the weeding is eliminated. The weeds start, but if pulled or hoed or actually lifted out of the mulch at the right time early in their growth, weeding is reduced to an absolute minimum.

This is not to be taken as a ruthless means of eliminating all annuals and many perennials from the garden. Rather it should be understood as a suggested shortcut for those who want flower beds, but are unwilling to give the time (or the money to buy someone else's time) to care for such beds properly. Space may always be left in such beds for plants requiring time-consuming care. This method also results in beautiful formal or informal beds of flowers and low shrubs of interest throughout the entire year with a minimum amount of effort.

There are hundreds of combinations of plants that can be made, varying with the location, type of soil, and part of the country where the project is to be maintained. Any gardener can make lists of both perennials and shrubs requiring a minimum amount of attention. The lists on pages 103–193 are of bulbs, perennials, and shrubs which we have grown over the past fifteen years in a garden nearby, fully protected on all sides by hemlocks, arborvitaes, specimen trees of crab apples,

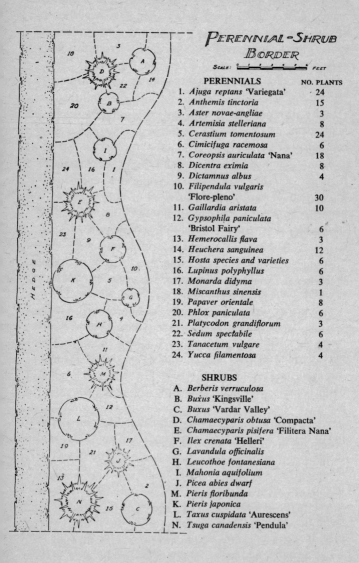

PERENNIAL-SHRUB BORDER

SCALE: ⊢━━━━━━━┤ FEET

PERENNIALS	NO. PLANTS
1. *Ajuga reptans* 'Variegata'	24
2. *Anthemis tinctoria*	15
3. *Aster novae-angliae*	3
4. *Artemisia stelleriana*	8
5. *Cerastium tomentosum*	24
6. *Cimicifuga racemosa*	6
7. *Coreopsis auriculata* 'Nana'	18
8. *Dicentra eximia*	8
9. *Dictamnus albus*	4
10. *Filipendula vulgaris* 'Flore-pleno'	30
11. *Gaillardia aristata*	10
12. *Gypsophila paniculata* 'Bristol Fairy'	6
13. *Hemerocallis flava*	3
14. *Heuchera sanguinea*	12
15. *Hosta species and varieties*	6
16. *Lupinus polyphyllus*	6
17. *Monarda didyma*	3
18. *Miscanthus sinensis*	1
19. *Papaver orientale*	8
20. *Phlox paniculata*	6
21. *Platycodon grandiflorum*	3
22. *Sedum spectabile*	6
23. *Tanacetum vulgare*	4
24. *Yucca filamentosa*	4

SHRUBS

A. *Berberis verruculosa*
B. *Buxus* 'Kingsville'
C. *Buxus* 'Vardar Valley'
D. *Chamaecyparis obtusa* 'Compacta'
E. *Chamaecyparis pisifera* 'Filitera Nana'
F. *Ilex crenata* 'Helleri'
G. *Lavandula officinalis*
H. *Leucothoe fontanesiana*
I. *Mahonia aquifolium*
J. *Picea abies dwarf*
M. *Pieris floribunda*
K. *Pieris japonica*
L. *Taxus cuspidata* 'Aurescens'
N. *Tsuga canadensis* 'Pendula'

magnolias, dogwoods, and the like. The trees and background shrubs on three sides of this garden (approximately 130' x 300') were faced with low borders. In the center were two irregular beds stretching three-fourths the distance of the garden and surrounded with grass walks.

The combination of bulbs (those which need no attention), perennials, and shrubs, all carefully mulched (mostly with pine needles), resulted in a beautiful, low maintenance garden at all seasons of the year. Space can always be found for some new plant, or, if we remain at home throughout the summer, for a few annuals if we are willing to give the additional time required to grow them. With such a garden one's interest is retained because it does not require a continual draining of time from other activities for excessive garden work.

SHRUBS

Once the trees are located on the plan and the flower borders have been drawn in, then the shrubs can be placed. Shrubs should be chosen for the same reasons as trees—for both utilitarian and aesthetic reasons. You must know the shrub types, heights, and habits to make the right selection. Lists of shrubs which will grow under varied conditions (shade, dry soil, wet soil, etc.) are given in Chapter 3 of this book, "Low Maintenance Plants," and they are also described in greater detail in the final section where all the plants discussed in the book are listed alphabetically and described.

The main objective in choosing shrubs should be to provide for the maximum of beauty and privacy with a minimum amount of cultural care. One should consider the reason for placing every shrub on the property. Is it to create privacy, add beauty to the garden, be a background for the flower border, shield a play area, compost pile, or vegetable garden, or is it to act as a buffer between lawn and street? There should be good reason for planting every shrub used, for open space for lawn and views is also a prerequisite of a good plan. Miscellaneous shrubs in the center of the lawn can serve merely as hazards when it comes to mowing.

Be certain to select some of the dual-purpose plants (pages 145–148). If the soil is known to be dry or wet, consult these lists in order to choose the plants that will do best under such conditions. Is the shrub to grow in the shade? If so, consult the list on page 159. Are special shrubs wanted for flowering or fruiting or for colored foliage? Are evergreens wanted? All these prerequisites should be considered, and the proper lists examined in order to help with the right selections.

Be certain of the heights of the shrubs selected. Never plant taller shrubs than are needed for this always creates work; the tops will have to be continually lopped off to keep the plants in scale which usually makes them unsightly. In a shrub border, plant the taller shrubs at the rear and the smaller shrubs in the front. Allow for flower and fruiting displays at several periods in spring, summer and fall. Shrubs that are 10 to 12 feet tall should usually be planted about 10 feet apart while shrubs only 3 to 4 feet tall should be planted about 3 feet apart. If planted closer they may become too dense to flower and fruit well. On the other hand, if privacy is the factor, the taller plants might be planted closer.

Selecting the right low maintenance plant for the right place is one of the best ways of reducing garden maintenance.

FOUNDATION PLANTING

Nowhere will mistakes in plant selection be more quickly obvious than in the foundation planting about the house. The main objective here is to "tie in" the house to the soil and the surrounding vegetation—to make them an obvious part of a unit. Though few houses look well without some planting about them, too much planting, or the selection of tall-growing shrubs that quickly blot out views from windows, is a common error.

The homeowner who wants a proper foundation planting should be warned against buying smaller evergreens for such planting unless he is familiar with their rate of growth and probable height at maturity. Sometimes it is difficult to resist buying small plants that in their present form will obviously fit very well into the scale of the planting about the house. Take as an example a three-foot plant of the Moss Retinospora, which when well grown and sheared in the nursery is a perfect, soft bluish green evergreen. However, in good soil it can grow a foot a year until it is over a hundred feet tall! After it is well on its way, when its obvious tendency for growing taller and taller becomes better known, the homeowner is compelled to spend more and more time in pruning it, and it becomes more and more difficult to keep within bounds. Such is not the way to make gardening easier.

In order to make a proper foundation planting, one should know the mature heights of the plants selected, and place them accordingly. For instance, taller shrubs should be placed at the corners of the buildings, where they would not obscure the windows. If there is a porch, terrace, or patio where privacy is wanted, tall plants should be used.

Plants selected for placing in front of windows should be dwarf or very low growing, and at maturity should not reach above the bottom of a window; better still, they should grow only to a point a foot below it.

Sometimes a tall plant is wanted on either side of

an imposing main entrance, but more often medium-sized shrubs are better. Certainly for all side entrances, shrubs that mature under four feet tall are desirable.

Where windows are widely spaced, taller shrubs may be used to cover part of the bare house wall as well as to provide a contrast with the lower plants used in front of the windows. Ground covers, bulbs, and occasionally flowers may be used in front of such plants for contrast in form and color.

Foundations, depending on their height, may well be hidden with low shrubs, or even a clinging vine or two, if desired. The chimney might well be planted with a clinging vine to add contrast to the rest of the planting. A twining vine, like the Five-leaf Akebia, may be planted to wind up the rainspout or to follow a specially provided wire support to give additional height to the entire planting.

It is not correct to say that all foundation planting should be made with evergreens; usually it is more interesting to have a few deciduous flowering shrubs as well. However, because the foundation planting should be effective during the entire year, evergreens should compose a good portion of it.

The height of plants, their spacing, even open areas between them to allow for shadows and interesting contrasts in different kinds of foliage, some bulbs and deciduous plants for flower, autumn color, and fruit—all these can be blended together to make an interesting planting. If the plants mature at the proper heights, if they have been planted sufficiently far apart to give them some individuality, and if some have been selected to provide color at different times of the year, then one will have a foundation planting that will always be interesting and at the same time very easily maintained.

WOODY VINES

Vines are a necessary asset in most gardens to lend beauty and to cover objectionable walls, fences, poles, wires, and other objects. Most are fast growing, once they are started in good soil, but in selecting them one should note their respective assets carefully. Some, like the Five-leaf Akebia and Bower Actinidia are fast-growing twining vines with small flowers that are none too conspicuous.

Others are flowering vines, like wisterias, honeysuckles, and clematis. These are usually chosen for their conspicuous flowers at certain times.

The clinging vines, like English Ivy, Climbing Hydrangea, and the so-called Boston-ivy, are all useful for clinging with rootlike holdfasts to surfaces of some sort, and do not have to be helped in this clinging process by man-made aids.

The few that climb by the use of tendrils (grapes) or twining leaf stalks (clematis) of course need some supporting wires or trellis for support, and sometimes must be aided by tying the longer shoots about the supports.

Clinging vines should only be planted for growing on stone or brick walls, for on wood walls they quickly aid in the disintegration of the wood. Many a house with exterior of shingle or wood has a stone or brick chimney on the outside from ground to roof, an ideal place for some of the slower growing forms of English Ivy. For larger surfaces, the Climbing Hydrangea is excellent, for although it may take two or three years after planting to become properly established, it then becomes vigorous and will cover much space. The same is true of the Boston-ivy.

The question of how many plants to place along a wall or fence for complete coverage depends on the rapidity with which the vine grows. Usually five feet apart (or less if one is in a hurry) is about right for fast-growing vines like Boston-ivy, Climbing Hydrangea, and the Trumpet-creeper. Then if the growth is too luxuriant, some of the vines can easily be eliminated. Slower growing types like English Ivy and Creeping Fig should be planted closer together, especially for quick effects.

Twining vines should be pruned occasionally if they become too rampant or too tall. There is really no special method involved—merely cut away the excess vine foliage.

Though trellises on which to train vines are sometimes necessary, wooden ones, at least, can become a problem because they require repeated painting. A chain link fence, always effective as a barrier, can be completely and easily covered with any one of the twining vines or those with tendrils. A rainspout at a corner of the house can provide a support for properly displaying an important twining vine. If the house must be painted, the entire spout (and vine) can be laid on the ground and replaced after the painting is done. It would be easier to cut the vine off about three feet above the ground when the spout is removed; but this pruning should be done before midsummer, for if it is done later there might not be sufficient time for the plants to grow new shoots that would mature properly before freezing weather sets in.

Selecting the proper vine for the proper place is a most important operation as a labor-saver. The vines recommended in the list on page 124 are the most easily grown and cared for, and if the proper selections are made they should thrive with little attention. The method of climbing—by twining, by clinging, or by attaching themselves by means of tendrils—is all clearly marked on this list.

18

HEDGES—LABOR-SAVERS
UNDER SIX FEET HIGH

The old-fashioned concept of the proper hedge plant is one that is inexpensive and fast growing. In order to be inexpensive it must be easily and quickly propagated, and if it is fast growing it must be sheared frequently. Probably the most popular and widely planted hedge plant has been the California Privet, which adequately fulfills both prerequisites.

If screening alone is desired, almost any nine-foot-high shrub could be selected and several planted in a line. If such plants were allowed to go untrimmed, however, they would look ragged and unkempt. Upon examining the need for hedges more closely, it usually appears that what one really wants is a low, formal line of foliage over which one can look, through which it is difficult for animals or humans to pass, and which will appear neat at all times. If this is the kind of hedge you want, it would be a good idea to consider the new hedge plants more closely before making your final selection. There are now plants available that require very little shearing, if any, once they are established.

Without any question, the cheapest way to plant a long hedge is to use the old-fashioned, quick-growing hedge plants. But the best, low maintenance, short hedge may well be of some of the new plants that grow to a certain height and then usually maintain themselves without constant shearing. Such plants are usually slower growing than the privets and more expensive. They may be selected for their ability to produce interesting flowers or fruits, or for their fine texture or even for their informal, regular habit of growth when left unsheared.

The more "informal" appearing the hedge can be, the less shearing will be required, with certain plants.

Others, like the dwarf forms of Japanese Barberry, are mounded in general habit, and always look as if they have been sheared when actually they have not.

There are some plants—like the Dwarf Eastern Ninebark—which, if used in a hedge, could be allowed to grow "informally," that is, unsheared, for as long as desired. This would result in a rather wide, fan-shaped type of hedge that could be most interesting because of its increased flowering and fruiting (when compared to what it would be like sheared) and also because of the graceful nodding of the upright branches in the wind. Such an informal growth would result in a wide hedge, probably as wide as tall. If this proved to be too wide, or if one wished the more "formal" sheared type of hedge, it could be easily and quickly attained merely by shearing the plants to the proper dimensions. In this way, with certain plants, one can have a "formal" (sheared) or an "informal" (flowering and fruiting) hedge at will.

In planning where to place the hedge, one should keep in mind that it never should be exactly on the property line, always a foot or so inside. The abutting property owner has the right to cut off or dig up any part of the hedge which encroaches on his side of the line. It is best to dig a ditch about 18 inches wide and 1½ feet deep, removing poor soil and replacing it with good soil. Hedge plants might best be bought 2 to 3 feet tall, but as noted above, larger sizes can be used if necessary. The reason for the smaller plants is that they cost less and are easier to establish.

Spaced 1½ to 3 feet apart, the deciduous types can be cut to within 6 to 12 inches of the soil immediately after planting. This is hard for many gardeners to do, but it forces the plants to send out new buds and shoots from near the base of the plant, thus making a dense hedge. Tall, spindly plants may eventually grow into a hedge, but they will be open at the bottom, allowing animals to go through. Another way to overcome this same hazard is to run a line of chicken wire, 2 to 3 feet tall, along the newly planted hedge line. This will help keep out animals and the wire can be left indefinitely, eventually rusting out as the plants grow thicker.

When pruning or shearing is necessary, the hedge should always be narrow at the top, wider at the base, thus allowing the valuable lower branches to develop properly with sufficient sunlight. If shearing is to be done (and some of the rounded hedge plants mentioned in the list on pages 136–140 do not require it), hedges are best trimmed just as their growth is nearly complete, usually in early June, a few weeks later with the evergreens.

Evergreen hedges are not as quick to recuperate from heavy pruning; hence they should not be cut back so severely at the start, merely lightly trimmed.

Hedges such as the red-leaved 'Crimson Pygmy' Barberry, 'Curly Locks' Box, 'Helleri' Japanese Holly and the Cushioned Japanese Yew, only need a "touching up" with the shears once every two or three years. More vigorous hedges like the Slender Deutzia, *Philadelphus* 'Avalanche' and *Viburnum opulus* 'Compactum' may need a shearing once a year, but these can also be allowed to grow (and flower and fruit) at will, without any shearing for a few years, to make delightfully informal hedges. Later they can be formally sheared if desired.

Study the list of labor-saving hedge plants on pages 136–140 and select some of these slow-growing low types that will make excellent hedges under the eye level in height. To plant fast-growing hedge plants (when the mature height is to be under the eye level) is only asking for more and more maintenance work.

VEGETABLES

If a vegetable garden is needed, it is possible that it will eventually outlive its usefulness; at which time, it may be seeded over and used for some other purpose.

In the midwinter planning season the idea of a vegetable garden seems attractive, but during midsummer, when the constant fight against drought, poor soil, weeds, insects, and disease is at its height, many people tend to have second thoughts. We have had a vegetable garden each summer for many, many years, varying in size from 50 feet x 100 feet to 100 feet x 300 feet, which you must admit is a sizable plot. With youngsters at home to care for it, there were not too many problems except to keep after the youngsters. When we had to do all the work ourselves, we drastically reduced the size of the garden.

Now we say each year that it is not worth the effort, modern packaging and frozen-food products being what they are. However, in the winter, when "spring-fever planting" has control of both of us, we usually again plan to plant more than we can use. Everyone must make his own decision on the merits of a vegetable garden. If, however, a vegetable garden is decided on, but you don't enjoy the work of it, take a tip from an old hand who has grown everything from peanuts to soybeans, and plant only the easy things like carrots, beans, corn, and tomatoes.

It is obvious that the size of the vegetable garden depends upon one's needs, the space available, and one's willingness to care for it. A vegetable garden 25 feet x 50 feet, if properly planned, can supply four people with vegetables from June to October, but the gardener looking for shortcuts is certainly not going to be bogged down with growing his own vegetables. If he is interested, the state experiment station has excellent free bulletins giving information about planting the right kind of garden in the right way.

FRUITS

Bush fruits are another addition to the home planting, but the size of the space available determines whether or not these are planted. For instance, one or two raspberry bushes would take up valuable space in a small garden, and all the fruits may well be taken by the birds. If space is available for twenty-five plants (about two to three feet apart in the row) without using land needed for more important assignments, then plan on the raspberries by all means. But remember: the fruits must be picked and the plants pruned, and all that is real work!

Fruit trees are interesting to read about in colorful catalogues, but such publications usually neglect to remind you that in order to bear suitable fruits such trees must be thoroughly sprayed four to seven times during the growing season at just the right times. Take the McIntosh apple as an example—this year these apples were selling at wayside stands in New England for $4.00 and up per bushel. If you are thinking of saving money by growing your own fruits, take a second look at the facts before you give up valuable space to this activity. If it is an interesting hobby you want, although often expensive and discouraging during the years the trees fail to fruit, plant the tree fruits; but if you wish to save labor, omit them from the planting scheme.

We like strawberries, blueberries, and grapes, and have the space to grow them and are willing to give the time and energy to do so successfully. When such fruits are grown and enjoyed, gardening is a real hobby. But they do require maintenance work.

Any garden may have special needs that have to be considered—possibly a rock garden or a hedge must be located, or a bank of rocky soil properly planned for in the easiest possible way. Are there any unsightly views that should be screened out with tall shrubs or trees? If the garage is separate from the house, should it be shielded with shrubs or a vine trellis? Are any permanent stone seats or small statues to be located and properly placed? If there are permanent walks, are they to be paved, or are stepping-stones and gravel sufficient?

Very important, too, is to remember to allow for easy access to every part of the property: leave room for trucks to deliver coal or oil; have a place for stacking wood, if fireplaces are to be used; and, what is more important (and often overlooked), if any trucking is to be done over the property (of manure, soil, stone, coal, wood, and so on), always leave space available for such passage at the most strategic places. The smaller the garden, the more one should give careful consideration to the possibility of the movement on the property at some time in the future.

Finally, the question often arises—how should one obtain local advice. The novice can, if he prefers, go to his local landscape architect or to his nurseryman, if he is one who has talented landscape advice available. To the experienced individual, or the one who has had considerable plant training, such advice may not be needed. Or one can refer to various reference books, articles, and experiment station publications, all of which should be studied carefully to sift all the pertinent facts concerning the type of planting desired. For those planning a garden for the first time, professional advice at the beginning sometimes saves many a headache and much money later on. For others who like to learn from their own mistakes, planning their own place is a challenge. Regardless of which attitude is taken, it pays to consider carefully all these items in advance, on paper, before any actual plantings are made. In other words, first have a plan, and make certain that it is the best possible one that can be devised. Once the plan has been decided on, try to stay with it and avoid costly, last-minute changes. Undoubtedly, having a good plan before planting is one of the best shortcuts to having a successful and easily cared for garden.

HOW TO USE THE HARDINESS MAPS

The Hardiness Maps included in this book make it easy for you to come to a quick decision about which plants can be grown in your area. All plants in this book have been given a hardiness rating geared to these maps.

Plant hardiness is a highly complex factor, and depends on temperature, rainfall, and soil. Since it is impossible to show these three variables simply for an area as large as the United States, the best practical method is to show hardiness ratings on the basis of average annual minimum temperatures. This gives a fairly accurate idea of where certain plants will grow, and is the method used satisfactorily by the author in other reference books as well as here.

Those familiar with hardiness zones realize that altitude plays its part too; the higher up a tall mountain one goes, the lower the average annual minimum temperature and hence the fewer plants that can be grown. The zone number given for the plants discussed in this book does not indicate that they can only be grown in the one band across the land; they may be grown in a colder zone, but only with a great deal of protection.

They can also be grown in several warmer zones, at least until rainfall, summer heat, and possibly soil conditions become limiting factors.

To use the maps to best advantage, first determine the hardiness zone in which you live. Then, in checking the lists and noting the hardiness zone numbers for each plant, you can see at a glance what plants you should expect to grow. If, for instence, you live in the Boston, Massachusetts area, you should be able to grow all plants listed for Zone 5. Also, it is very important to remember, you can also grow all plants listed for colder zones, i.e. Zones 2, 3, and 4. As for the plants listed in the next warmer zone, i.e. Zone 6, you might be able to grow a few of them, but they would require a great deal of winter protection. They might survive some winters and be killed by others. It would be practically worthless to attempt to grow plants listed for still warmer zones, i.e. Zones 7 to 9.

The hardiness zone ratings are not infallible, but they are a means of telling in advance, with a reasonable degree of accuracy, the plants that can be grown in any certain area. This of course saves much effort in hit-or-miss experimental maintenance.

2

Shortcuts and
Aids in Maintenance

The modern gardener can take advantage of the many shortcuts and aids to gardening that are available today. Centuries of growing plants by dedicated gardeners everywhere has resulted in volumes of information. Modern engineering and chemistry both contribute their full share of aid. Plant explorers have searched the world for new and better plants. Government experiment stations throughout America annually make sizeable appropriations for experimental work, research which helps the homeowner with his own gardening problems. In effect, the modern gardener can, if he wishes, materially reduce expense and personal labor by using these many sources now available to him.

In approaching low maintenance gardening, there are three basic factors to consider. Planning, the first and often the most important element, has already been discussed. Garden shortcuts and aids will be discussed in this section. Finally, the selection of the right low maintenance plants that are now available to the public (or soon will be) for specific situations is taken up in the third main section of this book.

Few gardeners will want to avail themselves of all these shortcuts, and the majority may not wish to confine themselves to growing only the low maintenance plants discussed in the last section. All, however, will find herein some information of value to them in making low maintenance gardening a more pleasant and interesting experience.

PLANTING

The objective in every planting is to have healthy, well-grown plants that are always in vigorous condition. You will not, I'm afraid, find any shortcuts at planting time. Many years ago, L. H. Bailey said that it was always better to prepare a five dollar hole for a fifty-cent shrub rather than to plant a five-dollar shrub in a fifty-cent hole. There is a great deal of truth in this; far too often, with plants just obtained from the nursery, one hurries to plant them quickly to finish the job.

It is far better to prepare the holes for the plants in advance and thus to find out the kind of soil where the plants are to be permanently placed. If it is poor—composed chiefly of gravel or very sandy soil—it should be removed to a depth of at least 18 inches, depending on the size of plant used; with trees or large balled evergreens the soil may have to be excavated deeper. The hole should be at least two feet wider than the roots of the new plant, so that when the roots are placed normally in the hole they can be comfortably spread out (not jammed in together) and have a foot on all sides in which to enlarge properly.

Well-rotted manure or decomposed compost might be placed in the bottom of the hole, two inches of soil added on top, and the plant carefully set in the hole on top of that. Then good soil is firmed in about the normally spread-out roots, and a slight depression left at the top of the hole to catch and hold water until the plant becomes fully established. Care should be taken not to plant when the soil is muddy, for in firming such soil it may dry out into an almost bricklike consistency. Also, the young plants should be set out at exactly the same depth they were in the nursery row prior to digging. When planting is completed, then in order to keep the young plants from drying out during the first years of growth, they should be properly mulched. See Mulching (p. 57).

WATERING

The young plants should be thoroughly watered in at once—really soaked in—and water applied to them when necessary during the *next two years* so that at no time does the soil actually dry out in periods of drought.

The use of water wands (gadgets that permit water to leak out without the force or pressure that one finds in an open hose) are ideal. Soil soakers—long, porous hoses that when attached to a hose allow the water to ooze out slowly—are also excellent. A good deal of water is needed to soak into the soil to reach a depth of 12 to 18 inches, and when applied by "pressure" watering, much of it quickly runs off. In fact, letting the water soak slowly into the soil, by either of these two methods, or by the use of sprinklers kept in one position for a long time, is the best method of watering anything whether it be lawn, newly planted shrubbery, or a flower bed.

The gardener who makes a big show of watering with a pressure hose, going quickly from one spot to the next, is really wasting time as well as water. Water applied in this fashion seldom goes into the soil more than a fraction of an inch, and because it is on the surface, it quickly evaporates without even reaching the roots of the plants. It is a good idea to test the method you use, timing the soaker or sprinkler, and then digging into the soil to see how far the water has penetrated, since soils differ in the rapidity with which they soak up water. To be effective, the water must get down to the plant roots.

There may be places about the grounds where water outlets would be a most desirable asset. It is not necessary to use metal pipe for these outlets, which must be either drained in the fall or else installed below the frost line. The best modern shortcut is to use plastic pipe. It is a good idea to set these in the ground so that they can be drained, but this is not necessary. They need be inserted only a few inches below the soil level, and once in the ground they can last for many years without breaking. They are highly practical and economical as well.

Various watering devices are available in all makes and types. We even fell for an ad which asked, if there was a rectangular bed, why waste water? The obvious thing to do was to buy the device advertised, which spread water on the ground in a regulated rectangular pattern. We bought it; but later we realized that any device with a back-and-forth motion does the same thing, and can be regulated by the amount of water pressure.

Watering, like planting, should be done with care, and if done correctly will be worth the time expended. If done with "a lick and a promise" the time and money can be considered wasted.

BANK PLANTING

The chief objective in bank planting is to select vigorous-growing species which will root along procumbent stems on or near the soil surface. This will tend to hold the soil in place and keep it from washing away during heavy rains. Many banks are unsuitable for growing grass; either the gradient is too steep or the soil is irregular and covered with rocks and large boulders, making it difficult or impossible to maintain a lawn.

The soil on the bank should be as good as possible. Mix in compost or well-rotted leaves or manure. If the soil is very sandy, add peat moss to help the soil retain moisture.

If grass must be planted, there are roughly woven, light burlaplike rolls of open-mesh woven material available that can be laid and then pegged down over the seeding. This is left on to eventually rot away. It ensures a good start for the grass by keeping the soil from washing away in rains until the grass becomes firmly established. If the grade is too steep for this, and grass must be grown, then sods of grass should be laid down. These are bought in rolls of living grass and pegged down to keep them in place at the start, but one should remember that the gradient can become too steep to mow any grass properly, regardless of how it is started. Recognizing such situations for what they are, and planting bank plants instead of grass, results in low maintenance later.

Often it is easiest in the long run to forget growing grass on banks and use fast-growing bank plants selected from the list (pages 134–135). Plant well, in good-sized holes, and space the plants so they will give a reasonably good cover in two or three years. The Memorial Rose, as one example, is fast growing, rambles over rocks and boulders, and its rooting can be hastened if a few shovelsful of soil are placed over the longer runners to aid rooting at those places. The plants should be spaced 3 to 4 feet apart.

Junipers might be planted 2 to 3 feet apart; Forsythia 'Arnold Dwarf' and *Stephanandra incisa* 'Crispa' about the same. This last is an excellent new plant for bank planting and can be easily pruned back to any height if it grows too high. Periwinkle clumps on the other hand might be spaced a foot or less apart. The nursery or garden center where the plants are purchased can save problems later by telling you how far apart to space the plants chosen.

After planting and watering well, then mulch (see Mulching, p. 57) for mulching is a necessity on any bank planting. This mulch should be periodically renewed whenever needed. It is the best low-maintenance insurance on bank plantings for it aids in keeping the soil moist and the plants growing.

Soil, soil mixture, steepness of the bank, and the speed with which a cover is needed, all govern the type of plant selected and the planting distances to be used for bank planting.

SHADE PLANTING

Trying to grow plants in the shade can be a frustrating experience. Shade can vary from continual light shade to intermittent shade caused by buildings, to very dense continual shade. The deeper the shade, the fewer the plants which will survive.

Shade caused by low, overhanging tree branches is also accompanied by tree roots close to the surface of the soil which can have a serious effect on the growth of plants. The roots of Norway Maples and beech trees, as examples, will absorb most of the available moisture and nutrients, so that plants placed beneath them have little chance to grow normally.

Under such circumstances instead of experimenting with different plants and suffering successive losses, select a few of the sturdiest in the list of plants withstanding shade (pages 158–162), such as Japanese Pachysandra, barberries, or yews. If they fail, simply give up the situation as too difficult. Spread crushed stone over the area, or use paving stones. There are some situations where plant growing is practically impossible, and the sooner one recognizes such situations for what they are, the more time one will have to devote to more rewarding areas of the garden.

All the plants in the list on pages 158–162 will withstand some shade, some more than others. One can select several types that would be suitable and worthy of trial. Give them the best of soil, moisture, and fertilizer conditions to offset the growth-slowing effect of the shade. A little effort in properly selecting plants for the shaded areas about the home grounds will definitely result in low maintenance later.

GROUND COVERS

Ground covers are low, woody, or herbaceous plants that grow rapidly and are dense enough to cover bare ground. Only a very few are considered substitutes for a grass lawn, since few of them can survive being walked on. There are areas in most gardens where a low ground cover is most useful—in the shade (page 158); in dry areas (page 151); in wet soil (page 155); on a bank (page 134)—in fact any place where it is difficult or undesirable to maintain grass. Extreme care should be made to select the correct type of ground cover initially. Know its height, what it looks like, whether it's evergreen, and whether it will grow in the site selected. Quick information about these will be found in the alphabetical listing (pages 197–358) and also on pages 127–133.

The majority of the low maintenance ground covers in the list (pages 127–133) can be grown in the full sun; thirty-one will withstand partial shade, and these are marked with an (S).

Good soil is a necessity and the best way to provide it is when the initial planting is made. Remove poor soil, to a depth of 4 to 6 inches, depending on the size of the plant, and then provide good top soil. Mix in well-decomposed humus or rotted leaves, compost or manure, even peat moss if there is nothing better, as this aids the soil in retaining moisture. Also, if necessary, mix in a fertilizer recommended by the nurseryman or garden center, but be sure to read the directions on the bag so you will know how much to apply. A "complete" fertilizer of the granular chemical kind labeled 5–10–5 (5 percent nitrogen, 10 percent phosphoric acid and 5 percent potash) is often available. This could be mixed with the soil before planting at 3 to 5 pounds per hundred square feet. If the best possible soil is given at the start, the ground cover will grow quickly and can be expected to be truly low maintenance.

Spacing the plants depends, of course, on the kind of plants selected. Many of the herbaceous plants could be spaced one per square foot, but Hostas might easily be allowed 2 square feet for each plant. Vigorous plants like the Memorial Rose and junipers might be allowed 3 to 4 square feet at the start. The pachysandras, thymes, and bugleweed might be spaced only 6 inches apart, especially if a quick cover is desired. Get approximate planting distances from the store where you buy plants. This prevents problems later!

Mulching the new bed is always an excellent way to reduce maintenance later for it reduces weed growth and water loss from the soil. See Mulching (page 57) for full information.

Do not let the new planting dry out during the first year of summer droughts. Winter protection, especially through the first winter, is a must. This can take the form of a good mulch, or possibly pine boughs or straw thrown lightly over the plants to protect them from too much winter sun and the alternate freezing and thawing of the soil in the winter which sometimes results in actually pushing the young plants out of the soil. If this occurs, they should be replanted immediately.

Fertilizing after the first winter sometimes may be helpful. Apply the fertilizer before the plants start growth in the spring, at rates recommended on the container. Water the fertilizer at once so that none remains on the foliage. Many find the easiest way of fertilizing is by use of a fertilizer cartridge attached to the garden hose. If this method is chosen, the directions with the cartridge should be followed exactly.

The quickest possible way to save time, trouble, and expense is to take time at the start to select the right ground cover for the right place. Then plant in good soil, mulch well, and keep the soil from drying out.

LAWN SUBSTITUTES

There are many homeowners seeking shortcuts to having a good lawn. It should be emphatically stated at the start that there is no material that will appear as neat or be as serviceable as good, well-cut grass. True, it must be cared for—fertilized, watered, and cut—but if these things are carried out well there is no plant better suited for lawns than grass. There are different kinds of grasses and different grass mixtures for varying situations, but all require reasonable care in order to look well. Given this care, they serve indefinitely.

There is always the perfectionist who never can rest until every dandelion seedling and every bit of Crab Grass has been painfully pulled from his lawn. He spends all his spare time on his hands and knees, and welcomes visitors in order to inveigle them into helping him. If he enjoys this, it is probably satisfactory for him, but it can certainly discourage visitors!

About the only shortcut in lawn maintenance is to acquire the state of mind that enables one to see all the good things about the lawn, while at the same time overlooking completely its many little shortcomings. For instance, the lawn never looks better than in the early spring. The first task is to fertilize, a process that invariably results in a greener lawn, faster growing grass, and hence more labor in cutting. Can one be satisfied with a second-rate lawn requiring less maintenance time—that is, no fertilizer—or must one aim for the best, year after year? It is a momentous question that every gardener will have to answer for himself.

Weekly cutting, or approximately that, is another hurdle. Closer cutting makes for a more uniform lawn but it does take time. Can the gardener be satisfied with higher grass in the lawn, cut every two weeks, possibly with little piles of clippings left here and there? These piles turn brown as they die and can be so dense that they kill small spots of grass underneath. Can the owner bring himself to a state of mind where such a lawn doesn't bother him? Admittedly, if the lawn is in an inconspicuous place, less cutting may well be the rule.

When weeds like dandelion and Crab Grass begin to take over, is the gardener going to approve of the different color scheme and note the advantage of such a lawn, or is he going to fret until every last weed is pulled? All depends on the individual, and one might as well take stock of one's self and one's projected lawn before it is even planted, to try to predetermine the hazards of maintenance from the psychological point of view.

As old hands at gardening, both my wife and I have been through all phases of lawn maintenance. There used to be a time when every weed was religiously pulled, fertilizing was done every spring, and summer watering was a welcomed recreation. As time went on, and we learned that most of the summer droughts in our area did not actually kill the grass although they could mar it for some time, we came to the satisfying point of view that we were going to appreciate the change of appearance in our lawn from one season to another. I do not mean that we allowed dandelions to take over, but we took out the majority—if we wanted to or could inveigle one of the children to do it; otherwise we would try (if we had time and did not forget) some of the weed killers especially made to eliminate dandelions. If we remembered and did it—fine! But if we forgot or went on a trip when the work should have been done— that was also fine! Then we would be most interested in seeing what would happen to the lawn because we had not pampered it at the proper time. As the years rolled on, we learned how to compliment our friends on their beautiful lawns, and became satisfied in allowing ours to be the one they used for comparison. They liked that (and had the work). We also liked it, because it made them happy and we didn't have the work. We found that the lawn would not die. One summer we went away and left it for ten weeks without mowing. Fortunately, there was a drought, but even if there had not been, that lawn was due for a real labor-saving experiment. Admittedly, it looked pretty bad on our return, but the grass did not die (much) and then we had the pleasure of seeing how fast it recuperated with a minimum of care. So, a state of mind is the best shortcut to lawn maintenance.

Because lawns are being maintained under many and varied situations in this vast country, it is impossible to make all-inclusive statements about plants that might be used as grass substitutes. Under certain conditions, especially in the southern parts of the country, there has been a great demand for Zoysia grasses of one clone or another. These are more uniform and slower in growth and need less care. Zoysia lawns are planted by seed (2 pounds per 1000 square feet), sprigs, or plugs and the resulting lawns are so dense and tough that it is best to have heavy-duty, reel-type mowers. In the North, Zoysia turns brown in the winter after the first heavy frost and remains brown all winter. This makes it unsightly as well as a fire hazard, while a good stand of Kentucky Bluegrass usually remains green all winter long.

Dichondra repens is a lawn substitute widely used in the southwestern United States, but only in areas where winter temperatures do not go below 25°F. It is not a grass but a creeping broad-leaved perennial plant, a native of the West Indies, with small leaves less than one-quarter inch in diameter. A Dichondra lawn can either be started by seeding or by planting plugs of the growing plant. Seed is used at the rate of 2 pounds per 1000 square feet, preferably sown between March and May. It should not be sown in mixtures and does not need a nurse crop. If planted in plugs, these should be spaced 6 to 12 inches apart. However, a Dichondra lawn does need nearly as much attention as a grass lawn, although if it is in hot sun, with people walking on it continually, the times between mowing can be considerably longer than with a grass lawn.

Then there are the Lily-turf species (*Liriope*) which have been widely advertised as lawn substitutes. Unfortunately, many advertisements leave the uninitiated with the impression that these plants are the real answer to a lawn substitute. Here again, in certain areas of the South they may have their place, but most are not suitable for continued growth in the northern gardens of the United States. One species, *Liriope spicata,* is hardy in the North, but anyone who has grown it knows that if Quack Grass ever gets into a planting of *Liriope spicata* the entire area must be dug up and the Quack Grass deliberately separated from the Lily-turf, piece by piece, and the latter then replanted.

Over the years other types of plants have been tried in various areas with questionable success: Sandworts (*Arenaria* species); Roman Camomile (*Anthemis nobilis*); Common Yarrow (*Achillea millefolium*); Brass-buttons (*Cotula* species); Mayweed (*Matricaria* species); Procumbent Pearlwort (*Sagina procumbens*). Others have been given a certain amount of publicity, but when investigated carefully it has usually appeared that any success has been obtained in small local areas, under extremely local climatic conditions. For instance, one gardener on Nantucket Island off the southern Massachusetts coast became very discouraged with his grass lawn, for it usually dried up during the summer months in the sandy soil unless it was watered with unfailing regularity. Experimenting with a small spot of yarrow, he found that this plant could be cut with a lawn mower and that it would result in a fairly green surface during hot summer droughts without incessant watering. Later, he sowed his entire lawn with yarrow. He was rightly proud of his green "lawn" when those all about him were brown in summer. However, the atmospheric moisture was undoubtedly high in this small area, even though rainfall was deficient, and yarrow is apparently a plant able to utilize atmospheric moisture far better than many grasses. In areas where this atmospheric moisture is not available, a yarrow "lawn" might well have its drawbacks during serious summer droughts.

Local soils and climatic conditions, therefore, play an extremely important part in the success or failure of lawn substitutes. A certain amount of experimentation by the gardener, especially on small plots of a hundred square feet, may prove most helpful to him in making a later decision concerning what to plant in his lawn. In no case, however, should he plant thousands of square feet of a "lawn substitute" without first studying carefully all the good and bad points about it in his particular local area. Rather than waste too much energy and expense experimenting on large areas with plants of unknown performance, it would be much wiser to admit that, with all its faults, the right kind of grass creates the fastest growing and most serviceable lawn.

PRUNING

One of the best shortcuts to maintaining a home planting easily is to understand the few simple rudiments of pruning, and to prune—where necessary—early in the life of the shrub or tree. This saves major work later on. A small sapling eight feet tall (or less) showing a double leader should have one of the leaders removed as soon as it is first noticed, otherwise the fault will be growing bigger year by year until correcting it may easily become a costly major operation, whereas a snip of the hand shears in the first place would have done the job satisfactorily.

A little knowledge of what to prune and how to do it goes a very long way in helping plants grow into well-balanced specimens that are an asset in any garden. Conversely, the indiscriminate hacking of shrubs and trees at definite heights is the quickest means by which otherwise beautiful plantings are made unsightly. Here are a few of the general essentials:

As far as the growth of the plant is concerned,

pruning can be done at almost any time except in the early summer, for if done then, the new growth may not have sufficient time to mature before winter, and killing may result. However, as far as our interest in the ornamental qualities of plants is concerned, shrubs are divided into two groups, first, those that bloom in the early spring, like daphne, forsythia, and lilac, which might be pruned after they flower in order to obtain the full benefit of their flower the current year; and second, plants that bloom on the current year's wood, like hydrangea and Rose of Sharon, which can be pruned in the late winter or early spring and still be expected to bloom the same year. Trees are usually pruned in the late winter and early spring (with the exception of those that "bleed" profusely, like the birch, maple, or Yellowwood), for at this time, before the leaves appear, it is much easier to see which branches should be removed, and also it gives the tree the entire spring and summer to form new growth.

What to Prune

1. Dead, broken, or diseased branches.
2. Broken roots and one-third of the branches at transplanting time. Some roots are always cut when a plant is dug. A good general rule is to remove about one-third of the total linear branch length, when the plant is moved, by thinning out weak or damaged branches and correcting structural defects. This compensates for the loss of roots that have been cut in the transplanting operation, and always results in more vigorous plants at the end of the first year. This is difficult for the homeowner to do, since the new plant looks smaller than the original specimen purchased from the nursery, but it is always better for the plant in the end. When plants are to be moved from their native place in the

woods, it is advisable to root-prune (merely forcing a spade in the ground in a wide circle about the plant) one year in advance, to force the production of many roots close to the base so that the transplanting operation will be easier. Nursery-grown plants are usually root-pruned periodically.

3. Young trees should be pruned early. Timely corrective pruning saves trouble later. If the tree is one that normally has a single trunk, see that only one straight trunk develops and cut out any others that try to grow. Occasionally several branches grow out from the trunk at the same place, and these will always make weak crotches. All but one should be removed. Sometimes young shrubs should be "headed back" a bit to force them to grow more branches from the base. A forsythia, for instance, with just one leader would never become an interesting shrub. In other words, know how the tree or shrub will develop at maturity, and help it early in life by selecting the proper leaders, removing the others if necessary.

4. Correct structural defects. Never allow two equally vigorous leaders to develop on exactly opposite sides of the same trunk. This will always be a "weak" crotch, susceptible to splitting as the tree grows older. It may spoil the symmetry of the entire tree when this happens. There are several kinds of weak crotches to look for, but in general the greater the angle a branch makes where it leaves the trunk of the tree, the stronger the wood at that union. It is really very simple to watch the younger trees as they begin to grow, and with hand shears quickly remove secondary leaders, unnecessary crossing branches, and so on.

5. Cut suckers from the bases of grafted or budded plants. Many plants used in gardens, such as roses, crab apples, lilacs, and fruit trees, are either grafted or budded on another kind of understock. Usually, this is

never more than a foot or so from the ground. Hence, all suckers developing below this point should be removed as soon as they are observed, for if allowed to develop they will not only spoil the symmetry of the plant and sap the strength of the variety wanted, but will develop into an entirely different and usually undesirable plant. Roses especially produce frequent examples of understock growth, since many an ornamental rose is budded or grafted on *Rosa multiflora* as an understock. This is a vigorous-growing rose species, and once started into growth above ground it quickly takes over the entire plant. Frequently, when two kinds of blossoms or leaves are seen on one plant this is the reason. The understock suckers should be cut out as soon as they develop.

6. Rejuvenate old shrubs. A Mock-orange, privet, lilac, spirea, or many another shrub may grow too tall and become open and ungainly at the base. Most shrubs can be rejuvenated in one of two ways: either by cutting the entire shrub to six inches above the ground in the early spring and allowing it to develop as a new plant; or by thinning out the old wood, cutting some of the older branches off near the ground and allowing new ones to form, then repeating the process with a few more of the older branches the second and third years. Lilacs are often treated thus, for in this way they produce a few blooms each year of the change, while when they are cut to the ground they do not bloom for two or three years. Forsythias, privets, Mock-oranges, deutzias, and even lilacs treated in this way early one spring have flowered the following year. Usually one must wait another year or two for such shrubs to bloom when they have been cut back hard. It is essential to note, however, that many evergreens do not respond to such drastic pruning, although a few may. To be on the safe side, one should follow the general rule that evergreens should

be thinned but not be expected to grow back to good size if cut to the ground. Certainly few if any of the conifers will recuperate and reproduce new shoots when cut to the ground.

7. Hedges, screens, and windbreaks. These should be pruned with the objective of increasing their density, for if a twig is cut back a few inches it frequently sends out more than one new shoot to take the place of the one removed. This growth habit of plants can be utilized to force them to grow more dense.

8. Certain limbs for utility purposes. The lower limbs of street trees, or limbs that interfere with a certain view, walk, window or wire, must sometimes be removed.

9. Girdling root. Close observation of the base of trees which are growing poorly often discloses a girdling root; that is, a root partly on the surface of the soil or just beneath, that is growing in such a way as to choke or constrict the trunk of the tree or a larger root. Such girdling roots can do real harm and usually should be cut as near as possible to the trunk of the tree or at least at the point where they are doing the damage.

These, then, are the reasons for pruning. Be certain the reason for pruning is understood before it is done, for it is always a dwarfing process, and there are some plants that never need any. Study the situation and have a good reason for all pruning.

How to Prune

1. Make all cuts clean, with sharp tools.

2. Never leave any stubs. A short stub may never heal over and is always a source of infection. Make all cuts back to a bud, branch, or main trunk. The removal of a large limb should be done in 3 cuts. First, an under-cut is made on the bottom of the branch by sawing up

one-fourth or one-third through the limb about a foot from the trunk of the tree. Then the upper cut is started on the top of the branch, one to two inches beyond the first cut but toward the trunk, and sawed down until the limb falls. As the two cuts near each other and the limb begins to sag, its weight will break the wood at the enter and the limb will jump clear without stripping and tearing the bark down the tree trunk. Finally, the stump is removed by a cut flush with the trunk of the tree.

3. Paint all cuts over 1 inch to 2 inches in diameter with a special protective tree paint.

4. Disinfect tools after each cut on a diseased plant. A satisfactory disinfectant to have in a suitable can for this purpose is alcohol.

5. Shrub rejuvenation. Thin out the older branches over a period of a few years or cut the shrub to within a few inches of the ground in late winter or early spring. The obvious exception to this would be weak-growing shrubs or those which have been budded or grafted. Never cut any shrub off at a horizontal line several feet above the ground. This is an artificial practice outmoded for many years, and always results in unsightly specimens. Thin out here and there, cut one branch back hard and another not nearly so much, and thin out from the base simultaneously. In this way an old plant can be reduced in size, still look natural, and will produce new growth at different places from the ground on up to the top.

6. Shear hedges wider at the base than the top. Both evergreen and deciduous hedges should be sheared in such a way that they are wider at the base than at the top, thus allowing the important lower branches plenty of room, light, and air. If the hedge is pruned narrower at the base than at the top, the lower branches will often die from lack of light. Once these lower branches die on an evergreen hedge, it is practically

impossible to force any new ones to grow in the same place. Deciduous hedges, on the other hand, are mostly vigorous-growing plants, and when they become open at the base the entire hedge can be cut to within a few inches of the ground in the early spring and will quickly start a new, vigorous growth from the ground, thus forming a new hedge in a few years' time.

Pruning need not be difficult. It is important, however, that one understand exactly why the contemplated pruning is necessary and can visualize the probable results. Even yews and rhododendrons can be heavily pruned and old plants rejuvenated by the expert gardener who has previously studied what to do and when to do it.

FERTILIZING

Fertilizers are applied to make plants grow more vigorously and so to produce more leaf, stem, flower, root, and fruit. This should be remembered especially in fertilizing the lawn, for more growth means frequent grass cutting. With certain foundation plants, such as Canada Hemlocks that are to be restrained to six feet, more growth may create more work in pruning. More growth can certainly produce more work in shearing a hedge. Think twice before fertilizers are used, especially if garden labor is to be cut to a minimum.

At one time, before chemical fertilizers were developed, manure was the fertilizer most commonly used in gardening. If you live in a suburban community where manure is free or cheaply available, it is a most valuable aid to cultivation; like other organic matter, such as decomposing weeds, leaves, and so on, it releases available nitrogen and other nutrients into the soil as well as aiding the water-retention properties of the soil. It should be remembered, however, that a ton of average manure contains about the same amounts of nitrogen and potash as 100 pounds of 5–10–5 commercial fertilizer (5 parts nitrogen, 10 parts phosphoric acid, and 5 parts potash), although only about one-fourth as much phosphate. If manure is not available, a combination of rotting vegetable compost complemented with commercial fertilizer can achieve the same end results.

Tilth is frequently aided by the addition of organic matter to the soil; and usually manure, and commercial fertilizers as well, contain a certain amount of other elements that sometimes are deficient in the soil. Certainly one cannot have a vegetable garden on the same plot year in and year out, annually taking off crops of vegetables, without replenishing the soil with fertilizers in some way. Farmers practice crop rotation; the amateur vegetable gardener with only limited space must be satisfied with the simple addition of organic manures or commercial fertilizers.

Unquestionably, the proper application of the right kind of fertilizer at the right time is one of the easiest aids to insure vigorous plant growth. Many gardeners who are in a hurry fail to take the time to determine the proper amount or the proper kind of fertilizer to apply at any one time, and as a result of their efforts they may do more harm to the plants than good. There are a few simple fundamentals one should understand before applying large amounts of fertilizers to plants. These will be briefly summed up for the benefit of those who wish to review the subject.

Most plants grow in soil, and in the soils there are usually some 15 elements. Many of these are termed "trace" elements or "minor" elements, since they are usually present in most soils in minute quantities but sufficient for plant growth. The most important elements needed in the largest amounts for plant growth are nitrogen, phosphorus, and potassium. It is these that are the chief components of the so-called "commercial" fertilizer in the 5–10–5 ratio noted above.

Water in the soil (and in the atmosphere), warm temperatures, and light are also necessary ingredients for plant growth. In gardens out of doors we cannot do much about the temperature; we try to segregate those plants requiring some shade from those that will withstand full sun; and of course we can augment the water that comes from the skies in the form of rain.

Plants vary in their requirements for water, in their ability to withstand continually high temperatures and, as just pointed out, in the amount of direct sunlight they can withstand. Therefore, it is obvious why all plants cannot grow in all locations, even though the soil might be uniform, which of course it is not.

Presupposing that plants to be grown in a certain soil are known to be hardy in that area and will grow in the right kind of soils, what function does the soil serve and how does one go about "improving" it or adding to its general constituents the items necessary for good growth? To answer this, one should know that the soil is usually considered to be broken-down weathered rocks combined with decayed vegetative plant materials in which are living a myriad of microscopic organisms. Without these, it might be impossible to grow anything at all. Oxygen and water from the air filter down through these soil particles, dissolve chemical compounds as they do so, and aid in supporting the life of the soil organisms as well as the plants. Only when you know the composition of your soil, can you know what fertilizer to add effectively.

Soil Acidity

In addition to the nitrogen, phosphorus, and potash in the soil considered essential to growth, there are also calcium and magnesium, both of which are sometimes deficient. When there is not much calcium in the soil, it is "acid" in reaction; when calcium is prevalent in large quantities it is "alkaline" in reaction. The symbol of pH is used to designate the acidity or alkalinity of the soil, neutral soil having a pH of 7.0; below this figure the pH becomes increasingly acid, to pH 3.5, which is extremely acid. Soils become alkaline above pH 7.0 up to about pH 8.5 or more, which is very alkaline. Actually, the pH scale runs from 1 to 14.

As every experienced gardener knows, soils vary in different parts of the country. In New England they tend to be acid; in the areas of little rainfall in the Midwest they are alkaline, sometimes extremely so; in parts of the East and the West, they are both alkaline and acid. Hence a soil may be strongly acid or alkaline and unsuitable for the growth of certain types of plants. This is where soil testing aids the homeowner. Most state experiment stations have a soil-testing laboratory where small soil samples may be sent in for testing of the acidity. Usually recommendations are made, when the report is returned, of just what should be added to that soil to make it a proper medium for growing plants.

Most plants will grow best in a soil with a pH between 6.5 and 7.0, but apparently trees and shrubs are more versatile. In the Arnold Arboretum the soil tests about pH 5.5 and the majority of the woody plants do well. However, the so-called "acid-soil" plants, like azaleas, rhododendrons, and blueberries, will also grow well on soils even more acid.

To correct for soil pH variations, one adds lime to make the soil more alkaline, or aluminum sulfate (or powdered sulfur, which eventually forms sulfuric acid) to make the soil more acid. The amount depends on how much of a change is desired.

SOIL pH	APPROXIMATE AMOUNT OF GROUND LIMESTONE NEEDED PER 100 SQUARE FEET TO BRING SOIL UP TO A pH OF 6.5
Slightly acid (6.5–6.0)	10 pounds
Medium acid (6.0–5.5)	15 pounds
Strongly acid (5.5–5.0)	20 pounds
Very strongly acid (5.0 and less)	25 pounds

It is advisable to use ground limestone—sometimes ground dolomitic limestone where it is available, because this will have a trace of magnesium in it which may be deficient in some soils.

In order to make the soil more acid, aluminum sulfate can be used at the following suggested rates:

ACIDITY OF SOIL USED AT START	ALUMINUM SULFATE PER 100 SQUARE FEET
Medium acid (pH 5.5 to pH 6.0)	2¾ pounds
Slightly acid (pH 6.5 to pH 7.0)	5½ pounds
Neutral to strongly alkaline (pH 7.0 to pH 8.0)	8¼ pounds

Also, flowers of sulfur can be used to make the soil more acid. This material is cheap and easily available, but it takes much longer to be effective than aluminum sulfate does. In any event, when flowers of sulfur is used it might best be applied in summer, worked into the soil at once, and watered in heavily. It has been suggested that it be applied at 1 to 1½ pounds per 100 square feet for each half pH the soil is to be lowered. Since it is slow in becoming effective, one should be cautious about not adding too much. It might be best to apply it conservatively and test the soil again in several months rather than to use a very large amount all at once.

The first step having been taken, and the soil acidity checked and corrected where necessary, one then considers the matter of fertilizers. If they are to be added, and if the growth of existing plants is not what it should be and an increase is desired, the next steps follow in sequence.

Kinds of Fertilizer

There are many types available on the market: some are sold under specialized trade names; some are special mixtures for acid-soil plants like the azaleas and rhododendrons; and of course there are the various types of manures. It is not our purpose to discuss this subject in detail, since the experienced gardener will know what is best for his needs. For the inexperienced gardener the easiest thing is to obtain one type of fertilizer and try to adapt it for his various garden needs.

Fertilizers under trade name usually come in bags with directions for applications. Many commercial mixtures, such as those used in large amounts on farm land, do not come with directions but merely as marked mixtures with the exact ingredients listed on the outside of the bag as is required by law.

If a 10–10–10 is to be used, it will be applied at one-half the rate of a 5–10–5, for the former has twice as much nitrogen as the latter. If one buys sodium nitrate for instance, it is an extremely powerful fertilizer, and one should have experience with the very small amounts that should be used. There are others in this

51

category also. It is easiest to settle on a fertilizer of a standard mixture, like 5–10–5, at least in the first few years of gardening experience.

Another important thing to determine at the start is the amount of fertilizer one is using. Guessing at amounts often results in either no aid to the plants or in injury from overapplication. Measuring fertilizer is easier than weighing each amount used. It has been determined that such common garden fertilizers as a 5–10–5 or 6–10–4, superphosphate, or some others can be considered to measure out to one pint equaling about one pound. Other calculations may be necessary for other fertilizers, but this is certainly the easiest method to determine exactly the amount of fertilizer one is working with.

Method of Application

The method of applying the fertilizer may have to be varied, depending on the type of plant material. Undoubtedly, broadcasting by hand is the easiest, and a little experimentation is all that is needed to learn how to do this evenly. Applying fertilizers irregularly will quickly show up in alternate streaks of vigorous and poor growth on the lawn, and leaving small piles of fertilizer that should have been broadcast evenly is the quickest way to cause plant injury.

Sometimes, as may be the case in the vegetable garden or around specimen plants, the fertilizer is wanted only for certan plants and not for the whole area; hence it can be applied in bands or circles about such plants, care being taken to apply it evenly over the wide surface where the roots are. Care must also be taken not to leave it on the foliage of valued plants. This will result in the injury or death of the leaves.

Because of this type of injury, which is often hard

to avoid, commercial fertilizers should be applied shortly before a rain or else watered in with a hose immediately after application.

In the long rows of plants in the vegetable garden the fertilizer can be applied as a side dressing merely by distributing it along the sides of the rows. It is often a good idea, if burning the young foliage is to be avoided, to make two light applications of fertilizer two weeks apart rather than one very heavy application. This is easily done by determining the amount to be used and applying half of it to one side of the row at a time.

As mentioned previously, fertilizers can be applied by means of cartridges attached to the garden hose, and when this method is used care should be taken to apply the fertilizer evenly, as called for by the manufacturers of the fertilizer cartridges.

When plants are under irrigation, as in the Far West, fertilizers are frequently applied in the irrigation water itself, calling for a careful study of amounts of fertilizer to use and the even distribution of the water.

The method frequently advocated for applying fertilizers to trees by means of holes punched or bored in the soil is most easily accomplished with machines. Using a crowbar is not easy work and will not appeal to the gardener who is in a hurry. He can either pay to have experts apply the fertilizers to his trees by the punched-hole method—sometimes it is actually blown into the soil by compressed air—or he can take the easy way out and apply it broadcast. The only difficulty (if it is considered such) with the broadcast method of tree fertilizing is that sometimes the tree is growing in a beautiful lawn and the grass may be burned by heavy application.

This is not always a serious obstacle, for the grass will usually grow back quickly, especially if the fertilizer is well watered in immediately. Another way to circumvent burning is to divide the amount into two or three applications, about a week or two apart, each one to be thoroughly watered in. This method is simple, easy, and takes little time.

Finally, we read much now about foliar fertilizer applications—fertilizers in solution sprayed on the foliage. This may have merit in some instances, but it takes equipment and certainly is not a time-saver to the gardener, for many applications have to be made to equal the effects of one soil application.

When to Apply Fertilizers

Fertilizers should be applied early in the growing season. After all, it does take time for the material, when applied broadcast to the surface of the soil, to be dissolved by water, taken down into the soil, translocated to the leaves of the plant, and used in the formation of increased growth, flower, or fruit production. The time the fertilizer is applied will vary, too, with the kind of plant.

Deciduous trees and shrubs should be fertilized early in the spring, just before growth starts. This gives these plants a long growing season to utilize the fertilizers to best advantage. In most areas, they can also be fertilized any time after early mid-September, the objective being to make the fertilizers available to the plant roots until the ground freezes, when the roots are no longer active. This is usually for a long time after the leaves have dropped from the plants. It is obvious that fertilizing in midwinter has little value in areas where the ground freezes.

Deciduous trees and shrubs should not be fertilized between early summer and fall, for fertilizing at this time may stimulate late vegetative growth that will not have a sufficient period to mature properly by the time the leaves fall in the autumn, and such a condition will result in winter injury to those plants.

Evergreens may best be fertilized only in the early spring, just before the growth has started. Although some plantsmen may do it in the fall, this is not a healthy practice generally.

How Much Fertilizer to Apply

Trees: The first year a small tree is planted, it may need an application of fertilizer. If this be the case, one pound of a 5–10–5 or a 6–10–4 could be applied broadcast around the base for each inch in diameter of trunk. If the tree is small, this is applied in a band several feet wide starting 6 to 8 inches from the trunk.

The rates for established deciduous trees for the same types of commercial fertilizer are 2 to 4 pounds per inch in diameter (half that amount for a 10–10–10, which of course has twice as much nitrogen), slightly less for evergreens. The area fertilized is from a line on the ground at the perimeter of the branches and two-thirds of the way toward the trunk.

Shrubs: The amount of fertilizer applied depends on the size of the shrub. For small evergreen shrubs, 2 to 4 pounds of a 5–10–5 per 100 square feet is probably satisfactory. We use this type of fertilizer at the Arnold Arboretum, and have a standard practice of applying from 3½ pounds up to as much as 18 pounds of 5–10–5 per shrub, the larger amounts being for shrubs 15 feet or more tall and as much across.

It is imperative that acid-soil plants like azaleas, rhododendrons, blueberries, and the like have acid soil of about pH 4.5 to 5.5 in which to grow. Help in maintaining this is supplied with the use of acid mulches like peat moss and pine needles. Mulches of maple and elm leaves do not have an acid reaction. Acid-soil plants in the foundation planting around a brick or stucco house may eventually suffer because, over a period of time, the splashing rain will dissolve a certain amount of lime in the mortar which may raise the soil acidity to neutral or alkaline conditions.

Occasionally limestone may be needed around azaleas and rhododendrons in which the pH has gone as low as pH 3. If this is the case, then 40 to 50 pounds of ground limestone might be added per 1,000 square feet so that the pH will be raised nearer to 4.5; then the plants will be able to obtain proper amounts of nitrogen and iron. If the soil is only slightly less acid, but still under pH 4.5, then add only half the above-mentioned amount to bring the soil nearer a pH of 4.5.

Flower Garden: Since many kinds of plants tend to make up the flower garden, it is difficult to give a specific fertilizer recommendation that is perfectly adjusted to all plants. However, using the 5–10–5 or the 6–10–4 as examples, probably 2 to 3 pounds per 100 square feet would be the amounts to try. For special plants in the flower bed the fertilizer should be applied in bands several inches wide on the soil, ringing the base of each plant.

Bulbs will respond to these fertilizers if applied at the same rate as flowers in general. Sometimes this amount is split three ways, one-third applied at time of planting, one-third when the first growth comes out of the ground, and one-third at time of flowering.

Vegetable Garden: Soil reaction is important to vegetables. For instance, we could never grow beets in our garden, could not even get them to germinate, until we learned that they require an almost neutral soil (together with asparagus, cauliflower, celery, lettuce, muskmelon, and spinach). To our acid soil we applied a special application of ground limestone to the row where beets were to be seeded, and following this practice we have had beets every year.

Organic matter is important, too, and can be applied when the garden is plowed each spring. Commercial fertilizers (5–10–5) at the rate of 3 to 5 pounds per 100 square feet, or better still at rates recommended by the local state experiment station, are about right. The smaller amount would be on heavy fertile soils and the larger amounts on light soils. In the vegetable garden the broadcast method (or the side-dressing method) is easiest on the plants, and safest.

MULCHING

A mulch is any material that can be applied to the soil surface without injuring the plants, which reduces water loss from the soil and prevents weed growth. To be practical, it should be inexpensive, easily obtained, and easy to use—although it is difficult to find materials that fulfill all three qualifications completely. Gardeners who have taken the initial time, trouble, and expense to experiment with the best mulch for their garden, find that not only is garden labor materially reduced, but that the mulches are actually beneficial to the growth of their plants.

The first advantage of using mulches is that one has to water less. Mulches reduce the amount of water lost from the soil, cutting down on the amount of watering needed both in short dry spells, and in periods of extended summer droughts.

Another important function of certain mulches is to lower the temperature of the surface soil during extremely hot weather. Soil studies with accurate temperature recordings have proved that under a two-inch mulch of sawdust, for instance, the surface of the soil may be as much as 30° cooler when air temperatures are over 100°F. This means the plant roots have a more uniform temperature in which to grow. Conversely, soil temperatures under mulches in the cold nights of early fall are raised, thus allowing the plants to grow better during this difficult period. This becomes increasingly important in the late fall and early winter, for many mulches prevent the daily freezing and thawing of the surface soil that can result in the heaving of small plants and the breaking of many of their fine feeding rootlets. The roots of plants will continue to grow in soil as long as soil moisture is available. When the soil water freezes, and hence is unavailable to the roots, they stop their growth. Hence it is obvious that a winter mulch aids in the longer growth of roots during this trying period. In the spring the reverse is true; a mulch prevents the soil from thawing out prematurely on the warm days that are followed by night temperatures that drop to well below freezing, thus preventing roots from beginning growth too soon.

For the busy gardener, however, the most obvious advantage of using a mulch is that it prevents weeds from growing—how effectively, depends on the depth and type of mulch used. There will always be certain vigorous weeds that will grow through peat moss or pine needles, for instance, but these can easily be pulled by hand. Black polyethylene film, on the other hand, prevents all weeds from growing.

Some mulching materials add substantial nutrients to the soil after they have begun to disintegrate, thus making them excellent soil amendments. A note of warning must be sounded here, however; nitrifying bacteria are much more active under a mulch, more so under some than others. This means that for the first year or so these bacteria are using up the nitrates already present in the soil at a great rate and many mulches, like sawdust, should never be applied without fertilizing heavily before putting down the mulch to make up for this initial loss. If this is not done, plants may appear yellowish and stunted during the first year of growth, which is probably the reason why many gardeners, after only one trial, have given up mulching as detrimental. However, after the first year or so, the nitrates under a mulch are greatly increased because of the dying soil bacteria, and the plants have a much better medium in which to grow. In general, in fact, mulching aids the tilth (soil texture) and this, too, is a result to be sought by all those growing plants. There are some gardeners who keep a continual mulch on their gardens at all times. One elderly lady has had a hay mulch on her garden for fourteen years, and reports the results have been excellent in every way.

Undoubtedly, then, mulching is an important aid to low maintenance gardening, as long as the right type of mulch is used for the soil and the plants being grown. The gardener, should, however, be aware of some of the dangers of incorrect mulching.

In the first place, a good mulch should not prevent air from getting to the roots of the plants that need it. Many plants, like azaleas and rhododendrons, have most of their feeding roots in the upper few inches of soil. These need moisture, of course, but they also need a certain amount of air. If a heavy mulch of sawdust were applied to a depth of six to eight inches and allowed to pack down hard, or if maple leaves were allowed to pack down, the plants would suffer from lack of air. A light application of sawdust, or a few inches of oak leaves (which do not pack down so hard as those of maple) would be an effective mulch.

Mulches, too, have different reactions when breaking down in the soil. Peat moss, pine peedles, and oak leaves may leave an acid reaction in the soil—to be desired when growing acid-soil plants like azaleas and rhododendrons, but not for all plants. Other materials, like elm and maple leaves, tend to make the soil slightly alkaline.

Mulches are excellent places for disease spores to winter over in and multiply. Because they can also harbor insects and rodents, if serious infestations of any of these pests occur, one of the first control measures is to remove and burn the mulching material. In a reasonably "clean" garden, however, one in which pests are not allowed to gain much headway without strong control measures being taken, it is usually not the mulch that is seriously at fault.

How should you go about choosing the best mulch for your garden? It is impossible to recommend two or three "best" mulches from the many available; the location, weather conditions in the area, cost, and results to be accomplished will all have to be considered. At the Arnold Arboretum in Boston, Massachusetts, for instance, we have tried many things, changing from year to year depending on the availability of mulching material. None have proved harmful to the trees and shrubs; all have proved beneficial.

Cost has been a primary consideration, as it is for most people, and cost is usually closely associated with availability. If one were mulching plants in the great corn-growing areas of the central United States, one would hardly consider using a seaweed mulch, since ground corncobs would be easily available. In areas where local peat is available, one would not go to the expense of shipping in spent hops or cocoa shells. Other factors that should be considered are: how well will the mulch withstand fire; will it scatter in the wind; what will it look like when it is in place? The best plan is to investigate the cheapest type of mulching material available locally, and to use what will do the job best.

APPEARANCE

Because every planting, whether in a public park or home garden, should be neat, a mulching material should be selected that, once applied, remains in a neat condition regardless of high winds, heavy rains, or disturbance by birds or animals. For instance, a mulch of spent hops should remain in a neat condition, but at the Arnold Arboretum there are frequently large flocks of pigeons that find some food material in the hops and continually pick them over and spread them about. Some gardeners like buckwheat hulls, claiming that they make a neat appearance in any garden and so are worth using.

WATER-RETAINING CAPACITY

This is an important point, since a natural mulch retains water. A mulch may also be of some material, like alumnium foil, or polyethylene film, that prevents water from evaporating from the soil but retains no water itself. Of course some, like peat moss and ground corn-cobs, will do both.

EASE OF APPLICATION

In pine-growing areas, pine needles are frequently used, as they are in our own garden. There are many white pines on the place, and each year we have a family project of raking up a sufficient number of the needles in the fall, when they drop from the trees, and applying them to the garden. They cost nothing, are very easily applied, and are about as serviceable as any other mulch we can obtain. They certainly are more easily applied in the diversified perennial border than mulching paper could be.

LENGTH OF TIME SERVICEABLE

It may not always be feasible or advisable to apply the same mulch (that is, pine needles, sawdust, oak leaves) year after year to the same bed. One good mulching may last for several years, and the length of time the material can be expected to perform its duty is important. Theoretically, a mulch of aluminum foil between straight beds of plants or about single trees or shrubs may be expected to last for many years; actually, the wind may rip it loose, vandals may take it, or dogs and small children may dislodge it in short order. Hence a material should be chosen that can be expected to last for several years under expected local conditions.

SUITABILITY

It is seldom advisable to apply a mulch of maple leaves to a bed of rhododendrons and azaleas because maple leaves tend to pack tightly into a thick cover, thus preventing needed air and moisture from circulating easily among the roots. Also, maple leaves can leave an alkaline reaction in the soil, detrimental, in the long run, to plants like rhododendrons and azaleas which prefer acid soil.

Another example would be the use of buckwheat hulls about small succulents that grow flat on the ground. Being black, the buckwheat hulls may absorb sufficient heat on hot summer days to injure those parts of the leaves coming in contact with them. It might be far better in this case to use crushed gray stone.

FIRE HAZARD

In public places there is always the possibility that someone may set fire to a very dry mulch. Peat moss can become powder dry in the hot summer. If a lighted cigarette stub is thrown on such material, especially in a high wind, fire will quickly result and can be extremely difficult to put out. In many home plantings the fire hazard is not an important one.

DEPTH AND TIME OF APPLICATION

In applying any mulch, one must keep in mind the fact that the roots of plants need a certain amount of pure air, as do the leaves. When soils are wet and then are so thoroughly tamped that, as they dry out, they compact into a bricklike substance without air spaces between the soil particles. This results in death or injury to the plants, merely because of lack of air to the roots.

A mulch must allow water to seep through it to the soil beneath, as well as a small amount of pure air. Some mulching materials (for instance, paper pulp) cake when they are dry, thus reducing the amount of air allowed through. Others, like coffee grounds, are so fine that if a deep mulch is applied (5 to 6 inches) little air may reach the soil below, and hence the mulch would do more harm than good when applied so thickly. Dried oak leaves, on the other hand, might be applied 5 inches thick. It really depends on the kind of material used. There are no definite rules for the exact thickness of all mulches, since even the soil itself varies, although a thicker mulch might be applied to a sandy or gravelly soil, for example, than would be necessary on a heavy clay soil. In general, however, it might be said that 2 to 3 inches of mulching material is satisfactory in many cases.

Actually, experience is the best teacher as to the

depth of mulches. They should be deep enough to kill the weeds and prevent the soil from drying out, but not so deep that they prevent pure air from reaching the surface soil.

In placing a very wet mulch like spent hops direct from the brewery on extremely hot days, one should be certain that the materials do not touch the plant stems. Being thoroughly wet, when the temperature is well above 90°F., such mulches tend to absorb heat to such an extent that they can actually kill the plant parts with which they come in contact. In applying spent hops a few years ago, we found a lilac with stems two inches in diameter at the base that had been quickly killed merely because the hops had been piled around the base of the plant on a very hot day. In applications of this nature, be certain that the mulching materials do not come within a foot or more of the stems of the plant, and thus avoid serious injury.

Some materials can harbor rodents. For instance, last summer we were using black polyethylene film as a material around the base of Oriental Crab Apples to kill quack grass. The film was brought right up to the trunk of the trees. It killed the quack grass, but in late fall it was noticed that field mice were starting to hibernate under the film. Fortunately, plenty of food was available for them until that time; but in the winter, when food becomes unavailable to them, "protecting" their runs and nests in this fashion by the use of polyethylene film is practically ensuring mouse injury to the young tree trunks. In order to prevent this, the film was removed and poison grain placed about each tree as necessary insurance against injury.

Mulching materials can be applied at any time when available. To do the most good they should be applied well before summer droughts and before the time weed growth starts actively. Also, to do the most good as a winter protection, mulches should be applied well before the time the ground freezes in the fall.

Mulching Materials

The following is a list of some of the mulching materials that have been used or are available in various parts of the country. Some are better than others; but in many situations where poor soil and summer drought combine to make growth poor, any one of these materials used as a mulch should result in better plant growth than when no mulch at all is used.

Bark: Some large lumber companies grind up the bark of certain trees, making this material available for mulching purposes. So, in certain areas of the country it is possible to obtain redwood bark, pine bark, yellow birch bark, and others. Some even go so far as to grind the materials into particles of different diameters so that one may obtain an "all-purpose," "fine grit," "pea," or "chestnut" size. Obviously these would have merit for different purposes and might well be experimented with in areas where they are economically available.

Buckwheat Hulls: A good mulch where available economically, buckwheat hulls do not pack down like leaves, but remain light and well aerated, not absorbing much water themselves, and so allowing small amounts to trickle down to the soil underneath. They are black, and take two years or more to decompose. They are best applied 1 to 2 inches in depth, a 50-pound bag covering approximately 65 square feet to a depth of one inch. Apparently weed seeds do not seem to germinate in them, but, as in other mulches, weeds can grow through them from the soil beneath. These may be spindly, and are easily pulled, if done in time.

Winds do not seem to blow buckwheat hulls, and if a water wand is used when watering, the water can easily be placed beneath the mulch. When applied this way, the entire mulch seems to raise up a bit as the water spreads over the soil, the mulch returning to its proper place after the water has soaked into the ground. With this type of watering (without pressure), and the ability of buckwheat hulls to reduce soil water loss markedly, it is unnecessary to water plants under such a mulch more than every 10 to 14 days, even in the severest of summer droughts.

Cocoa Shells: These are the shells from the cocoa bean, and have been used as soil amendments for several years. As received direct from the cocoa- or chocolate-producing plants, they are very dry, light, and easily handled. They retain moisture for long periods, and are rather slimy to walk on after about six months in the open, but the excessive leaching of potassium salts can be injurious to some plants (particularly azaleas and rhododendrons) where the material is used as a very deep mulch.

However, when used judiciously, cocoa shells apparently do little harm and considerable good. They have nearly as much nitrogen as dried chicken manure and more than dried cow manure. When applied as a mulch at a depth of not more than 2 to 3 inches, beneficial results should appear, especially from the comparatively high nitrogen. When worked into the soil, cocoa shells result in the better growth of many kinds of plants, woody and herbaceous alike. Though cocoa shells may not be the perfect mulch, they bear serious consideration if they can be obtained inexpensively, for with their high content of nitrogen, phosphoric acid, and potash (N P K) they serve the dual purpose of fertilizer and mulch.

Coffee Grounds: When coffee beans were bought at the grocery store and ground at home, it was an old-fashioned custom to place coffee grounds about garden plants and house plants, and the results were said to be excellent. Today, with instant coffee, coffee grounds are available only from the few factories processing coffee beans. Because these coffee grounds are very fine, they cake readily when exposed to the weather. This prevents normal amounts of pure air from reaching the plant roots. As a result, coffee grounds should not be used as a heavy mulch but always as a light mulch an inch or so in depth. It is doubtful if they are as beneficial to the soil as are some of the other mulching materials.

Corncobs (ground): Often a very cheap item in rural areas, it has several advantages as a mulch when applied 2 to 3 inches deep. However, because it has been found that when corn and cobs are ground together they can be fed to steers and hogs in the form of mash, this material may become scarce for mulching purposes.

Grass Clippings: Clippings from the lawn are sometimes so thick that they must be raked off. These can be used as a mulch, but if applied too green and too deep they heat up considerably, and become a dense mat through which the proper amount of air and water fail to penetrate. They may be put to a better use by being mixed with dried leaves or garden trash in the compost heap so that eventually they reach the garden soil as compost rather than as pure mulch.

Ground Tobacco Stems: In certain southern areas this material can be obtained inexpensively. It is coarse, and has not been entirely satisfactory on rose beds because the diseased leaves can fall down and become lodged in the material, thus providing new infestations of the black-spot disease. However, because it is refuse from the tobacco plant it will undoubtedly aid in the restraining of insect attacks, and so has merit as a mulch in areas where it can be obtained inexpensively.

Leaves: One of the most common of mulching materials, dead leaves are always available wherever trees and shrubs are grown. Because there has been much agitation against burning them, more and more gardeners are being trained to use them either as a winter mulch on the garden or in compost operations. The leaves from some species of trees are often better than those from certain others for mulching materials. Take, for instance, the leaves of the Sugar and Norway Maples, as well as the poplar. These pack flat and tight on the soil surface, thus excluding sufficient air and moisture when applied to any appreciable depth. This type of mulch is particularly harmful to rhododendrons and azaleas, the roots of which are close to the soil surface and need plenty of air and moisture.

On the other hand, oak leaves are ideal for mulching. They do not pack nearly as tightly as those of maple; they seem to retain a fluffy character in the mulch that is conducive to good aeration and allows ample penetration of rain water into the soil.

Some who grind leaves up in a leaf mulcher feel that the results are far superior to merely applying the dead leaves themselves. It is probably true that the cut-up material does not tend to blow as readily as large leaves do, and this may be an advantage in some places.

As noted before, as leaves from some species of plants decompose (notably oaks and pines), they tend to leave an acid reaction, one of the reasons why they are the best kind of mulching material for azaleas and rhododendrons; while those from others (notably elm) may leave an alkaline reaction. It should always be kept in mind that there is little about the garden more combustible than dried leaves and that they will blow away in a high wind. The larger the leaves, the more unsightly the general aspect of the mulch. If these hazards are not serious in the garden, use the leaves as a mulch by all means.

Peanut Shells: These make another good mulch in areas close to the southeastern parts of the United States where peanuts are grown and processed. They are light and easily handled, and some tests in the production of greenhouse tomatoes show that they are well suited for mulching this crop in the greenhouse. In fact, shipping charges were so low (because of the light weight) that they have been sold in Massachusetts and Ohio in recent years for use in growing commercial tomato crops. It is conceivable that if they are not completely free of peanuts, if used outdoors they might prove a great attraction to rodents. Here again, availability and cost are the chief factors in their use. Since they contain .95 percent nitrogen, they do have some fertilizing value.

Peat Moss: The merits of peat moss are well known, and it is probably one of the most widely used mulching materials, although it is certainly not the least expensive. It is impossible to make specific statements about contents, since there are all kinds of peat in use. The least expensive are those that come from the local peat bogs, frequently containing considerable amounts of soil. The most uniform are those that have been processed and come from large deposits in Michigan, Canada, or Europe. The gardener with only a small garden is usually willing to pay premium prices to obtain uniform material of a light brown color that looks well after it has been applied and contains relatively few (if any) weed seeds.

It has merit when mixed with certain types of soils, but woe to the gardener who thinks that because a little amount is good for the soil, a large amount can be better! When completely dry, it takes an extremely long time for a large amount of dry peat to absorb moisture, the reason why young plants planted in almost 100 percent peat may die in a long drought where plants in the normal soil nearby may not. The small amounts of rain in a dry summer fail to soak through a great depth of dry peat, although they may do so in the soil. Mixed with a goodly amount of soil, however, peat moss does not become such a hazard as only peat alone.

Native peats can be bought by the bag, the bushel, or the truckload, while processed peats are usually dried and pressed into bales for easy shipping. Bales are available in different sizes, some containing 4 cubic feet and weighing about 55 pounds, others 6 cubic feet and weighing about 95 pounds, and others 7½ or 8 cubic feet. To estimate the amount of this material needed, a 95-pound bale of pressed peat, broken up and well moistened, will cover approximately 300 square feet of soil surface in a layer one inch thick.

Some peats have 98 percent organic matter and have been advertised as "lasting in soil service up to ten years." This is probably an optimistic estimate, but it shows that they cannot be expected to break down very soon. They have been estimated to hold anywhere from 600 to 1200 percent water when compared on a dry-weight basis, so their water-absorbing qualities are high indeed. But, as noted above, completely dry peat absorbs water very slowly, so that it is best to moisten peat well before it is applied to dry soil. It is usually acid in reaction, 3.6 to 6.8 pH being the normal range.

It is suggested that peat-moss mulches be applied from 1 to 3 inches deep, depending on the reason for using the mulch. The deeper mulch would of course tend to keep more weeds from growing, although even at the three-inch depth there will be some that eventually have to be pulled out after a period. During winter, when used as a protective mulch, an even deeper application of up to four inches might well be in order.

Pine Needles: A great part of the gardening public lives in areas where pine needles are available, and these make excellent and often very inexpensive mulching materials, especially in areas where they may be had merely for the raking and hauling. They are acid in reaction and hence ideal for use on acid-loving plants like azaleas and rhododendrons. The particular gardener will note that there is a difference in quality of mulch made by needles from the different species of pine. White Pine, for instance, has soft flexible needles that make a very fine mulch, while those of Red Pine are more coarse and may not deteriorate for three or four years. White Pine needles could be used in mulching the smaller plants and Red Pine in mulching the shrubs and the trees.

In general, pine needles do not absorb much moisture themselves, but let the rain quickly filter down through to the soil, one of the reasons why they are so good for the surface-rooted azaleas and rhododendrons that need air as well as moisture about their roots. Weed seeds also will have a difficult time germinating in a pine mulch, especially during dry weather when the mulch dries out.

Another advantage of the pine needles is the fact that they can be easily lifted with rake or fork. If weeds do grow through, as they will, a prompt lifting of the mulch with a pitchfork, and then laying the needles down again in the same place but covering the weeds growing from the soil, can aid materially in discouraging them from too much growth.

Still another advantage is the fact that these mulches can be easily raked off in the spring, if desired, piled, and then used later where needed. We have been using a White Pine mulch at the same place in the garden, renewed every other year or so, for as much as eight years, with excellent results. Commercial fertilizers applied to the mulch surface are quickly washed into the soil by rain or water from the hose, and so they are not held in the mulch to encourage root growth above the soil level. If the soil becomes too acid because pine needles are used continuously on the garden, sufficient lime can easily be applied and washed through the needles to the soil, bringing the soil pH up to the desired level. Needless to say, this also is an excellent qualification for pine mulches in the garden.

If applied three or four inches deep, pine needles act as a splendid insulation on the soil against high temperatures in the summer. This, combined with the crisscross effect of the needles, resulting in good soil aeration, makes pine needles one of the best of mulching materials.

Polyethylene Film: Science has provided horticulture with this excellent material that can be used for all kinds of purposes in storing, shipping, and propagating plants. Its value stems from the fact that gases like nitrogen, carbon dioxide, oxygen, and others can pass through it without much difficulty, but water and water vapor cannot. The clear film is of no value as a mulch, merely because sunlight passes readily through it, and weeds grow almost as well underneath it as they do in the open soil.

However, black polyethylene has all the properties of the clear plastic except for the fact that it excludes the light. Used as a mulch it has possibilities, but also one great drawback—it will hold the moisture in the soil, but it will not let water into the soil unless special steps, which will be described later, are taken. Experiments show that this mulching material if handled properly will last as a mulch for many years. It comes in several thicknesses, but for mulching purposes a thickness of .015 inches is probably satisfactory.

Normally, water travels by capillarity in the soil, both up and down and sidewise, but the movement from side to side is very slow. Consequently, in very dry periods, with a large area covered by this film, it is understandable that the soil can be deficient of moisture underneath it, no matter how often water is applied from sprinkler or hose. This difficulty can be overcome simply, in either of two ways: If hose watering is desired, merely see to it that the hose is held for a considerable length of time at the base of the plant where it comes through the film, thus allowing water to spread around underneath the film and to all parts of the area, eventually soaking down into the soil. The chief difficulty with this method is that it creates special work and the technique can easily be faulty, that is, not enough water or not often enough.

By far the simplest method is to use an ice pick or screwdriver to poke holes in the film after it is in place on the ground, especially in the lower spots to which the water drains. If the holes are at about six-inch intervals, possibly closer in the depressions, sufficient water will be allowed through to keep the soil moist in all but the driest of summers. For prized, newly planted specimens, a combination of these two practices, together with checking on the soil under the polyethylene during the dry periods, will suffice.

Another advantage in using the polyethylene film is that it will quickly kill the grass over which it is placed. Grass is always an important competitor of the newly planted tree or shrub for soil moisture and nutrients. At the end of the summer, or in the fall if need be, the plastic film can be lifted and stored for use again the next year, but this only creates work and it is far more satisfactory to leave it around the plant permanently.

Salt Hay, Hay, Straw: These three materials have always been used for mulching, especially with agricultural crops and fruits, but to be effective they should be 8 to 10 inches deep. They are still used to some extent in the garden, but their chief difficulties are that they are bulky, often unkempt, and can bring into the garden a large amount of weed seeds. Also, they can harbor mice. For winter use as protecting materials they still have their place, but in most gardens, especially the small, well-kept ones, other neater mulching materials are usually used. However, in mulching fruit trees and small fruits there is nothing better or more economical. Many experiments over the years have definitely proved that, after the first three years, nitrates are considerably higher under the hay mulch; soil moisture is raised; growth is better; and yield is better than those of trees grown under cultivation. The rodent hazard must be met forthrightly, and a vigorous program of placing wire mesh about the base of the tree trunks and placing poison grain about the trees to combat the mice should yield favorable results. In other words, heavy hay mulching is a satisfactory system of orchard management, the chief regulating factor being the cost of application.

Sawdust: At many lumber mills about the country sawdust can be obtained at very little cost, and these sources of cheap mulching material should not be overlooked. The type of tree from which the sawdust comes makes little difference in the long run, whether it is pine, oak, maple, or birch. As a mulch, applied at a depth of about two inches, it will aid markedly in reducing weed growth, in preventing water evaporation from the soil, and in reducing soil temperatures during the hot summer months.

Many studies have been made with various kinds of sawdust. The most important fact to keep in mind is that for the good of the plants a generous application of a complete fertilizer should be made to the soil before the sawdust is applied.

There is always a reduced amount of available nitrogen in the soil under sawdust, especially the first year after application. This has been clearly noted in many experiments, resulting in reduced growth of plants when compared with those having no mulch. This is also true with other mulching materials, but especially with sawdust. The defect can be offset with the application of fertilizer *before* mulching. If applied after the sawdust is in place, the nutrients may be held in the sawdust and hence may be unavailable to the plant roots for a long period.

Experiments with mulching commercial blueberry plantings have proved that a two-inch sawdust mulch (if preceded by an application of fertilizer) increases yield over a three-year period. No great differences were found between hardwood and softwood sawdust, except that the latter does not tend to break down so quickly. Nor are there any harmful effects (to the plants) from the resins in the softwood sawdust.

After several years, when the sawdust has deteriorated, it can be worked into the soil as a means of "soil improvement." However, in the heavily planted perennial garden where soil digging is not advisable, merely applying more sawdust is all that is necessary. As it breaks down and becomes humus, it serves its purpose in the surface soil, and more applied on top—if not too deep—fulfills the purpose of a continual mulch.

Spent Hops: Spent hops have proved quite successful. The Arnold Arboretum has been fortunate in being comparatively near two breweries having an ample supply of spent hops to dispose of and can obtain them merely by hauling at regular intervals. These hops had the following analysis:

Water	87.67%
Nitrogen	.40
Organic matter	11.49
Ash	.49
pH	4.8

This material was used for over ten years. There are several drawbacks, for it is obvious that since they are obtained from a brewery they have an extremely high water content. (For every 238 pounds of dry material, we were hauling 1,740 pounds of water.) They also have an objectionable odor which is noticeable on a warm day but disappears in about two weeks after application. Third, spent hops attract pigeons and rodents.

The merits of spent hops far outweigh their disadvantages when used as a mulch. Because they are wet when first applied, they do not blow away on a windy day. And, what is more important, even when dry (after weeks of drought) these hops will not burn appreciably. Time and again it has been noticed that plants mulched with spent hops have not been injured by surrounding grass fires. The fire has burned up to the edge of the mulch, and stopped. Because of this, we have actually used spent hops for mulching as a fire preventive.

Although slightly more acid than our soil, the spent-hops mulch has been applied to practically all the kinds of trees and shrubs in the Arboretum except a dozen of the outstanding lime-requiring plants. We have seen no ill effects from their use except when applied on days preceding high temperatures and when the hops are heaped around the base of a small tree trunk or shrub with numerous stems. When this occurs and the temperatures are high, the material does heat noticeably and can kill stems several inches in diameter. Hence, the only precaution to be taken in applying this material is to keep it a foot or so away from the basal stems of trees and shrubs.

The spent-hops mulch is applied 4 to 6 inches thick and lasts about two years before disintegrating appreciably. Quack grass and other vigorous weeds will eventually grow through it, but this mulch is ideal for conserving soil water and has necessarily been applied at all seasons of the year without injury to plants.

Sugar Cane: This material has been offered by some of the sugar mills in the South after the cane stalks have been pressed and subjected to very high temperatures. Usually it is ground—it has a pH value of from 4.5 to 5.2, has a water-holding capacity of over 340 percent, and supposedly decomposes into almost pure humus. Recommendations for a mulch suggest that it be applied about two inches thick on the soil surface. This is another mulching material for extensive use in areas in the sugar-producing parts of the country.

Wood Chips, Wood Shavings: With the advent of brush-chipping machines, wood chips have become a very important mulching material, especially in large parks and arboretums where there is always pruning work being done. They are applied usually about 2 to 3 inches deep, but here, as with sawdust, it is advisable to give the soil an ample application of high-nitrogen fertilizer or complete fertilizer before the chips are applied. They last at least two years, sometimes longer, birch chips of course disintegrating before pine and oak chips.

They are coarse, allowing for the easy wetting of the soil from light rains. They do not burn readily, will not blow (like much lighter shavings), and go a long way in conserving soil moisture. At the same time, because they are coarse they allow good soil aeration. They should be used wherever available, but because they are heavy, shipping costs are too high to make it economically feasible to ship them any great distances. If a local supply is available, the chances are that it will pay to use this material as a mulch. We have found coarse wood chips lasting (as a mulch on the ground) at least three years. It is unwise to use elm wood in the making of the chips since such material could conceivably aid in spreading the Dutch Elm disease.

Wood shavings burn more readily and are blown by high winds more easily than wood chips, but if neither of these drawbacks proves serious then they too can be used as mulching material.

These are only some of the mulching materials available. Others occasionally used are aluminum foil, sprayed asphalt, cranberry vines, fiber glass, gravel or crushed stone, walnut shells, roofing papers, seaweed, and ground banana stalks. It should be pointed out, however, that it might be inadvisable to use new or untried materials for mulching purposes until they have been tried or assessed by some of the state agricultural experiment stations. In general, materials that conserve soil moisture and at the same time allow sufficient soil aeration prove satisfactory, for these act as valued time savers in weed control for the busy gardener. If, later, they decompose and add essential chemicals to the soil, so much the better, for then they serve the dual purpose of mulch and fertilizer as well.

HERBICIDES

Chemical weed killers should head every list of labor-saving devices for the gardener. Now no one need kneel on the ground, laboriously digging out each weed in the lawn, for there is a chemical spray that with two or three applications will eradicate a major part of the broad-leaved weeds from the lawn. Poison ivy, being one of the most pernicious of woody weeds in eastern gardens and woodlands, can also be killed by chemical sprays. Unwanted saplings or "brush" along the roadside, the woods walk, the stone fence, or under the cross-country power lines has been effectively and cheaply killed for many years now by proper spray procedures. Most stumps can also be effectively killed merely by spraying them with a highly concentrated chemical herbicide of the right kind.

There are so many herbicides being offered and the publicity about them makes weed elimination sound so easy, that the homeowner who makes one application (possibly at the wrong time) is very disappointed if all the weeds are not killed at once. In fact, his first failure may be responsible for his treating all herbicides with great skepticism. They must be properly used at the proper time, and when this is done they can well be among the best labor-savers and money-savers in garden maintenance. In general, chemical herbicides can be divided into three groups: those that are selective in killing only certain types of plant growth; those that kill or at least seriously injure all types of plant growth; and finally those that, when applied to newly cultivated soil, kill the germinating weed seeds.

Selective Herbicides

This is by far the most important group, for here are those that will kill the broad-leaved weeds in the lawn without injuring the grass, or the woody seedlings and brush without injuring the grass. Recently, herbicides have been developed that when applied to certain grasses will kill those grasses without apparently injuring the woody plants close by. Some have been found to be adaptable for use in keeping down the weed population in carrots, strawberries, or asparagus, and most recently we were most pleased to find one that was supposed to be effective in killing the grass in raspberries without injuring the raspberries!

The 2,4-D [2,4-dichlorophenoxy acetic acid] sprays are highly volatile, once applied. They are used chiefly to kill broad-leaved lawn weeds and do not injure grass. They should be applied on a mild day when there is no wind, for their injurious effect to trees and shrubs is now very well known, since severe injury to trees can occur when even a slight drift of wind sends some spray on the foliage. One young arborist, supposing the spray tank filled with material for killing insects, sprayed the trees and shrubs on a property only to be sued shortly thereafter when all the plants started to die. Actually, his tank had been full of 2,4-D weed killer. These materials are so highly toxic to broad-leaved plants that it is always advisable to keep a separate sprayer for this purpose, good protective insurance in using any weed killer, but especially those containing 2,4-D.

When 2,4-D sprays are applied to the lawn, the nozzle should be close to the grass and extreme care should be taken that the spray does not hit shrubs or trees. If, on a windy day, a gust of wind blows the spray into a tree close by, that tree will show severe injury within a few days. In fact, the mere evaporation of heavy doses of this material to herbaceous weeds under trees or shrubs has been known to seriously injure the woody plant parts growing above but not touched with the spray. Extreme caution must be taken, especially in the period of late spring when all growth is lush and succulent, for injury can be expected to certain oversensitive plants like *Malus ioensis* 'Plena' within fifty feet of where the material has been used, depending on the direction of the wind, even after application. In fact, the odor has lasted about an area for as long as sixty days, so that it is obvious why oversensitive plants may be injured even though they are not touched with the actual spray at spraying time.

There are several methods of applying herbicides to the lawn. They can be mixed with the proper amount of water and then used from a hand-pump sprayer for spot application. Or they can be applied (according to directions that come with the material) in a hand sprayer which is attached to the garden hose. If there are not too many broad-leaved weeds in the lawn, the 2,4-D herbicide can be mixed with the proper amount of water and carried around in a bucket. It is applied by simply using a stick to which a sponge is atttached and dabbing the weeds with the wetted sponge. Finally, there have been three-foot bars of wax manufactured containing 2,4-D and these are merely pulled over the weedy spots in the lawn on a hot sunny day when the temperatures are above 80°F.

In using herbicides one should know that certain ones (2,4-D) are volatile and leave no residue in the soil, but others like "Amazine" (ammonium sulfamate), or "Ammate" and "Simazine" do leave a residue in the soil for varying amounts of time, and the accumulation of this residue over a period of years after repeated applications can result in unexpected injury to various plants. Also, if these are applied on a bank, followed by heavy rainfalls, injury can occur to plants wherever the run-off from that bank occurs—sometimes a hundred feet or more away from the spot where the material was originally applied. So, know the herbicides you choose to use and their residual characteristics, and use them accordingly.

KILLING GRASSES

There are materials on the market that kill certain kinds of grasses without injuring woody plants close by. We have been most interested in this particular problem in the Arnold Arboretum, and probably everyone is who tries to grow plants in an area where Witch Grass thrives. We set out young woody plants on the grounds, digging a sizable hole and of course placing the sod removed in the bottom of the hole to rot and thus afford nutrients for the young plant. However, in a very few months, unless we mulch the plant or hoe about it (which is always expensive) Witch Grass grows in vigorously. It is not long before this is competing for moisture and nutrients with the young plants, and sometimes it can actually kill the young plant that is not properly established. Dalapon sprayed on the grass kills the grass but does not injure the plant.

Crab Grass is always a bad lawn weed, for which there now are effective controls (materials now named "Balax," "Bandane," "Dacthal," DSMA, MSMA, etc.). Annual Bluegrass is controlled with "Betasan." "Silvex" is another material especially effective in controlling buttercup, chickweed, dandelion, Ground Ivy, pennywort, plantain and Poison Ivy, among others. Another chemical currently available under the trade name of "Casoron G4" (a dichlobenil weed and grass killer) at this time of writing is one of the best weed and grass killers around established woody plants. It is a white granulated powder, applied in November after the ground has frozen. We have used the current material at the rate of 1 ounce per 22 square feet and it has killed all the grass and weeds in the nursery row for nearly a full year. Supposedly it is non-cumulative in the soil, but recently there have been instances of its accumulation in the soil after being applied annually for many years in the same plot.

These are just current examples of chemicals available for specific weed-killing jobs, but they must be sought out and used according to directions. Careful compliance with the remarks on the can or package will forestall serious trouble. I remember all too well my experience in first trying out a new Witch-Grass killer. I had been struggling with the Witch Grass about my grapes for years, and welcomed the opportunity of a spray that would eliminate the pest easily. I applied the material at the proper time and in the proper way, but on arriving at the end of the row found I still had half a tank full of spray. Being of a thrifty nature, and anxious to do a thorough job, I went back over the same row with the remainder of the spray. We were very pleased in the next few days when the Witch Grass began to die, but not so satisfied when, six weeks later, the grapes began to die from the material that had been applied at twice its recommended strength!

STUMPS

Stump killing is very simple: merely mix a goodly amount of concentrated "brush killer" (the current rates are 3 pints of a commercial brush killer in 10 gallons of fuel oil, kerosene or discarded crankcase oil) and brush it or spray it generously on the stump in question. Most commonly used brush killers now contain 2,4,5-TP [2-2,4,5-trichlorophenoxy propionic acid]. This can be done at any time of the year, but it is best to do it immediately after the stump has been cut. It is advisable to daub the material on the sides of the trunk left exposed above the ground as well as on the cut surface. It is a simple matter to clean out a few woody seedlings in the garden by merely cutting them down and then with a paintbrush and a can of mixed brush killer daub the stubs generously with this material. They will eventually die. This approach eliminates the necessity of digging out the roots. Also, for a fee, arborists have heavy machines to chip down stumps to inches below the ground line, thus saving the expensive digging out and removal of the whole stump.

PRE-EMERGENCE SPRAYS

Pre-emergence sprays can be applied to the soil, after it has been cleaned of weeds, to prevent the germination of new weed seeds. Some of these are effective for several months and have merit where the woody plants, even though small, are well established. There are many of these chemicals available, some of them harmful to certain woody plants but not to others. As far as the home gardener is concerned, he should approach this group with a completely experimental point of view. At the present time there is no material available that can be sprayed up and down the rows of the newly planted vegetable garden which will kill the germinating weed seeds but which, on the other hand, will allow all the vegetable seeds to germinate and grow properly.

BRUSH KILLERS

The current "brush killers" usually contain a mixture of 2,4-D [2,4-dichlorophenoxy acetic acid] and 2,4,5-TP [2-2,4,5-trichlorophenoxy propionic acid]. This combination has been found to be more effective in killing woody plants than either chemical alone. These materials are finding wide use in spraying areas along highways, railroad right-of-ways, and the brush beneath power lines. The best time to apply brush killers is while the plants are still in active growth during the late spring, when the leaves are young and succulent. When foliage applications are made in the late summer, the percentage of killing is often not so great.

Brush killers can also be mixed with fuel oil or kerosene and sprayed on the basal parts of woody brush when it is dormant. However, it is essential to cover *all sides* of the stems to get a good killing. Sometimes a good approach is to use the dormant spray in late fall or winter, followed up in late spring with the foliar spray to kill any shoots that have grown in the interim. Such spraying usually gives excellent control.

It might well be that the best time-saver would be to adopt a philosophical attitude toward many weeds. Take, for instance, those in the lawn. The perfectionist wants to rid his lawn of every plant that differs from the kinds of grass he is growing, and is willing to spend hours and hours in so doing. I knew of a small group of dwellings in which there was one such individual who spent all his spare time weeding his lawn while his neighbors were out golfing and doing numerous other things they wanted to do. A cursory examination of the lawns in front of these houses showed the comparative results in a prominent way. Those with poor lawns were continually being urged to follow the excellent example set by the man with the perfect lawn. After several months of trying attempts to do so, the heads of the other households sent a delegation to the enthusiastic weeder to ask him to please cease from attaining such perfection in his lawn so that they could spend their spare time doing other things.

To some, a few dandelions in front of the house is a challenge; to others they are merely a spot of yellow. A little effort with 2,4-D or a digging tool can eliminate most of these weeds, but the gardener who has learned how to live with such things, eradicating the worst if and when there is a little time—but only if and when he chooses—is the one who will get the most pleasure out of life. In the flower garden, and possibly even in the vegetable garden, one can practice weed control more effectively with mulches.

The low-maintenance-minded gardener had best study his specific needs himself and then investigate the weed killers currently available. Using the wrong one, or the right one in the wrong way, could let him in for some decidedly high-maintenance replacement problems!

PESTICIDES

Because of the general interest in air, soil, and water pollution, there are an increasing number of regulations concerning the use of pesticides. The gardener using pesticides should be certain that they are cleared with regard to state and federal laws and, if uncertain, should check with the state Pesticide Board or the local County Agricultural Extension Agent. The right pesticide, applied at the right time, is the quickest way to control or eliminate the pest concerned. It is not necessary to have a whole closet filled with sprays and dusts for specific pests, since some like Malathion, easily control a number of different kinds of pests when applied at the right time. In fact one might well obtain a general purpose mixture, which is usually a wettable powder or dust containing one or more insecticides and fungicides, and is used to control several common pests. New formations and mixtures are continually appearing, some in the form of aerosol cans. A good way to be sure you are using the right pesticide at the right time is to obtain the most recent recommendations from your state agricultural experiment station. Most gardens have similar common-pest problems, and the majority of these can be controlled with easily available pesticides or general pesticide mixtures.

CHEMICALS THAT KILL ALL GROWTH

There are some of these on the market. Their use is usually restricted to the weeds and grass that come up in the roadway or between the bricks on the terrace or in the walk—in places where it does not matter if a poison is retained by the soil. Most of the weed killers already discussed do not leave toxic materials in the soil for any length of time. This group of chemicals may well leave toxic residues in the soil that would not be harmful in gutters or roadways, but certainly would be decidedly harmful in garden soil. There are also other materials like Stoddard's Solvent or Sovasol (a cleaning fluid) which when applied to grass kills only the above-ground portions, not the roots. It will kill foliage of woody plants in a few hours' time, but not the woody stems that send out new leaves later. Its best use is for the control of annual weeds, especially purslane. The best time to spray these fast-growing summer pests is when they are only a quarter-inch high, and Sovasol kills them within a few hours. It is highly volatile and leaves no toxic material in the soil.

There are precautions to be taken with weed killers, as everyone knows who has considered using them. Take as an example the eradication of Poison Ivy. If it is growing in the open field, there are several quickly applied "killer" compounds that prove satisfactory. However, when the Poison Ivy is growing in shrubbery or under trees one must remember the fact that roots of other plants are underneath those of the Poison Ivy or intermingled with them, and a soaking of the soil with a destructive weed killer can damage both types of plants. Even when the foliage is supposed to be merely "slightly moistened" with the weed killer, damage can result to the roots of other plants, as we found out the hard way several years ago when we were first trying out one of the experimental materials.

The plot we selected for trial was in the woods under some fine young pine trees with trunks six inches in diameter. The chemical killed the Poison Ivy all right, even with just a hasty moistening of the foliage, but six weeks later we noticed that the White Pines were severely damaged, and later they died. We repeated the experiment elsewhere with the same results, and so have never again used this material as a weed killer in areas where we want selective killing of only certain types of plants.

Many a gardener will find among the available weed killers some that are selective which he can use for a particular purpose, and they will act as time-savers. One should obtain the latest information on such materials from the nearest state experiment station, where impartial tests are usually conducted. Also, there are always articles covering the uses of new weed killers in horticultural publications.

CHEMICALS TO PREVENT GROWTH

Recently work has been done at several of the state experiment stations with chemicals that are supposed to prevent or retard growth. Wouldn't it be wonderfully convenient to have some soluble chemical that could be sprayed on plant material to "arrest" growth at some particular stage? For instance, let a lawn grow to just the right height and proper degree of luxuriousness, then spray to keep it that way for the remainder of the season.

Such chemical solutions may be forthcoming at some future date. However, those tried up to the present time, chiefly maleic hydrazide and alpha-naphthalene-acetic acid, cannot be used promiscuously on all plants with the same results. Some have "arrested" growth for a period of anywhere from a week to several months. However, the results have varied greatly. Current weather conditions can affect the results materially; in addition, the aftereffects of repeated sprays of the same materials on the same plants or the same area of soil may have injurious effects.

Consequently, as far as short-cutting certain garden operations like pruning or cutting grass, it is inadvisable to depend on the chemicals that have been used experimentally for this purpose up to the present.

Chemicals have been used to control the flowering and fruit set of some kinds of fruit trees; to destroy the blossoms of the fruiting forms of the Ginkgo, Honeylocust, Horse-chestnut and ash so that the objectionable fruits will not be formed. It was found with lilacs, however, that in order to apply the spray at the proper time, the flower blossoms would have to be prematurely injured. Chemicals have also been used to inhibit the sprouting of plants held in storage for lengthy periods. Since work with these materials is still in the experimental stages, one should obtain the latest information from the nearest agricultural experiment station before attempting to use them. Application must be made at certain definite strengths and at specific times for specific plants if desired results are to be obtained, or actual injury, sometimes serious, can be done to the plants.

KILLING POND WEEDS

There are times when water lilies become naturalized in ponds and grow so vigorously that they completely cover the water surface, becoming pests instead of ornamentals. Cattails and arrowheads also can become established in the border of a shallow pond, and quickly take over to such an extent that they become most objectionable. Sodium arsenite has been used to rid pools of these pests without injuring the fish.

The current brush killers (2,4-D plus 2,4,5-PT including Dowpon) have also proved successful, used at the same rates of dilution recommended for killing brush. These are lightly sprayed on the exposed above-water surfaces of the plant parts during the active growing season. It is most important to spray in the late spring or early summer when the plants are growing actively, for succulent, vigorous, growing leaves absorb the materials better and result in a better kill. Using the same material late in the summer may have few apparent results, but timely applications can eradicate many water plants that become pests.

Large ponds have been successfully sprayed by helicopter. Two pounds of acid equivalent, 2,4-D, and 2 pounds of acid equivalent 2,4,5-PT are used in a one gallon mixture, and this in turn was mixed with 2 gallons of water and sprayed from the helicopter at the rate of 3 gallons of this mixture per acre. When this spray was applied in early summer, excellent control of water lilies was obtained by October.

Small pools covered with algae (and without fish) can be "cleaned" with the use of potassium permanganate at 4 parts per million of water, or copper sulfate at the rate of 2 pounds per million gallons of water. Though this will certainly kill any fish in the pool, and may be strong enough to injure water lilies present, it has its value for pool cleaning.

However, before using any of these materials on ponds, especially those with outlets to streams, one should check with the local Pest Control Board to ascertain the restrictions against treating such pools with chemicals. Many boards have strict rules now as the result of the recent water pollution laws that have been enacted in many states.

LABOR-SAVING MACHINES

The individual desires of the gardener as well as his needs, true and fancied, will govern the types of garden machinery that are accumulated over the years. The man who enjoys gardening for the fun and exercise he gets out of it will have few gadgets—few unless he also happens to be afflicted with an inquisitive mechanical twist, in which event he may eventually buy them all. Of course, the size of the garden determines whether or not large expenditures should be made for complicated machinery that is used infrequently. New types and makes of machines appear every year, and one has only to read the ads in the major horticultural magazines to know what such machines are and where they can be obtained.

Any machine reduces hand labor, but the main criterion is whether it stays in working order long enough, without repair, to pay for its purchase price. Thereby hangs many a sad tale, but each individual has to cross this mechanical-obstacle bridge some time or other, and whether he buys more than he can use is not a problem we can deal with here. There are only a few things that can be said in this connection.

Lawn Mowers: The popular types now being used in the greatest numbers are those with horizontally revolving blades. These can be dangerous if safety measures are not taken, but they come in so many sizes and models that anything from grass to seedling trees and shrubs nearly an inch in diameter can be cut with them. They are also ideal for cutting low ground covers and can do the job at a higher level than the old-fashioned reel-type mowers. Another advantage is that keeping them sharpened for clean cutting is relatively simple, since all that is needed is a file, emery wheel, or grindstone. The reel type of mower, on the other hand, is comparatively difficult to sharpen and keep properly adjusted.

However, in buying a mower with a rotary type of blade one should be certain to obtain a machine that does not leave the cut grass in one small line or strip, but rather has enough power to blow the grass clippings and distribute them over a wide area. The reason for this is simple, but it is one I had to learn by firsthand experience.

When one owns a rotary-blade mower, the tendency is to let the grass grow taller and to mow less frequently. When the heavy clippings are deposited in a thin line by the mower, they may be so dense that they kill the living grass underneath. When this happens, bare spots quickly occur, followed by the intrusion of Crab Grass and other lawn weeds. Thus a beautiful lawn can be ruined in a few short weeks. This actually happened to ours, and the situation was augmented by the fact that the lawn was inadvertently fertilized (it really did not need fertilizer), thus making the grass clippings heavier. The use of a reel-type mower would have helped to spread the clippings evenly, as would some type of blowing mechanism with a rotary blade mower.

Labor can also be eliminated if the grass is not fertilized too much or too often. Some people like to maintain a perfect lawn of green grass, and in order to do so must fertilize, water, and cut frequently. There are many situations where such a lawn adds to the overall landscape picture, and the time and money spent in its maintenance are considered well spent. On the other hand, there are lawns not in this classification; there are areas where green grass is appropriate and necessary, but as long as it is green and not too tall, and as long as it does not die out in spots, it serves its purpose well. Such lawns need not be fertilized too frequently or cut too often. The rotary mowers are ideal for cutting these, since many of them can be adjusted to cut easily at higher levels than one would ordinarily use to cut with a reel-type mower. Lawn sweepers and riding sulkies are only a few of the mower "accessories" we are continually being urged to buy to make this one garden chore easier.

Speaking from experience, I have seen our large lawn in its ups and downs over the last twenty-five years. When our children were at home to mow it, it was sometimes cut too often, merely so an energetic youngster could earn a little extra spending money. As they grew older it became more and more of a chore, regardless of the cash reward at the end of the job. Now that I am left with it, and it takes all of two hours to cut, naturally I am experimenting with all sorts of heights at which it may be cut, and with machines as well, to see how long the grass can grow and then be cut without making raking a necessity. Needless to say, under this regime it has not been fertilized for many years, and when summer drought brings out dead spots it is merely a matter of interest to note how long it takes for grass to grow back in again once the rains come. It is not what many would call a perfect lawn, but it is green most of the time, and it is cut.

Leaf Shredders: The restrictions on burning in the open, now forced upon many communities in order to alleviate air pollution, bring up the problem of what to do with dead leaves in the fall. For years it has been recommended that these be placed in the compost heap to be used later for soil improvement. Now, many a homeowner is forced to do so. Many types of leaf shredders are available that are great aids in doing this work. One we bought was advertised as being able to reduce 20 bushels of dry leaves into one bushel—and it did just that. Instead of using all the shredded material on a compost pile, we put a two-inch layer of shredded leaves about the plants in the garden in the fall, at the time they were shredded. This mulch aided materially in bringing plants through the winter in better condition, and as they rotted during the following year, they greatly improved the soil. Shredded material left over from this operation was put in a compost pile at the back of the garden together with weeds and lawn clippings. This operation has greatly improved the growth of all our plants.

Brush Chippers: Some leaf shredders are powerful enough to chip brush as well as leaves. If there is need of much brush chipping each year, these larger machines might be considered. One should, however, carefully estimate the amount of brush he will have each year, as well as the size of the branches, to determine whether a large machine, that is pretty heavy and hard to move around and store, is going to be worth the expenditure.

Fertilizer Spreaders: If the lawn is to be fertilized, a simple, pushable, fertilizer spreader is a good investment. They are available with standard calibrations for most of the standard fertilizers.

Soil Cultivators: There are many garden gadgets for working the soil, both man-operated and machine-operated. Certainly the right machine can eliminate a great deal of hand labor. This is especially true with the mechanical rotary hoes. The larger the garden area that needs to be redug each year, the more important a machine becomes. It must be kept in mind that almost every community has such machines for hire, with or without operators. Years ago, when the suburban homeowner planned his vegetable garden, he would have to make arrangements with the nearest farmer to have the garden plowed by a team of horses. Today the rotary hoe takes their place and saves all the spading and digging and hoeing.

Other Garden Machines: The small, engine-operated dusters and sprayers available can deteriorate fast unless cared for properly. The same is true of fertilizer spreaders. Small chain saws do make work easy on the tree-covered suburban grounds, and many a gardener purchases one even though careful consideration would show him that he did not have enough work to justify the expense of buying one. Here again it might be cheaper to rent a machine or even have the work done; but chain saws, regardless of whether they are operated by electricity or gasoline engines, do make work easier and faster.

If one desires a careful edge kept on the perennial border, there are inexpensive gasoline or electrically operated edgers available. It takes a little practice to keep the edge straight with these machines, but once the task is mastered one can edge a border or walk using far less physical exertion than with the spade and hoe.

Clipping the hedge need not be so strenuous either. Electric shears are available, operated with the house current. These mechanically operated shears can be used on certain types of hedges that do not grow too vigorously. These tools are assets, and save the sore arms that result from a few hours' effort with the old-fashioned hedge shears. Better still, of course, would be to use hedge plants that grow only to a certain height. More will be said elsewhere about these most desirable plants (see pages 136–140).

Wheelbarrows or garden carts made of aluminum save extra exertion and should be bought wherever they can be used appropriately.

There is always a machine-minded addict who wants to sell himself a bill of goods. This is the man who finally invests in a combination tractor affair that will dig the garden and cultivate it, that will mow the grass and at the same time pull a riding sulky, that will plow the snow on walk or driveway (the advertisement never mentioned how much snow or how heavy), and that will also saw wood. Well, there are such machines, but the smaller they are, the less they will do all these things effectively. One should thoroughly understand his own needs, and then be certain the machine he is considering can do the job or jobs effectively, before he tries to short-cut some needed exercise by yielding to the machine age completely.

The individual who wants to reduce hand labor by the use of mechanical devices can have a field day deciding which machines to purchase. Ultimately a realization of his own ability (or inability) to do the work will dictate to him what form his purchases should take.

VACATIONING HOUSE PLANTS

All house plants are not amenable to being given a vacation outdoors unattended during the summer, but fortunate is the person who can select types that are. A shaded spot where the soil is good and does not dry out proves best. Where such a spot is not available, it may be impossible to place house plants outdoors, for the hot summer sun can quickly dry up or burn many tender plants.

Our situation is rather fortunate, for we have selected a cool spot near the house under a large and dense Canada Hemlock. Every other year we add generous amounts of manure to the soil, so that there is plenty of organic matter. The location is within reach of the hose so that it can easily be watered during droughts. Otherwise, the plants receive no attention.

They are set out as soon as all danger from frost is over; taken out of their pots, they are merely set in the soil and cut back, for usually some have grown long and lanky during the winter months indoors. Nothing much is done to them until about the first of September, when they are potted, but still left outdoors in the same place to become acclimated. Just before frost they are brought into the house—it's as simple as that.

It should be pointed out that experience and many trials have shown us the proper spot, and we have confined ourselves to growing types of plants that can be handled this way. Having given considerable care to house plants indoors for eight months of the year, we are ready for a vacation from these chores, and frequently the plants are ready for a vacation from our somewhat haphazard care! In any event this system works well, and is about the easiest possible arrangement that can be made for the "vacation" period of house plants. Some of the plants growing well under this nice arrangement are:

Aspidistra elatior	Aspidistra
Begonia semperflorens	Wax Begonia
Cacti species	Cacti
Chlorophytum elatum	Spider Plant
Cissus incisa	Grape-ivy Treebine
Crassula argentea	Jade Plant
Dracena species	Dracena
Fatshedera lizei	Fatshedera
Ferns—several genera and species	Ferns
Ficus elastica	Indian Rubber-plant
Hedera helix	English Ivy
Kalanchoe species	Kalanchoe

Peperomia obtusifolia	Oval-leaf Peperomia
Persea americana	Avocado
Philodendron species	Philodendron
Plectranthus oertendahlii	Swedish Ivy
Sansevieria species	Sansevieria
Saxifraga stolonifera	Mother-of-thousands
Tolmiaea menziesii	Piggy-back Plant
Zebrina pendula	Wandering Jew

3

Low Maintenance Plant Lists

The plants in the following lists have been selected because of their low maintenance needs. Few have serious pests, although it will be admitted by everyone that certain plants may have local pests on occasion. The ones listed have not had serious pest troubles in our experience. It has been most disconcerting to eliminate some of the best of the ornamentals from the following lists (such as azaleas, euonymus, roses, and rhododendrons) merely because they may have had one or two serious pests or were overly particular concerning soil requirements. Their elimination merely points up the fact that they do require special care, and because of this have no place in this book on easy maintenance.

The hardiness zones given refer to the hardiness map on the inside book covers. This is the same map used by the author in *Wyman's Gardening Encyclopedia*. Most gardeners are accustomed to using this map by this time, and realize that when a plant is listed as hardy in Zone 4 it will usually be hardy in Zones 5 to 9; in other words, it can also be grown farther South until summer heat or drought, rather than winter cold, become the modifying factors. Also, it may be possible to grow the same plant in certain sheltered spots in colder regions. No zonal map of hardiness is complete, and many local variations in altitude or climate must be taken into consideration when selecting plants for any garden.

Time of bloom given is that for the vicinity of Boston, Massachusetts. The blooming period can be set ahead the farther south one goes.

Plants normally blooming together in Boston, Massachusetts; Rochester, New York; Detroit, Michigan; Chicago, Illinois; and Seattle, Washington; would bloom approximately so many weeks earlier in the following places:

New York, New York; Columbus, Ohio; Philadelphia, Pennsylvania; London, England	2 weeks
Washington, D.C.; Lexington, Kentucky; Asheville, North Carolina	3 weeks
St. Louis, Missouri	5 weeks
Augusta, Georgia	8 weeks

and in Portland, Maine, and southern Canada, they would bloom 1½ weeks *later*.

Available low maintenance plants are divided into the following lists in this chapter, for quick selection. All are listed alphabetically and described in Chapter 4, pages 197–358. It is well to keep these lists in mind when hunting for a plant to fulfill a particular need.

Obviously, the heights of plants are extremely important in making plans for a garden or landscape planting. In small gardens with low-foundation plantings, the shrubs under 3 feet high are the most important;

Number of Plants (or Groups) Listed

Bulbs	53
Perennials	106
Woody Vines	37
Ground Covers	87
Bank Plants	31
Labor-saving Hedge Plants Under 6 Feet Tall	60
Low Woody Plants for Accent in the Perennial Garden	41
Dual-purpose Plants	30
Plants for Dry Soils	49
Plants for Wet Soils	34
Plants for Shade	110
Plants for City Gardens	65
Shrubs—Flowering and Fruiting	81
Trees—Flowering and Fruiting	38
Trees and Shrubs with Colored Foliage	59
Plants Creating Work	54

you will seldom need any that are over 4 to 5 feet high —just under eye level is best. The larger the garden, of course, the larger the shrubs that are needed to afford the correct landscape proportions.

Especially valuable to owners of small one-story homes are the small trees under 35 feet at maturity, the newer trees that are proving popular in modern plantings. Some of the larger trees are also given, but it is the smaller ones that are meeting favor on every side, for they are often less exepnsive, and are easier and cheaper to care for. They do not grow out of scale, and if they must eventually be removed for one purpose or another, the removal costs are lower.

Selecting low plants for the low house is extremely important. The reader is urged to go through the alphabetical list (pages 197–358) carefully when he is seeking a plant to serve at a definite height. The various size groups and number of plants in each group as are follows:

Shrubs under 1½ feet	70
Shrubs 1½–3 feet	66
Shrubs 4–5 feet	68
Shrubs 6–9 feet	141
Shrubs 10–15 feet	62
Shrubs 15 feet and over	40
Trees 20–35 feet	77
Trees over 35 feet	178

The author offers the plant lists on the following pages as a helpful method of making quick selections of good, low maintenance plants for specific purposes. He realizes that there may be insect or disease pests attacking some of these plants in local areas, and that those experienced in horticulture will know of other low maintenance plants that might be listed either on a local or on a national scale. However, offering such lists —even though full agreement may never be reached concerning them—will aid independent thinking and experimentation on the subject, which is certainly all to the good.

Letters given at the left hand side of the scientific names of these plants in the following lists and in the A to Z listing (Chapter 4, pages 197–358) are provided for quick identification of plant properties:

E—Woody plant with evergreen foliage

E-D or D-E—Woody plant that is either deciduous or evergreen, depending on location

H—Herbaceous plant, the foliage dies to the ground in winter

B—Bulbs or bulblike plants

   (If no E, H, or B is given, the plant is a deciduous woody plant.)

x—Placed before a plant name means the plant is of hybrid origin.

' '—Single quotes—as 'Barbara Ann'—indicate that

the plant is a clone or cultivar which will not breed true from seed, but must be asexually propagated by cutting, budding, or grafting.

Time of Bloom given (between the Flower Color and the Hardiness Zone) is for the approximate time the plant blooms in the vicinity of Boston, Massachusetts. (See page 100 for approximate time of bloom in other areas.)

LOW MAINTENANCE BULBS AND BULBLIKE PLANTS

Every garden needs its full complement of bulbs in the flower borders, in the foundation plantings about the house, or naturalized in the open where they will be conspicuous when they bloom in the spring.

The soil should be well prepared to a depth of at least 6 inches (and sometimes deeper in the case of large bulbs). If they are to be interplanted among shrubs or perennials, dig a hole and remove all the poor soil. Mix in advance some good soil with a little decayed leaf mold and fertilizer. Sometimes bone meal is suggested. This mixture can be carried around in a bucket if only a few bulbs are to be planted in each spot. Place some of this good soil mixture at the bottom of the hole, then place the bulb on top of this mixture at the proper depth and fill in with the same good mixture.

The depth of planting, in general, is about two and a half times the width of the bulb. This means that the bottom of some of the larger bulbs is 6 inches or more under the soil surface.

The time to plant most bulbs is in the fall, usually by mid-October, but there are exceptions. In the list that follows, the Summer-hyacinth (*Galtonia candicans*) and the Tiger-flower (*Tigridia pavonia*) might best be planted in the spring. Late summer is the best time to plant some of the fall blooming crocuses and the Common Autumn-crocus (*Colchicum autumnale*) as well as the Autumn-amaryllis (*Lycoris squamigera*).

When planting is completed it is well to apply a good mulch (see Mulching, pp. 57–78) for this helps to protect the bulbs during the winter and prevents some of the more shallow-planted types from being pushed out of the soil by the alternate freezing and thawing of the ground during the colder months. It may be that in some areas rodents will eat a few of certain species, but this is one of the minor hazards that one will have to put up with.

Plant well, in good soil, at the proper time and right depths, mulch well, and then forget them. It is remarkable how bulbs will continue to surprise you each year with their bright blossoms—and minimum care.

LOW MAINTENANCE BULBS

SCIENTIFIC NAME	HEIGHT	FLOWER COLOR	TIME OF BLOOM	HARDI-NESS ZONE *	COMMON NAME
Allium albopilosum	3'	lilac	May	4	Stars-of-Persia
Allium flavum	2'	yellow	August	2–3	Yellow Onion
Allium giganteum	4'	blue	June	5	Giant Onion
Allium moly	1½'	yellow	June	2–3	Golden Garlic
Allium senescens glaucum	4–8"	pink	July	3	
Arisaema triphyllum	12–18"	green	June	4	Jack-in-the-pulpit
Bulbocodium vernum	6"	rose	April	5	Spring Meadow Saffron
Camassia cusickii	3'	blue	May	5	Cusick Camas
Camassia leichtinii	2'	blue	April	5	Leichtlin Camas
Chionodoxa luciliae	3"	white, blue	April	4	Glory-of-the-snow
Colchicum autumnale	6"	purple	October	4	Common Autumn-crocus or Meadow Saffron

* Remember, you can grow most of the plants listed for zones *colder* than yours.

LOW MAINTENANCE BULBS (continued)

SCIENTIFIC NAME	HEIGHT	FLOWER COLOR	TIME OF BLOOM	HARDI-NESS ZONE *	COMMON NAME
Convallaria majalis	8"	white	May	2–3	Lily-of-the-valley
Crocus sativus	3–6"	white	fall	6	Saffron Crocus
Crocus speciosus	3–6"	blue	September	5	
Crocus susianus	3–6"	yellow	March	4	Cloth-of-gold Crocus
Crocus vernus	3–6"	white, blue	March	4	Common Crocus
Crocus zonatus	3–6"	rose	fall	5	
Eranthis hyemalis	3"	yellow	April	4	Winter Aconite
Erythronium americanum	1'	yellow	March	3	Common Fawn-lily
Erythronium dens-canis	6"	rose	March	2–3	Dogtooth Fawn-lily
Erythronium grandiflorum	2'	yellow	March	5	Lamb's Tongue Fawn-lily

* Remember, you can grow most of the plants listed for zones *colder* than yours.

Fritillaria meleagris	1'	red, yellow	April	3	Guinea-hen Flower
Galanthus elwesii	1'	white	March	4	Giant Snowdrop
Galanthus nivalis	8"	white	March	3	Snowdrop
Galtonia candicans	3–4'	white	August	5	Summer-hyacinth
Hyacinthus orientalis	15"	white, red, blue, yellow	April	6	Common Hyacinth
Lilium amabile	3–4'	red	June	2–3	Korean Lily
Lilium auratum	3–12'	white, red	August–September	4	Goldband Lily
Lilium canadense	2–5'	yellow, red	July	3	Canada Lily
Lilium candidum	3½'	white	June	4	Madonna Lily
Lilium pumilum	1½'	red	June	3	Coral Lily
Lilium regale	4–6'	white	July	3	Regal Lily
Lilium speciocum	4–5'	red, white	August	4	Speciosum Lily
Lilium superbum	6–10'	orange	July–August	5	Turkscap Lily
Lilium tigrinum	3–4'	red	July	3	Tiger Lily

LOW MAINTENANCE BULBS (continued)

SCIENTIFIC NAME	HEIGHT	FLOWER COLOR	TIME OF BLOOM	HARDI-NESS ZONE *	COMMON NAME
Liriope spicata	8–12″	white	July–August	4	Creeping Lily-turf
Lycoris squamigera	2′	lilac	August–September	5	Autumn-amaryllis
Muscari armeniacum	1′	blue	May	4	Armenian Grape-hyacinth
Narcissus asturiensis	3–5″	yellow	April	4	Asturian Daffodil
Narcisssus bulbocodium	15″	yellow	April	6	Petticoat Daffodil
Narcissus cyclamineus	8″	yellow	April	6	Cyclamen Daffodil
Narcissus incomparabilis	1′	yellow	April	4	Nonesuch Daffodil

* Remember, you can grow most of the plants listed for zones *colder* than yours.

Narcissus jonquilla	1½'	yellow	April	4	Jonquil
Narcissus odorus	1'	yellow	April	6	Campernelle Jonquil
Narcissus poeticus	1½'	white	April	4	Poet's Narcissus
Narcissus pseudo-narcissus	15"	yellow	April	4	Daffodil
Narcissus tazetta	1½'	yellow	April	8	Polyanthus Narcissus
Narcissus triandrus	1'	white	April	4	Angels-tears
Ornithogalum umbel-latum	1'	white	May–June	4	Star-of-Bethlehem
Scilla hispanica	20"	blue	April	4	Spanish Squill
Scilla sibirica	6"	blue	March	2–3	Siberian Squill
Tigridia pavonia	1½'	yellow-purple	summer	6	Tiger-flower, Mexican Shell-flower
Trillium grandiflorum	12–14"	white	April–June	4	Snow Trillium

LOW MAINTENANCE PERENNIALS

There are many perennials being grown in America today and the following list of 106 low maintenance plants includes only a small portion of the whole. Missing are many valued garden perennials like Delphinium, Sweet William (actually biennials), Shasta Daisy, Columbine hybrids and the like, with which we have struggled and given up for one reason or another. Possibly our problems were entirely local.

Most perennials can be transplanted either in the spring (before they start to grow) or in the fall. Give them good soil and a mulch (see Mulching, pages 57–78)—especially if fall transplanted—to keep the alternate freezing and thawing of the soil from actually pushing them out of the soil. Water well after transplanting and during summer droughts. The perennials listed are those we have found to be satisfactory during the past fifteen years. Throughout this period our perennials have all been growing in one garden, regularly mulched each fall and fertilized each spring. Many of the same plants we started with 15 years ago are still flourishing—ample proof that these are not fickle types, producing good flowers one year and disappearing the next. It will be noted also that these provide a colorful display of bloom from earliest spring until frost.

None have had serious insect or disease problems, in our experience, hence spraying for pest control is not practiced. When frost kills the above-ground parts, however, the entire garden is quickly scythed and raked clean. This kind of sanitary culture takes little time and may prevent considerable trouble the following year.

The following perennials can make a beautiful garden by themselves. The list can be expanded after one has personally experimented with other plants under local conditions.

PERENNIALS

SCIENTIFIC NAME	HEIGHT	COLOR OF FLOWER	TIME OF BLOOM	HARDI-NESS ZONE *	COMMON NAME
Achillea millefolium Rosea	6″–2′	pink	July–September	2	Pink Yarrow
Achillea ptarmica	2′	white	July–August	2–3	Sneezewort
Ajuga genevensis	6–9″	blue	May–June	2–3	Geneva Bugle
Ajuga reptans	4–12″	blue, purple	May–June	2–3	Bugleweed, Carpet Bugle
Ajuga reptans 'Variegata'	4–12″	white	May–June	2–3	White Carpet Bugle
Alyssum saxatile (See *Aurinia saxatilis*)					
Anchusa azurea	3–5′	blue	June–July	3	Italian Alkane, Italian Bugloss

* Remember, you can grow most of the plants listed for zones *colder* than yours.

PERENNIALS (continued)

SCIENTIFIC NAME	HEIGHT	COLOR OF FLOWER	TIME OF BLOOM	HARDI-NESS ZONE *	COMMON NAME
Anthemis tinctoria	3'	yellow	July–August	3	Golden Marguerite
Aquilegia canadensis	3'	yellow, red	July–August	2–3	American Columbine
Arabis albida 'Flore-pleno'	6–10"	white, pink	April–May	3	Double Wall Rock-cress
Arabis caucasica	4–10"	white	April–May	6	Caucasian Rock-cress
Artemisia lactiflora	4–5'	white	August–October	3	White Mugwort
Artemisia schmidtiana 'Nana'	4"	white	August–October	3	Silvermound Artemisia
Asclepias tuberosa	3'	orange	August–September	2–3	Butterfly Milkweed

* Remember, you can grow most of the plants listed for zones *colder* than yours.

Name	Height	Color	Bloom		Common Name
Asperula odorata	8″	white	May–June	4	Sweet Woodruff
Aster frikartii 'Wonder of Staffa'	1½–2′	white, purple	July–November	4	
Aster novae-angliae	3–5′	pink	August	2–3	New England Aster
Aster novi-belgii	3–5′	white, purple	September–October	2–3	New York Aster
Astilbe japonica varieties	2′	white, red	June	5	Japanese Astilbe
Aurinia saxatilis	6″	yellow	April–May	3	Golden-tuft
Baptisia australis	3–4′	blue	May–June	2–3	Blue Wild Indigo
Caltha palustris	1′	yellow	April	3	Marsh Marigold
Campanula carpatica	1′	blue	July	3	Carpathian Bellflower
Campanula latifolia	3′	blue	July	3	Great Bellflower
Campanula percisifolia	3′	blue, white	July–August	3	Peach-leaved Bellflower
Centaurea dealbata	2′	red, white	June–September	3	Persian Centaurea

PERENNIALS (continued)

SCIENTIFIC NAME	HEIGHT	COLOR OF FLOWER	TIME OF BLOOM	HARDI-NESS ZONE *	COMMON NAME
Centaurea montana	2'	blue	May–July	2–3	Mountain Bluet
Cerastium tomentosum	3–6''	white	June	2–3	Snow-in-summer
Cheleone lyonii	3'	pink, purple	July–August	3	Pink Turtle-head
Cimicifuga racemosa	6–8'	white	June–September	2–3	Snakeroot, Cohash Bugbane
Coreopsis auriculata 'Nana'	6''	yellow	June–August	4	Dwarf Eared Coreopsis
Coreopsis verticillata	2½'	yellow	July–August	6	Threadleaf Coreopsis

* Remember, you can grow most of the plants listed for zones *colder* than yours.

Coreopsis lanceolata	2'	yellow	July–August	3	Lance Coreopsis
Dianthus plumarius	1½'	pink, white	May–June	3	Grass Pink, Cottage Pink
Dianthus gratianopolitanus	4"	pink	July	3	Cheddar Pink
Dicentra eximia	1–2'	pink	May–September	2–3	Fringed Bleeding-heart
Dicentra formosa	1'	pink	May–September	2–3	Pacific Bleeding-heart
Dicentra spectabilis	2'	pink	May–June	2–3	Common Bleeding-heart
Dictamnus albus	3'	white, purple			
Doronicum causasicum	2'	yellow	July	2–3	Gasplant
Echinacea purpurea	3½'	red, purple	May–June	4	Caucasian Leopardsbane
Echinops exaltatus	3–12'	blue	July–August	3	Purple Echinacea
Echinops ritro	1–2'	blue	July–September	3	Russian Globe-thistle
			July–September	3	Small Globe-thistle

PERENNIALS (continued)

SCIENTIFIC NAME	HEIGHT	COLOR OF FLOWER	TIME OF BLOOM	HARDI-NESS ZONE *	COMMON NAME
Epimedium alpinum rubrum	6–9″	red, yellow	May–June	3	Red Alpine Epimedium
Epimedium grandi-florum	9″	red, yellow	May–June	3	Long-spur Epimedium, Bishop's-hat
Epimedium pinnatum	9–12″	yellow	April–July	5	Persian Epimedium
Euphoibia epithy-moides	1′	yellow	summer	4	Cushion Euphorbia
Eupatorium macu-latum	6–10′	purple	August	2–3	Joe-pye-weed
Filipendula-ulmaria variegata	6′	white	June–July	2–3	Variegated Queen-of-the-meadow

* Remember, you can grow most of the plants listed for zones *colder* than yours.

Gaillardia aristata	2–3'	yellow, red	July–August	2–3	Common Blanket-flower
Geranium sanguineum	12"	red	May–August	3	Blood-red Geranium
Geranium sanguineum 'Prostratum'	6"	red	May–August	3	Dwarf Blood-red Geranium
Gypsophila paniculata 'Bristol Fairy'	3'	white	July	2–3	Double Baby's-breath
Gypsophila repens 'Rosea'	18"	pink	June–August	3	Rosy Creeping Gypsophila
Helenium autumnale	6'	yellow	July–August	3	Common Sneezeweed
Helianthus tuberosus	12'	yellow	August–September	3	Jerusalem Artichoke
Hemerocallis flava	3'	yellow	June	3	Lemon Daylily
Hemerocallis fulva	2½–3'	orange, red	July–August	2–3	Tawny Daylily

PERENNIALS (continued)

SCIENTIFIC NAME	HEIGHT	COLOR OF FLOWER	TIME OF BLOOM	HARDI-NESS ZONE *	COMMON NAME
Heuchera sanguinea	1–2'	red	May-September	3	Coral-bells
Hosta decorata	1–2'	blue	July	3	Blunt Plantain-lily
Hosta fortunei	2'	lavender	July	3	Fortune's Plantain-lily
Hosta lancifolia 'Albo-marginata'	1½–2'	lavender	August	3	Variegated Narrow-leaved Plantain-lily
Hosta plantaginea	10"	white	August	3	Fragrant Plantain-lily
Hosta sieboldiana	18"	lilac	July	3	Siebold Plantain-lily
Hosta undulata	2–3'	lavender	July	3	Wavy-leaved Plantain-lily
Iberis sempervirens	12"	white	April–May	3	Evergreen Candytuft
Iris kaempferi	2'	white, red, blue	June–July	4	Japanese Iris

* Remember, you can grow most of the plants listed for zones *colder* than yours.

118

Iris sibirica	2'	purple	June	3	Siberian Iris
Liatris spicata	1–6'	purple	September	3	Spike Gayfeather
Linnum perenne	2'	blue	June–August	4	Perennial Flax
Lupinus perennis	2'	blue, pink, white	May–July	4	Wild Lupine
Lupinus polyphyllus	2–5'	blue	June–September	3	Washington Lupine
Lychnis chalcedonica	2–3'	red	June–July	3	Maltese Cross
Lythrum salicaria	3'	red, purple	June–September	3	Purple Loosestrife
Macleaya cordata	6–8'	white, pink	July–August	3	Plume-poppy
Mertensia virginica	2–3'	blue	June–July	3	Virginia Bluebells
Monarda didyma	3'	red	June–August	4	Bee-balm
Monarda fistulosa	2–3'	lavender	August	3	Wild Bergemot
Oenothera missourien-sis	1'	yellow	June–August	4	Ozark Sundrops

PERENNIALS (continued)

SCIENTIFIC NAME	HEIGHT	COLOR OF FLOWER	TIME OF BLOOM	HARDI-NESS ZONE *	COMMON NAME
Ornamental Grasses					
Arrhenatherum elatius tuberosum	1'			3	Tuber Oat-grass
Cortaderia selloana	8–20'			8	Pampas Grass
Erianthus ravennae	8–12'			5	Ravenna Grass
Miscanthus sinense	10'			4	Chinese Silver Grass
Pachysandra procumbens	6–12"	white	April	4	Allegheny Pachysandra
Paeonia officinalis	3'	white, red	May–June	3	Common Peony
Papaver orientale	2–4'	white, red	May–June	2–3	Oriental Poppy
Penstemon barbatus	3–6'	red	June–August	2–3	Beardlip Penstemon

* Remember, you can grow most of the plants listed for zones *colder* than yours.

Name	Height	Color	Bloom		Common Name
Phlox paniculata	2–4'	white, red, purple	June–September	4	Garden Phlox
Phlox subulata	6"	white, red	March–May	2–3	Moss-pink
Physalis alkekengi	2'	white	August	2–3	Chinese Lantern, or Strawberry Ground-cherry
Platycodon grandiflorum	2½'	white, blue	June–September	3	Balloonflower
Pulmonaria officinalis	1'	white, red	May	2–3	Common Lungwort
Pulmonaria saccharata	6–18"	white, blue	May	2–3	Bethlehem-sage
Ranunculus repens pleniflorus	2'	yellow	May–August	3	Double Creeping Buttercup
Salvia azurea	3–4'	blue	August–September	4	Blue Sage
Santolina chamaecyparissus	1½–2'	yellow	July–August	6–7	Lavender-cotton

121

PERENNIALS (continued)

SCIENTIFIC NAME	HEIGHT	COLOR OF FLOWER	TIME OF BLOOM	HARDINESS ZONE *	COMMON NAME
Sedum—many species	3″–3′	white, yellow, red	summer	3–7	Stonecrop
Sedum spectabile	18″	pink, red	August–October	3	Showy Sedum
Sempervivum tectorum	1′	pink	summer	4	Hen-and-chickens
Tanacetum vulgare	3′	yellow	July–August	3	Common Tansy
Thalictrum rochebrunianum	4–6′	lavender	July–September	4	Lavender-mist
Thalictrum speciosissimum	3–6′	yellow	summer	5	Dusty Meadow-rue

* Remember, you can grow most of the plants listed for zones *colder* than yours.

Thermopsis montana	2'	yellow	June–July	3	Mountain Thermopsis
Tradescantia virgini-ana	3'	blue, purple	July–August	4	Virginia Spiderwort
Veronica longifolia subsessilis	2½'	blue	July	4	Clump Veronica
Veronica spicata	1½'	blue, pink	June–August	3	Spike Speedwell

LOW MAINTENANCE WOODY VINES

Cl—climbs by clinging with rootlike holdfasts
Tend—climbs by means of attaching tendrils to support
Tw—climbs by twining
Leafstalks—climbs by attaching leafstalks to support

SCIENTIFIC NAME	METHOD OF CLIMBING	HARDI-NESS ZONE *	COMMON NAME
Actinidia arguta	Tw	4	Bower Actinidia
Actinidia chinensis	Tw	7	Chinese Actinidia
Actinidia kolomikta	Tw	4	Kolomikta Actinidia
Akebia quinata	Tw	4	Fiveleaf Akebia
Ampelopsis arborea	Tend	7	Pepper-vine
Anisostichus capreolata	Cl	6	Crossvine
Aristolochia durior	Tw	4	Dutchman's-pipe
Bignonia capreolata (see *Anisostichus capreolata*)			
Bougainvillea spectabilis	Tw	10	Brazil Bougainvillea

* Remember, you can grow most of the plants listed for zones *colder* than yours.

Campsis grandiflora	Cl	7	Chinese Trumpetcreeper
Campsis radicans	Cl	4	Trumpetcreeper
Campsis tagliabuana	Cl	4	'Madame Galen' Trumpetcreeper
Clematis paniculata	Leafstalks	5	Sweet Autumn Clematis
Clematis virginiana	Leafstalks	4	Virgin's Bower
Cobaea scandens	Tend	9	Cup-and-saucer Vine
Doxantha unguis-cati	Cl	8	Cat-claw Vine
Ficus pumila	Cl	9	Creeping Fig
Gelsemium sempervirens	Tw	7	Carolina Jessamine
Hedera canariensis	Cl	7	Algerian Ivy
Hedera helix	Cl	5	English Ivy
Hydrangea anomola petiolaris	Cl	4	Climbing Hydrangea
Kadsura japonica	Tw	7	Scarlet Kadsura
Lonicera henryi	Tw	4	Henry Honeysuckle
Lonicera japonica 'Halliana'	Tw	4	Hall's Honeysuckle
Lonicera sempervirens	Tw	3	Trumpet Honeysuckle
Muehlenbeckia complexa	Tw	5	Wirevine
Parthenocissus henryana	Cl	8	Silver Vein Creeper
Parthenocissus quinquefolia	Cl	3	Virginia Creeper
Parthenocissus tricuspidata	Cl	4	Boston-ivy

LOW MAINTENANCE WOODY VINES (continued)

SCIENTIFIC NAME	METHOD OF CLIMBING	HARDI-NESS ZONE *	COMMON NAME
Passiflora caerulea	Tend	7–8	Passion-flower
Pilostegia viburnoides	Cl	7	
Polygonum aubertii	Tw	4	Silver Fleece-vine
Pueraria lobata	Tw	6	Kudzu-vine
Trachelospermum asiaticum	Tw	7–8	Yellow Star-jasmine
Vites coignetiae	Tend	5	Glory-vine
Wisteria floribunda	Tw	4	Japanese Wisteria
Wisteria sinensis	Tw	5	Chinese Wisteria

* Remember, you can grow most of the plants listed for zones *colder* than yours.

LOW MAINTENANCE GROUND COVERS

As a quick aid, a letter has been placed in front of every plant denoting the following, for these are very important items in the selection of ground covers.

E—with evergreen foliage
H—herbaceous plant that dies to the ground over winter
D—woody plant that drops its leaves over winter
(S)—withstands partial shade

SCIENTIFIC NAME	HEIGHT	HARDI-NESS ZONE *	COMMON NAME
H Ajuga reptans (S)	4–12″	2–3	Bugleweed
E Arctostaphylos uva-ursi	6–12″	2	Bearberry
D Aronia melanocarpa (S)	1½–3′	4	Black Chokeberry
H Arundinacea variegata	2–3′	6	Dwarf Whitestripe Bamboo
H Arundinaria viridi-striata	1½–2½′	6	Dwarf Japanese Bamboo
H Asarum caudatum (S)	7″	4	British Columbia Wild Ginger

* Remember, you can grow most of the plants listed for zones *colder* than yours.

LOW MAINTENANCE GROUND COVERS (continued)

SCIENTIFIC NAME	HEIGHT	HARDI-NESS ZONE *	COMMON NAME
E *Asarum europaeum* (S)	5"	4	European Wild Ginger
H *Asperula odorata* (S)	8"	4	Sweet Woodruff
H *Campanula carpatica*	1'	3	Carpathian Bellflower
E *Cerastium tomentosum*	3–6"	3	Snow-in-summer
H *Convallaria majalis* (S)	8"	2–3	Lily-of-the-valley
H *Coreopsis auriculata* 'Nana'	6"	4	Dwarf Eared Coreopsis
H *Coronilla varia* 'Penngift'	2'	3	Penngift Crown Vetch
D *Cotoneaster adpressa*	2'	4	Creeping Cotoneaster
D *Cotoneaster adpressa* 'Park Carpet'	1'	4	Park Carpet Cotoneaster
E *Cotoneaster dammeri*	1'	5	Bearberry Cotoneaster
E *Cotoneaster dammeri* 'Skogsholmen'	1'	5	Skogsholmen Cotoneaster

* Remember, you can grow most of the plants listed for zones *colder* than yours.

D, E *Cotoneaster horizontalis*	3'	Rock Spray
E *Crassula radicans*	6"	
E *Crassula schmidtii*	3"	Schmidt Crassula
D *Cytisus decumbens*	8"	Prostrate Broom
E *Dianthus gratianopolitanus*	4"	Cheddar Pink
H *Dicentra eximia*	1–2'	Fringed Bleeding-heart
E *Dichondra repens*	3"	Dichondra
D *Diervilla lonicera*	3'	Dwarf Bush-honeysuckle
E *Echeveria* species	3–12"	Echeveria
H *Epimedium grandiflorum* (S)	9"	Long-spur Epimedium or Bishop's-hat
H *Euphorbia cyparissias*	1'	Cypress Spurge
D x *Forsythia* 'Arnold Dwarf'	3'	'Arnold Dwarf' Forsythia
E *Galax aphylla* (S)	6–12"	Galax
E *Gaultheria shallon*	1½'	Salal
E *Gaylussacia brachycera*	18"	Box-huckleberry
D *Genista pilosa*	1'	Silky-leaf Woadwaxen
H *Gypsophila repens* 'Rosea'	6"	Rosy Creeping Gypsophila
E *Hedera helix* (S)	6–8" (Vine)	English Ivy
H *Hemerocallis fulva*	2'	Tawny Daylily

129

LOW MAINTENANCE GROUND COVERS (continued)

SCIENTIFIC NAME	HEIGHT	HARDI-NESS ZONE *	COMMON NAME
E *Heuchera sanguinea*	1–2'	3	Coral-bells
H *Hosta*—species and varieties (S)	1–3'	3	Plantain-lily (Funkia)
D *Hydrangea anomala petiolaris* (S)	2' (Vine)	4	Climbing Hydrangea
D *Hypericum buckleyi*	1'	5	Blue Ridge St. Johnswort
E *Hypericum calycinum* (S)	1–1½'	6	Aaron's Beard St. Johnswort
D *Indigofera incarnata alba*	1½'	5	White Chinese Indigo
D *Indigofera kirilowii*	3'	4	Kirilow Indigo
E *Juniperus chinensis sargentii*	1'	4	Sargent Juniper
E *Juniperus conferta*	1'	5	Shore Juniper
E *Juniperus horizontalis*	12–18"	2	Creeping Juniper
E *Juniperus horizontalis* 'Douglasii'	12–18"	2	Waukegan Juniper

* Remember, you can grow most of the plants listed for zones *colder* than yours.

E *Juniperus horizontalis* 'Plumosa'	12–18"	2	Andorra Juniper
E *Liriope spicata* (S)	8–12"	4	Creeping Lily-turf
D, E *Lonicera henryi* (Twining vine) (S)		4	Henry Honeysuckle
D *Lonicera japonica* 'Aureo-reticulata' ('Twining Vine) (S)		4	Yellownet Honeysuckle
D, E *Lonicera japonica* 'Halliana' (Twining Vine) (S)		4	Hall's Honeysuckle
E *Mahonia repens* (S)	12"	5	Creeping Mahonia
H *Mentha piperita*	1–2'	3	Peppermint
H *Nepeta hederacea* (S)	3"	3	Ground-ivy, Gill-over-the-ground
H *Pachysandra procumbens* (S)	6–12"	4	Allegheny Pachysandra
E *Pachysandra terminalis* (S)	6"	5	Japanese Pachysandra
E *Pernettya mucronata*	1½'	6–7	Chilean Pernettya
D *Phlox subulata*	6"	2–3	Moss Pink, Ground-pink
H *Polygonum affine*	6–9"	3	Himalayan Fleece-flower
H *Polygonum cuspidatum compactum*	3'	4	Low Japanese Fleece-flower

LOW MAINTENANCE GROUND COVERS (continued)

SCIENTIFIC NAME	HEIGHT	HARDI-NESS ZONE *	COMMON NAME
H Polygonum reynoutria	4–6″	4	Reynoutria Fleece-Flower
E Polygonum vaccinifolium	9″	7	Rose Carpet Knotweed
E Potentilla tridentata	2–12″	2	Wineleaf Cinquefoil
H Prunella vulgaris	2″–2′	3	Common Self-heal
H Ranunculus repens pleniflorus (S)	6–12″	3	Double Creeping Buttercup
D Rhus aromatica	3′	3	Fragrant Sumac
D Rosa wichuraiana	1′	5	Memorial Rose
E Rosmarinus officinalis 'Prostratus'	3′	8	Low Rosemary
H Sasa disticha	2–3′	6	Dwarf Fernleaf Bamboo
H Sasa variegata	1–3′	5–6	Variegated Bamboo
E Sedum spurium (S)	6″	3	Two-row Stonecrop

* Remember, you can grow most of the plants listed for zones *colder* than yours.

E *Sempervivum tectorum*	6–12″	4	Hen-and-chickens
D *Teucrium chamaedrys*	10″	5	Chamaedrys Germander
H *Thymus lanicaulis*	4″	3	Woolly-stem Thyme
E *Thymus serpyllum* (S)	1″	3	Mother-of-thyme or Creeping Thyme
E *Thymus serpyllum lanuginosus* (S)	2–3″	3	Woolly Mother-of-Thyme
H *Thymus vulgaris*	6–8″	5	Common Thyme
H *Tiarella cordifolia* (S)	6–12″	3	Allegheny Foam-flower
D *Vaccinium angustifolium* (S)	8″	2	Lowbush Blueberry
H *Vancouveria hexandra* (S)	1½′	5	American Barrenwort
E *Veronica chamaedrys*	1′	3	Germander Speedwell
H *Veronica incana*	2′	3	Woolly Speedwell
H *Veronica officinalis*	1′	3	Drug Speedwell
E *Vinca minor* (S)	6″	4	Periwinkle, Myrtle
H *Viola* species (S)	6″	2–7	Violets
D *Xanthorhiza simplicissima* (S)	2′	4	Yellow-root

LOW MAINTENANCE BANK PLANTS

H = Herbaceous E = Evergreen. Those not marked are deciduous.

SCIENTIFIC NAME	HEIGHT	HARDI-NESS ZONE *	COMMON NAME
Akebia quinata	vine	4	Fiveleaf Akebia
E *Arctostaphylos uva-ursi*	6–12"	2	Bearberry
Berberis thunbergii	7'	4	Japanese Barberry
Bignonia capreolata	vine	6	Cross-vine
Clematis paniculata	vine	5	Sweet Autumn Clematis
Clethra alnifolia	9'	3	Summersweet
Cornus sericea (*C. stolonifera*)	7'	2	Red Osier Dogwood
Cotoneaster horizontalis	3'	4	Rock Spray
Diervilla lonicera	3'	3	Dwarf Bush-honeysuckle
Forsythia 'Arnold Dwarf'	4'	5	
Forsythia suspensa sieboldii	9'	5	Siebold Forsythia
E *Hedera helix*	clinging vine	5	English Ivy

* Remember, you can grow most of the plants listed for zones *colder* than yours.

Indigofera kirilowii	3'	Kirilow Indigo	4
E *Juniperus horizontalis* varieties	12–18"	Creeping Juniper	2
E *Leucothoe fontanesiana*	6'	Drooping Leucothoe	4
E *Lonicera henryi*	twining vine	Henry Honeysuckle	4
DE *Lonicera japonica* 'Halliana'	twining vine	Hall's Honeysuckle	4
Muehlenbeckia complexa	twining vine	Wirevine	6
Myrica species	9–36'	Bayberry	2–7
Parthenocissus species	vine	Creeper	3–8
H *Phalaris arundinacea picta*	2–4'	Ribbon-grass	3
H *Polygonum reynoutria*	4–6"	Reynoutria Fleece-flower	4
Pueraria lobata	vine	Kudzu-vine	6
Rhus aromatica	3'	Fragrant Sumac	3
Rosa wichuraiana	1'	Memorial Rose	5
E *Rosmarinus officinalis* 'Prostratus'	3'	Low Rosemary	8
Stephanandra incisa 'Crispa'	1½–3'	Dwarf Cutleaf Stephanandra	5
Symphoricarpos species	3–6'	Coralberry	2–5
E *Vinca minor*	6"	Periwinkle	4
Vitis coignetiae	vine	Glory-vine	5
Xanthorhiza simplicissima	2'	Yellow-root	4

LABOR-SAVING HEDGE PLANTS UNDER SIX FEET HIGH

E = Evergreen. Those not marked are deciduous.

SCIENTIFIC NAME	HEIGHT	HARDI-NESS ZONE *	COMMON NAME
E D x *Abelia grandiflora*	5'	5	Glossy Abelia
Aronia melanocarpa	1½–3'	4	Black Chokeberry
E *Berberis buxifolia nana*	18"	5	Dwarf Magellan Barberry
Berberis candidula	2'	5	Paleleaf Barberry
E D *Berberis concinna*	3'	6	Dainty Barberry
Berberis koreana	6'	5	Korean Barberry
Berberis thunbergii 'Crimson Pygmy'	3'	5	Crimson Pygmy Barberry
Berberis thunbergii 'Erecta'	7'	5	Truehedge Columnberry
Berberis thunbergii 'Globe'	2½'	5	Dwarf Japanese Barberry
Berberis thunbergii 'Minor'	4'	5	Box Japanese Barberry

* Remember, you can grow most of the plants listed for zones *colder* than yours.

E *Berberis verruculosa*	4'	5	Warty Barberry
E *Buxus microphylla* 'Compacta'	1'	5	Compact Littleleaf Box
E *Buxus microphylla* 'Curly Locks'	2'	5	Curly Locks Box
E *Buxus sempervirens* 'Handsworthiensis'	1½'	5	Handsworth Box
E *Buxus sempervirens* 'Suffruticosa'	3'	5	True Dwarf Box
E *Buxus sempervirens* Vardar Valley	4'	5	Vardar Valley Box
Chaenomeles japonica alpina	1'	4	Alpine Japanese Quince
E *Chamaecyparis pisifera* 'Filifera Nana'	2'	3	Dwarf Thread False Cypress
E *Chamaecyparis pisifera* 'Plumosa Nana'	2'	3	Dwarf Plume False Cypress
Colutea arborescens 'Bullata'	2'	5	Dwarf Bladder-senna
Deutzia gracilis	3–6'	4	Slender Deutzia
E *Euonymus alatus* 'Compactus'	5'	4	Dwarf Winged Euonymus
E *Ilex crenata* 'convexa'	9'	4	Convexleaf Japanese Holly
E *Ilex crenata* 'Glass'	4'	4	Glass Japanese Holly

137

LABOR-SAVING HEDGE PLANTS UNDER SIX FEET HIGH (continued)

SCIENTIFIC NAME	HEIGHT	HARDI-NESS ZONE *	COMMON NAME
E *Ilex crenata* 'Green Island'	4'	5	Green Island Japanese Holly
E *Ilex crenata* 'Helleri'	4'	5	Heller's Japanese Holly
E *Ilex crenata* 'Kingsville'	4'	5	Kingsville Japanese Holly
E *Ilex crenata* 'Stokes'	4'	5	Stokes Japanese Holly
E D *Lavandula officinalis* 'Nana'	12"	5	Dwarf True Lavender
Ligustrum obtusifolium regelianum	4'	4	Regel Privet
Ligustrum vulgare 'Lodense'	3'	4	Lodense Privet
Lonicera alpigena nana	3'	5	Dwarf Alps Honeysuckle
E *Lonicera nitida*	6'	7	Box Honeysuckle
D E *Lonicera pileata*	4'	5	Privet Honeysuckle
Lonicera tatarica 'Leroyana'	5'	3	Leroy Honeysuckle
Lonicera tatarica nana	4'	3	Dwarf Tatarian Honeysuckle

* Remember, you can grow most of the plants listed for zones *colder* than yours.

Lonicera xylosteum 'Claveyi'	6'	4	Clavey's Honeysuckle
E *Pernettya mucronata*	1½'	6–7	Chilean Pernettya
x *Philadelphus* 'Avalanche'	4'	5	Avalanche Mock-orange
Physocarpus opulifolius 'Nanus'	2'	2	Dwarf Eastern Ninebark
E *Picea glauca* 'conica'	4–12'	4	Dwarf White Spruce
Potentilla fruticosa	4'	2	Bush Cinquefoil
Rosa spinosissima	3'	4	Scotch Rose
E *Skimmia japonica*	4'	7	Japanese Skimmia
E *Skimmia reevesiana*	1½'	7	Reeve's Skimmia
Spiraea albiflora	1½'	4	Japanese White Spirea
Spiraea bumalda alpina	1'	5	Dwarf Alpine Spirea
x *Spiraea bumalda* 'Crispa'	2'	5	Crisp Bumalda Spirea
Spiraea cantoniensis	3'	6	Reeve's Spirea
Spiraea decumbens	1'	5	Decumbent Spirea
Spiraea japonica ovalifolia	18'	5	Oval-leaf Japanese Spirea
Stephanandra incisa 'Crispa'	1½–3'	4	Dwarf Cutleaf Stephanandra
Symphoricarpus orbiculatus	3–6'	2	Indian Currant or Coralberry
E *Taxus cuspidata* 'Densa'	4'	4	Cushion Japanese Yew
E *Taxus cuspidata* 'Nana'	10'	4	Dwarf Japanese Yew
E x *Taxus media* 'Brownii'	9'	4	Brown's Yew

LABOR-SAVING HEDGE PLANTS UNDER SIX FEET HIGH (continued)

SCIENTIFIC NAME	HEIGHT	HARDI-NESS ZONE *	COMMON NAME
Viburnum opulus 'Compactum'	5–6'	3	Compact European Cranberry-bush
Viburnum opulus 'Nanum'	1–3'	3	Dwarf European Cranberry-bush
Viburnum trilobum 'Compactum'	3'	2	Dwarf American Cranberry-bush

* Remember, you can grow most of the plants listed for zones *colder* than yours.

LOW WOODY EVERGREENS FOR ACCENT IN THE PERENNIAL GARDEN

If one has decided to follow through with the idea of reducing labor in the perennial garden by including low woody plants, almost any of the dwarf species and varieties could be used. Because the evergreens show to best advantage in winter, some of these should be among the first to be selected. During the lush growing period of late spring and summer, they may be completely hidden by the taller growing perennials, but after the perennials have died to the ground in the fall, and their tops have been removed, it is the dwarf evergreens that give such a planting much interest throughout the fall and winter. The following low maintenance woody evergreens are a few that are suggested for this purpose.

LOW WOODY EVERGREENS

SCIENTIFIC NAME	HEIGHT	HARDI-NESS ZONE *	COMMON NAME
Berberis buxifolia nana	18"	5	Dwarf Magellan Barberry
Berberis candidula	2'	5	Paleleaf Barberry
Berberis chenaultii	4'	5	Chenault Barberry
Berberis triacanthophora	4'	5	Threespine Barberry
Berberis verruculosa	4'	5	Warty Barberry
Buxus microphylla 'Compacta'	1'	5	Compact Littleleaf Box
Buxus microphylla 'Curly Locks'	2'	5	Curly Locks Box
Buxus sempervirens 'Handsworthiensis'	1½'	5	Handsworth Box
Buxus sempervirens 'Suffruticosa'	3'	5	True Dwarf Box
Buxus sempervirens 'Vardar Valley'	4'	5	Vardar Valley Box

* Remember, you can grow most of the plants listed for zones *colder* than yours.

Chamaecyparis obtusa 'Compacta'	7'	3 Compact Hinoki False Cypress
Chamaecyparis obtusa pygmaea	2'	5 Pygmy Hinoki False Cypress
Chamaecyparis pisifera 'Filifera Nana'	2'	3 Dwarf Thread False Cypress
Chamaecyparis pisifera 'Plumosa Nana'	2'	3 Dwarf Plume False Cypress
Gaultheria miqueliana	1'	5 Miquel Wintergreen
Gaultheria veitchiana	3'	7 Veitch Wintergreen
Iberis sempervirens	1'	3 Evergreen Candytuft
Iberis tenoreana	8"	5 Tenore Candytuft
Ilex crenata 'Glass'	4'	4 Glass Japanese Holly
Ilex crenata 'Green Island'	4'	5 Green Island Japanese Holly
Ilex crenata 'Helleri'	4'	5 Heller's Japanese Holly
Ilex crenata 'Kingsville'	4'	5 Kingsville Japanese Holly
Ilex crenata 'Stokes'	4'	5 Stokes Japanese Holly
Ilex rugosa	spreading	3 Rugose Holly
Juniperus chinensis 'Pfitzeriana'	10'	4 Pfitzer Juniper
Juniperus virginiana 'Globosa'	15'	2 Globe Red-cedar
Lavandula officinalis	3'	5 True Lavender
Mahonia aquifolium	3–6'	5 Oregon Holly-grape

LOW WOODY EVERGREENS (continued)

SCIENTIFIC NAME	HEIGHT	HARDI-NESS ZONE *	COMMON NAME
Pernettya mucronata	1½'	6–7	Chilean Pernettya
Picea abies—dwarf varieties	3–7'	2	Dwarf varieties of Norway Spruce
Pieris floribunda	6'	4	Mountain Andromeda
Pieris japonica	9'	5	Japanese Andromeda
Pinus strobus 'Brevifolia'	7'	3	Variety of Eastern White Pine
Pinus strobus 'Umbraculifera'	7'	3	Umbrella White Pine
Skimmia japonica	4'	7	Japanese Skimmia
Skimmia reevesiana	1½'	7	Reeve's Skimmia
Taxus baccata repandens	6'	5	Spreading English Yew
Taxus cuspidata 'Aurescens'	1'	4	Goldtip Japanese Yew
x *Tabus media* 'Brownii'	9'	4	
Tsuga canadensis globosa	8'	4	Globe Hemlock
Tsuga canadensis 'Pendula'	8'	4	Sargent Weeping Hemlock

* Remember, you can grow most of the plants listed for zones *colder* than yours.

DUAL PURPOSE WOODY PLANTS—FOR THE GARDEN AND FOR FLOWER ARRANGEMENTS INDOORS

In a household where one of the members likes to grow plants out of doors, and the other likes to arrange cut branches indoors, there is no reason in the world why a happy time cannot be had by both individuals, merely by selecting the right plants to serve both purposes well. And there are such plants. Take our experience as an example.

I had hoped that in our household we would both concentrate on growing plants out of doors and that no one would injure valuable specimens by cutting off branches for indoor arrangements. However, one day my wife came home starry-eyed to tell me she had registered in a flower-arranging course so she could make beautiful arrangements for our home. Much time was spent on that course, and succeeding ones. When a few hard-earned blue ribbons were shown me as a result of her efforts against extremely stiff competition, I had to admit that, from her view point, there was something to this after all. Her interest in the plants I was growing about the home grounds was given a great impetus by cutting my carefully grown specimens and turning her arrangements into blue ribbons.

As we thought it over, this combining of efforts, especially when she promised to stay with arranging the woody plants which I grew, gave each of us the opportunity of following our own interests, yet fulfilling the dual purpose of keeping our home horticulturally interesting inside and out. A great lot of water has gone over the dam since we made that momentous decision over twenty-five years ago, but it has kept both of us interested in our home, and a little of both ideas has worn off on our children.

As one becomes interested in flower arranging,

more and more plants are found that can be of value. Variegated-leaved plants like the Golden California Privet and the Vicary Golden Privet may have little importance in proper landscaping, but they certainly stand out in indoors arrangements. The large, coarse leaves of the Whiteleaf Japanese Magnolia, or the evergreen leaves of the Southern Magnolia, are striking when a few branches are shown off by themselves.

The Drooping Leucothoe is excellent in many kinds of arrangements, and lasts for weeks, always in excellent condition. The same is true of the Japanese Umbrella-pine and many of the other broad-leaved evergreens. A little clump of Galax, growing under the sheltering branches of a rhododendron, is always there to yield a few leaves for a corsage arrangement.

In fact, most of the broad-leaved evergreens recommended for other purposes in this book are excellent for arrangements. One does not use many of the narrow-leaved evergreens—like spruce, pine, hemlock and yew—but at Christmas time these plants come into their own when the flower arranger switches to making wreaths and all sorts of other displays for the holiday season. Deciduous flowering trees and shrubs are always available when in flower or fruit or autumn color, but these do not have the keeping qualities, indoors, of the broad-leaved evergreens. A few of the woody plants we have found most interesting will be found in the following list.

DUAL PURPOSE PLANTS

E = Evergreen. Those not marked are deciduous.

SCIENTIFIC NAME	HEIGHT	HARDI-NESS ZONE *	COMMON NAME
Broad-leaved evergreens, especially:			
E *Aucuba japonica*	15'	7	Japanese Aucuba
E *Buxus species*	1½–4'	5	Box
E *Camellia japonica*	45'	7	Common Camellia
D E *Cotoneaster species*	10''–3'	4–5	Cotoneasters
E *Euonymus fortunei vegetus*	5'	5	Bigleaf Wintercreeper
E *Galax aphylla*	6–12''	3	Galax
E *Ilex species*	3½–36'	3–7	Hollies
E *Kalmia latifolia*	30'	4	Mountain-laurel
E *Laurus nobilis*	30'	7	Laurel, Sweet Bay
E *Leucothoe fontanesiana*	6'	4	Drooping Leucothoe

* Remember, you can grow most of the plants listed for zones *colder* than yours.

DUAL PURPOSE PLANTS (continued)

SCIENTIFIC NAME	HEIGHT	HARDI-NESS ZONE *	COMMON NAME
E *Magnolia grandiflora*	90'	7	Southern Magnolia
E *Pieris* species	6–12'	4–7	Andromedas
E *Pittosporum tobira*	10'	8	Japanese Pittsoporum
E *Prunus laurocerasus*	18'	6–7	Cherry-laurel
E *Vaccinium ovatum*	10'	7	Box Blueberry
E *Yucca filamentosa*	3'	4	Adam's Needle

Narrow-leaved evergreens, especially:

E *Cedrus atlantica* 'Glauca'	120'	6	Blue Atlas Cedar
E *Juniperus* species	1–90'	2–7	Junipers
E *Pinus* species	8–100'	2–5	Pines
E *Podocarpus macrophyllus*	60'	7	Yew Podocarpa
E *Taxus* species	1–60'	4–6	Yews

* Remember, you can grow most of the plants listed for zones *colder* than yours.

Deciduous trees and shrubs in flower and fruit, especially:

Cornus florida	40'	Flowering Dogwood
Cornus kousa	21'	Japanese Dogwood
Cornus mas	24'	Cornelian-cherry
Corylus avellana 'Contorta'	15'	Curly European Hazel
Cytisus praecox	6'	Warminster Broom
Cytisus scoparius	6'	Scotch Broom
E D *Lavandula officinalis*	3'	True Lavender
Ligustrum ovalifolium 'Aureum'	15'	Golden California Privet
Ligustrum vicaryi	12'	Vicary Golden Privet
Magnolia obovata	90'	Whiteleaf Japanese Magnolia

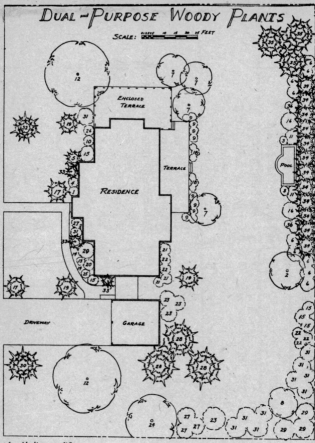

DUAL–PURPOSE WOODY PLANTS

SCALE: [----] 5 10 20 40 FEET

1. *Abelia grandiflora*
2. *Acer palmatum* variety
3. *Berberis verruculosa*
4. *Buxus* species
5. *Chamaecyparis obtusa* 'Filicioides'
6. *Cornus alba*
7. *Cornus florida*
8. *Corylus avellana* 'Contorta'
9. *Cotoneaster horizontalis*
10. *Cytisus praecox*
11. *Euonymus fortunei vegetus*
12. *Fagus sylvatica* 'Atropunicea'
13. *Galax aphylla*
14. *Hedera helix*
15. *Ilex crenata* 'Convexa'
16. *Illex glabra*
17. *Juniperus chinensis* 'Pfitzeriana'
18. *Juniperus horizontalis*
19. *Juniperus virginiana*
20. *Kalmia latifolia*
21. *Leucothoë (catesbaei)* 'Fontanesiana'
22. *Leucothoë catesbaei* 'Girard's Rainbow'
23. *Ligustrum ovalifolium* 'Aureum'
24. *Magnolia obovata*
25. *Mahonia aquifolium*
26. *Pieris floribunda*
27. *Pieris japonica*
28. *Pinus strobus*
29. *Prunus laurocerasus schipkaensis*
30. *Pseudotsuga menziesii*
31. *Rhododendron* species
32. *Sciadopitys verticillata*
33. *Taxus cuspidada*
34. *Thuja plicata*
35. *Tsuga caroliniana*
36. *Yucca filamentosa*

DRY SOIL PLANTS

E = Evergreen. Those not marked are deciduous.

SCIENTIFIC NAME	HEIGHT	HARDI-NESS ZONE *	COMMON NAME
TREES			
E *Cupressus macrocarpa*	75'	7	Monterey Cypress
E *Juniperus chinensis*	60'	4	Chinese Juniper
E *Juniperus rigida*	30'	5	Japanese Juniper
E *Juniperus scopulorum*	36'	5	Western Red-cedar
E *Juniperus virginiana*	90'	2	Eastern Red-cedar
Koelreuteria paniculata	30'	5	Golden-rain-tree
SHRUBS			
Acanthopanax sieboldianus	9'	4	Five-leaf Aralia
Artemisia species	1½–9'	2–5	Wormwoods, Sagebrushes

* Remember, you can grow most of the plants listed for zones *colder* than yours.

DRY SOIL PLANTS (continued)

SCIENTIFIC NAME	HEIGHT	HARDI-NESS ZONE *	COMMON NAME
Baccharis halimifolia	12'	4	Groundsel-bush
E D x *Berberis mentorensis*	7'	5	Mentor Barberry
Berberis thunbergii	7'	4	Japanese Barberry
Buddleia alternifolia	12'	5	Fountain Buddleia
Caragana arborescens	18'	2	Siberian Pea-tree
Chaenomeles japonica alpina	1'	4	Alpine Japanese Quince
Colutea arborescens 'Bullata'	2'	5	Dwarf Bladder-senna
Cotinus coggygria 'Purpureus'	15'	5	Purple Smoketree
Cytisus species	8"–6'	5–6	Brooms
Diervilla lonicera	3'	3	Dwarf Bush-honeysuckle
Elaeagnus angustifolia	20'	2	Russian-olive
Genista species	1–3'	2–6	Woadwaxen, Gorse
Hamamelis virginiana	15–24'	4	Common Witch-hazel

* Remember, you can grow most of the plants listed for zones *colder* than yours.

E *Hebe traversii*	6'	Travers Hebe
Hypericum calycinum	1–1½'	Aaron's Beard St. Johnswort
Indigofera species	3–6'	Indigo
Ligustrum species	1–18'	Privets
Myrica species	9–36'	Bayberries
E *Myrtus communis*	5–10'	Myrtle
E *Nerium oleander*	20'	Oleander
Physocarpus species	2–9'	Ninebarks
E *Pittosporum tobira*	10'	Japanese Pittosporum
Potentilla species	2"–6'	Cinquefoil
Rhus aromatica	3'	Fragrant Sumac
E *Rosmarinus officinalis* 'Prostratus'	3'	Low Rosemary
Sophora davidii	7'	Vetch Sophora
Viburnum lentago	30'	Nannyberry
E *Yucca filamentosa*	4'	Adam's Needle

HERBACEOUS PERENNIALS

Achillea millefolium rosea	6"–2'	Pink Yarrow
Achillea ptarrnica	2'	Sneezewort

DRY SOIL PLANTS (continued)

SCIENTIFIC NAME	HEIGHT	HARDI-NESS ZONE *	COMMON NAME
Anthemis tinctoria	3'	3	Golden Marguerite
Eupatorium maculatum	6–10'	2–3	Joe-pye-weed
Gaillardia aristata	2–3'	2–3	Common Blanket-flower
Gypsophila paniculata	3'	2–3	Baby's-breath
Helianthus tuberosus	12'	4	Jerusalem Artichoke
Hemerocallis fulva	2½–3'	2–3	Tawny Daylily
Liatris spicata	1–6'	3	Spike Gayfeather
Santolina chamaecyparissus	1½–2'	6–7	Lavender-cotton
Sedum species	3"–3'	3–7	Stonecrops
Tanacetum vulgare	3'	3	Common Tansy
Thymus serpyllum	1"	3	Mother-of-thyme

* Remember, you can grow most of the plants listed for zones *colder* than yours.

154

WET SOIL PLANTS

E = Evergreen. Those not marked are deciduous.

SCIENTIFIC NAME	HEIGHT	HARDI-NESS ZONE *	COMMON NAME
TREES			
Acer rubrum	120'	3	Red Maple
E *Calocedrus decurrens*	135'	5	California Incense-cedar
Liquidambar styraciflua	125'	5	Sweet-gum
E D *Magnolia virginiana*	6–60'	5	Sweet Bay Magnolia
Nyssa sylvatica	90'	4	Black Tupelo or Black Gum
SHRUBS			
Clethra alnifolia	9'	3	Summersweet
Cornus sericea	7'	2	Red Osier Dogwood
Enkianthus species	6–30'	4–5	Enkianthus

* Remember, you can grow most of the plants listed for zones *colder* than yours.

WET SOIL PLANTS (continued)

SCIENTIFIC NAME	HEIGHT	HARDI-NESS ZONE *	COMMON NAME
E *Gaultheria shallon*	1½'	5	Salal, Shallon
E *Gaylussacia brachycera*	18"	5	Box-huckleberry
E *Ilex cassine*	36'	7	Dahoon
E *Ilex glabra*	9–21'	3	Inkberry
Ilex verticillata	9'	3	Black Alder, Winterberry
E *Kalmia latifolia*	30'	4	Mountain-laurel
E *Leucothoe fontanesiana*	6'	4	Drooping Leucothoe
Myrica species	9–36'	2–7	Bayberries
Rhododendron aborescens	9'	4	Sweet Azalea
Rhododendron nudiflorum	6'	3	Pinxterbloom
Rhododendron vaseyi	6–9'	4	Pinkshell Azalea
Rhododendron viscosum	9'	3	Swamp Azalea
Spiraea tomentosa	4'	3	Hardhack Spirea

* Remember, you can grow most of the plants listed for zones *colder* than yours.

| *Vaccinium corymbosum* | 6–12' | 3 | Highbush Blueberry |
| *Viburnum cassinoides* | 6' | 2 | Withe-rod |

HERBACEOUS PERENNIALS

Asperula odorata	8"	4	Sweet Woodruff
Aster novae-angliae	3–5'	2–3	New England Aster
Astilbe japonica	2'	5	Japanese Astilbe
Caltha palustris	1–3'	3	Marsh Marigold
Cimicifuga racemosa	6–8'	2–3	Cohosh Bugbane
Eupatorium maculatum	6–10'	2–3	Joe-pye-weed
Helenium autumnale	6'	3	Common Sneezeweed
Helianthus tuberosa	12'	4	Jerusalem Artichoke
Lythrum salicaria	3'	3	Purple Loosestrife
Monarda didyma	3'	4	Bee-balm
Viola—several species	6"	2–7	Violets

TREES WITHSTANDING SHADE

E = Evergreen. Those not marked are deciduous.

SCIENTIFIC NAME	HEIGHT	HARDI-NESS ZONE *	COMMON NAME
Acer circinatum	25'	5	Vine Maple
Acer pensylvanicum	36'	3	Striped Maple
Acer spicatum	25'	2	Mountain Maple
Amelanchier species	25'–60'	4	Serviceberries
Cercis canadensis	36'	4	Eastern Redbud
Cornus florida	40'	4	Flowering Dogwood
E *Ilex* species	24'–70'	5–7	Hollies
E *Podocarpus macrophyllus*	70'	7	Yew Podocarpus
E *Tsuga* species	90'	4–5	Hemlocks

* Remember, you can grow most of the plants listed for zones *colder* than yours.

SHRUBS WITHSTANDING SHADE

E = Evergreen. Those not marked are deciduous.

SCIENTIFIC NAME	HEIGHT	HARDI-NESS ZONE *	COMMON NAME
D E *Abelia* species	5'	5–8	Abelias
Acanthopanax sieboldianus	9'	4	Five-leaf Aralia
Amelanchier species	6'–25'	4	Serviceberries
Aronia species	1½'–9'	4	Chokeberries
E *Aucuba japonica*	15'	7	Japanese Aucuba
D E *Berberis* species	2'–10'	5–7	Barberries
E *Camellia japonica*	8'–45'	7	Common Camellia
E *Chamaecyparis obtusa* varieties	2'–15'	3	Hinoki Cypress varieties
Chimonanthus praecox	9'	7	Wintersweet
Clethra alnifolia	9'	3	Summersweet

* Remember, you can grow most of the plants listed for zones *colder* than yours.

SHRUBS WITHSTANDING SHADE (continued)

SCIENTIFIC NAME	HEIGHT	HARDI-NESS ZONE *	COMMON NAME
Cornus species	1½'–24'	2–8	Dogwoods
Corylopsis species	10'–18'	5–7	Winter-hazels
Corylus species	15'–30'	3–4	Hazels
Fothergilla species	3'–9'	5	Fothergillas
E *Gaultheria shallon*	5'	5	Salal, Shallon
E *Gaylussacia brachycera*	18"	5	Box-huckleberry
Hamamelis species	10'–30'	4–5	Witch-hazels
Hydrangea macrophylla	12'	5–6	House Hydrangea
Hydrangea quercifolia	6'	5	Oak-leaved Hydrangea
Hypericum species	1'–6'	4–7	St. Johnswort
E *Ilex* species	9'–30'	3–6	Hollies
E *Illicium floridanum*	9'	7	Florida Anisetree
E *Laurus nobilis*	30'	7	Sweet Bay, Laurel

* Remember, you can grow most of the plants listed for zones *colder* than yours.

E *Leucothoe fontanesiana*	6'	Drooping Leucothoe
D E *Ligustrum* species	6'–30'	Privets
D E *Lonicera* species	3'–15'	Honeysuckles
D E *Magnolia virginiana*	6'–60'	Sweet Bay
E *Mahonia* species	10'–12'	Mahonias, Holly-grapes
E *Michelia figa (M. fuscata)*	15'	Banana-shrub
Myrica species	9'–36'	Bayberry, Wax-myrtle
Nandina domestica	8'	Nandina
E *Osmanthus fragrans*	30'	Sweet Osmanthus
E *Pieris* species	6'–12'	Andromedas
E *Pittosporum tobira*	10'	Japanese Pittosporum
E *Raphiolepis umbellata*	6'	Yeddo-hawthorn
Rhamnus frangula	18'	Alder Buckthorn
Rhododendron species	4½'–36'	Azaleas
Rhodotypos scandens	6'	Jetbead
E *Sarcococca ruscifolia*	6'	Fragrant Sarcococca
E *Skimmia japonica*	4'	Japanese Skimmia
Symphoricarpos species	3'–6'	Coralberry
E *Taxus* species	3'–60'	Yews
E *Thuja* species	3'–60'	Arborvitaes

SHRUBS WITHSTANDING SHADE (continued)

SCIENTIFIC NAME	HEIGHT	HARDI-NESS ZONE *	COMMON NAME
E *Torreya nucifera*	75'	5	Japanese Torreya
E *Tsuga canadensis* varieties	2'–10'	4	Common Hemlock varieties
D E *Vaccinium* species	8''–27'	2–7	Blueberries
Viburnum species	3'–12'	2–7	Viburnums
Xanthorhiza simplicissima	2'	4	Yellow-root

* Remember, you can grow most of the plants listed for zones *colder* than yours.

PERENNIALS WITHSTANDING SHADE

E = Evergreen. Those not marked are deciduous.

SCIENTIFIC NAME	HEIGHT	HARDI-NESS ZONE *	COMMON NAME
Ajuga species	4″–12″	4	Bugleweed
Anchusa azurea	3′–5′	3	Italian Bugloss
Aquilegia species	1′–3′	2–3	Columbines
Asarum species	5–7″	4	Wild Ginger
Aster species	1′–3′	2–3	Asters
Astilbe species	2′–3½′	5–6	Astilbe
Baptisia australis	3′–4′	2–3	Blue Wild Indigo
Cimicifuga racemosa	6′–8′	2–3	Snakeroot
Convallaria majalis	8″	2	Lily-of-the-valley
Dicentra eximia	1′–2′	2–3	Fringed Bleeding-heart
Dicentra spectabilis	2′	2–3	Common Bleeding-heart

* Remember, you can grow most of the plants listed for zones *colder* than yours.

163

PERENNIALS WITHSTANDING SHADE (continued)

SCIENTIFIC NAME	HEIGHT	HARDI-NESS ZONE *	COMMON NAME
Dictamnus albus	3'	2–3	Gasplant
Doronicum caucasicum	2'–5'	5	Leopardsbane
Epimedium species	9"	3	Epimediums
Eupatorium maculatum	6'–10'	2–3	Joe-pye-weed
Ferns—many	3"–5'	3–10	Ferns
Filipendula ulmaria	6'	2–3	Queen-of-the-meadow
E *Galax aphylla*	6–12"	3	Galax
Geranium sanguineum	12"	3	Blood-red Geranium
Helleborus niger	1'	3	Christmas-rose
Hemerocallis species	1½'–6'	3–7	Daylilies
Heuchera sanguinea	12"	3	Coral-bells
Hosta species	1'–3'	3	Plantain-lilies
Iberis sempervirens	12"	2–3	Evergreen Candytuft

* Remember, you can grow most of the plants listed for zones *colder* than yours.

164

Lychnis chalcedonica	2'–3'	Maltese Cross
Lythrum salicaria	3'	Purple Loosestrife
Mertensia virginica	2'–5'	Virginia Bluebells
Monarda didyma	3'	Bee-balm
Oenothera missouriensis	1'	Ozark Sundrops
Phalaris arundinacea picta	2–4'	Ribbon-grass
Platycodon grandiflorum	2½'	Balloonflower
Pulmonaria species	1'	Lungworts
Ranunculus repens pleniflorus	6–12''	Double Creeping Buttercup
Sedum species	2''–3'	Stonecrop
Tanacetum vulgare	3'	Common Tansy
Thymus species	2–4''	Thyme
Tiarella cordifolia	6–12''	Alleghany Foam-flower
Tradescantia virginiana	1'–3'	Virginia Spiderwort
Trillium species	12''–18''	Trilliums
Trollius species	2'	Globeflowers
E *Vinca major*	trailing	Big Periwinkle
Viola species	6''–12''	Violets

VINES WITHSTANDING SHADE

E = Evergreen. Those not marked are deciduous.

SCIENTIFIC NAME	HEIGHT	HARDI-NESS ZONE *	COMMON NAME
Akebia quinata	Vine	4	Fiveleaf Akebia
Ampelopsis species	Vine	4–7	Ampelopsis
E Hedera helix	Vine	5	English Ivy
Hydrangea anomala petiolaris	Vine	4	Climbing Hydrangea
Lonicera japonica 'Halliana'	Vine	4	Hall's Honeysuckle
Lonicera sempervirens	Vine	3	Trumpet Honeysuckle
Parthenocissus quinquefolia	Vine	3	Virginia Creeper
Pueraria lobata	Vine	6	Kudzu-vine
E Trachelospermum jasminoides	Vine	9	Star Jasmine
Vitis species	Vine	4–7	Grapes

* Remember, you can grow most of the plants listed for zones *colder* than yours.

TREES WITHSTANDING CITY CONDITIONS

E = Evergreen. Those not marked are deciduous.

SCIENTIFIC NAME	HEIGHT	HARDI-NESS ZONE *	COMMON NAME
E Abies concolor	120'	4	White Fir
Acer campestre	25'	4	Hedge Maple
Acer platanoides	90'	3	Norway Maple
Acer pseudoplatanus	90'	5	Sycamore Maple
Celtis laevigata	90'	5	Sugar Hackberry
Elaeagnus angustifolia	20'	2	Russian-olive
Fraxinus pennsylvanica lanceo- lata	60'	2	Green Ash
Ginkgo biloba	120'	4	Ginkgo
Gleditsia triacanthos "Inermis"	135'	4	Thornless Honey-locust
E Juniperus chinensis	60'	4	Chinese Juniper

* Remember, you can grow most of the plants listed for zones *colder* than yours.

TREES WITHSTANDING CITY CONDITIONS (continued)

SCIENTIFIC NAME	HEIGHT	HARDI-NESS ZONE *	COMMON NAME
Koelreuteria paniculata	30'	5	Golden-rain-tree
E Magnolia grandiflora	90'	7	Southern Magnolia
Magnolia soulangiana	15'	5	Saucer Magnolia
Magnolia stellata	20'	5	Star Magnolia
Malus species	8–50'	2–5	Crab Apples
Phellodendron amurense	30'	3	Amur Corktree
Quercus phellos	50'	5	Willow Oak
Quercus rubra	75'	3	Red Oak
Sophora japonica	75'	4	Japanese Pagoda Tree
E Taxus species	6–60'	4–6	Yews
Tilia cordata	90'	3	Little-leaf Linden
E Tsuga caroliniana	75'	4	Carolina Hemlock

* Remember, you can grow most of the plants listed for zones *colder* than yours.

SHRUBS WITHSTANDING CITY CONDITIONS

E = Evergreen. Those not marked are deciduous.

SCIENTIFIC NAME	HEIGHT	HARDI- NESS ZONE *	COMMON NAME
Acanthopanax sieboldianus	9'	4	Five-leaf Aralia
Acer ginnala	20'	2	Amur Maple
Acer palmatum	20'	5	Japanese Maple
Aronia arbutifolia	9'	4	Red Chokeberry
Berberis thunbergii	7'	4	Japanese Barberry
Caragana arborescens	18'	2	Siberian Pea-tree
Chaenomeles japonica alpina	1'	4	Alpine Japanese Quince
Cornus alba 'Sibirica'	9'	2	Siberian Dogwood
Cornus mas	24'	4	Cornelian-cherry
Cornus sericea	7'	2	Red Osier Dogwood
Deutzia gracilis	3–6'	4	Slender Deutzia

* Remember, you can grow most of the plants listed for zones *colder* than yours.

SHRUBS WITHSTANDING CITY CONDITIONS (continued)

SCIENTIFIC NAME	HEIGHT	HARDINESS ZONE *	COMMON NAME
Elaeagnus species	9–20′	2–4	Elaeagnus
Euonymus alatus	9′	3	Winged Euonymus
Forsythia species	4–9′	4–5	Forsythias
Hamamelis species	10–30′	4–5	Witch-hazels
Hibiscus syriacus	15′	5	Shrub Althea
Hydrangea species	3–30′	4–6	Hydrangeas
E *Ilex crenata varieties*	4–20′	4–6	Japanese Hollies
E *Ilex glabra*	9′	3	Inkberry
E *Juniperus species*	1–2′	2–4	Junipers
Lagerstroemia indica	21′	7	Crape-myrtle
E *Leucothoe fontanesiana*	6′	4	Drooping Leucothoe
D E *Ligustrum species*	3–18′	3–7	Privets
D E *Lonicera species*	3–15′	2–7	Honeysuckles

* Remember, you can grow most of the plants listed for zones *colder* than yours.

Magnolia stellata	20'	Star Magnolia
E Mahonia species	1–12'	Mahonias
Myrica pensylvanica	9'	Bayberry
Philadelphus coronarius	9'	Sweet Mock-orange
Physocarpus species	2–9'	Ninebarks
E Pieris species	6–12'	Andromedas
E Pittosporum tobira	10'	Japanese Pittosporum
Potentilla fruticosa	4'	Bush Cinquefoil
Rhamnus frangula	18'	Alder Buckthorn
Rhodotypos scandens	6'	Jetbead
Rosa rugosa	6'	Rugosa Rose
Rosa wichuraiana	1'	Memorial Rose
Spiraea bumalda 'Anthony Waterer'	2'	Anthony Waterer Spirea
Spiraea vanhouttei	6'	Vanhoutte Spirea
Symphoricarpos species	2–6'	Coralberries
E Taxus species	1–10'	Yews
V accinium corymbosum	6–12'	Highbush Blueberry
Viburnum species	1–12'	Viburnums
Xanthorhiza simplicissima	2'	Yellow-root

SHRUBS WITH ORNAMENTAL FLOWERS AND/OR FRUITS

E = Evergreen. Those not marked are deciduous.

Sp—spring	B—black	P—pink
Su—summer	Bl—blue	Pu—purple
F—fall	Br—brown	R—red
Wi—winter	G—gray	W—white
	O—orange	Y—yellow

SCIENTIFIC NAME	HEIGHT	HARDI-NESS ZONE *	FLOWER COLOR	FLOWER TIME	FRUIT COLOR	FRUIT TIME	COMMON NAME
D E *Abelia* species	3–6'	5–8	P, Pu	Su	—	—	Abelias
Amorpha canescens	4'	2	Bl	Su	—	—	Lead-plant
Aronia arbutifolia	9'	4	W	Sp	R	F	Red Chokeberry
E *Aucuba japonica*	15'	7	—	—	R	Wi	Japanese Aucuba

* Remember, you can grow most of the plants listed for zones *colder* than yours.

					W	F	
Baccharis halimifolia	12'	4	—	—	W	F	Groundsel-bush
D E *Berberis* species	2–10'	4–7	Y	S	R–B	F–Wi	Barberries
Buddleia alternifolia	12'	5	Pu	S	—	—	Fountain Buddleia
E *Camellia* species	4–5'	7	W–R	F–Sp	—	—	Common Camellia
Caragana arborescens	18'	2	Y	Sp	—	—	Siberian Pea-tree
Chaenomeles japonica alpina	1'	4	O	S	—	—	Alpine Japanese Quince
Chimonanthus praecox	9'	7	Y	Sp	—	—	Wintersweet
Clethra species	9–18'	3–5	W	Su	—	—	Summersweet
Cornus alba 'Sibirica'	9'	2	W	Sp	W	F	Siberian Dogwood
Cornus mas	24'	4	Y	Sp	R	Su	Cornelian-cherry
Cornus sericea	7'	2	W	Sp	W	Su	Red Osier Dogwood

SHRUBS WITH ORNAMENTAL FLOWERS AND/OR FRUITS (continued)

SCIENTIFIC NAME	HEIGHT	HARDI-NESS ZONE *	FLOWER		FRUIT		COMMON NAME
			COLOR	TIME	COLOR	TIME	
Corylopsis species	6–18'	5–7	Y	Sp	—	—	Winter-hazels
Cotinus coggygria	15'	5	—	—	G	Su	Smoketree
D E *Cotoneaster* species	1–3'	4–5	W	Sp	R	F	Cotoneasters
Cytisus species	1–6'	5–6	Y–Pu	Sp	—	—	Brooms
E *Daphne cneorum*	6"	4	P	Sp	—	—	Rose Daphne
Deutzia gracilis	3–6'	4	W	Sp	—	—	Slender Deutzia
Elaeagnus multiflorus	9'	4	—	—	R	Su	Cherry Elaeagnus
Elaeagnus umbellatus	12'	3	—	—	R	F	Autumn Elaeagnus
Enkianthus species	6–30'	4–5	W–R	Sp	—	—	Enkianthus

* Remember, you can grow most of the plants listed for zones *colder* than yours.

Name	Height	Zone	Flower	Season	Fruit	Fruit Season	Common Name
Exochorda giraldii wilsonii	15'	5	W	Sp	—	—	Wilson Pearlbush
Forsythia species	4–9'	4–5	Y	Sp	—	—	Forsythias
Fothergilla species	6–9'	5	W	Sp	—	—	Fothergillas
E *Gaultheria miqueliana*	1'	5	W	Sp	W	F	Miquel Winter-green
E *Gaultheria shallon*	1½'	5	W	Sp	B	Su	Salal, Shallon
Genista species	1–3'	2–7	Y	Sp	—	—	Woadwaxens
Hamamelis species	10–30'	4–5	Y–R	Sp, F	—	—	Witch-hazels
Hibiscus syriacus	15'	5	W, Bl, R	Su	—	—	Shrub Althea
Hydrangea species	3–30'	4–6	W–Bl	Su	—	—	Hyrangeas
Hypericum species	1–4'	3–6	Y	Su	—	—	St. Johnsworts
E *Iberis* species	8"–1'	3–5	W	Sp	—	—	Candytufts
E *Ilex cornuta*	9'	7	—	—	R	F–Wi	Chinese Holly
E *Ilex crenata* varieties	4–20'	4–6	—	—	B	F–Wi	Japanese Holly
E *Ilex glabra*	9'	3	—	—	B	F–Wi	Inkberry
E *Ilex rugosa*	1'	3	—	—	R	F–Wi	Rugose Holly

SHRUBS WITH ORNAMENTAL FLOWERS AND/OR FRUITS (continued)

SCIENTIFIC NAME	HEIGHT	HARDI-NESS ZONE *	FLOWER COLOR	FLOWER TIME	FRUIT COLOR	FRUIT TIME	COMMON NAME
Ilex verticillata	9'	3	—	—	R	F–Wi	Black Alder, Winterberry
E *Illicium floridanum*	9'	7	R	Su	—	—	Florida Anisetree
Indigofera species	3–6'	4–5	Pu	Sp–S	—	—	Indigo
E *Juniperus* species	1–10'	2–4	—	—	G	F–Wi	Junipers
E *Kalmia latifolia*	30'	4	W–P	Sp	—	—	Mountain-laurel
Kolkwitzia amabilis	10'	4	P	Sp	Br	F	Beautybush
Lagerstroemia indica	21'	7	P–R	Su	—	—	Crape-myrtle
D E *Lavandula officinalis*	3'	5	Pu	Su	—	—	True Lavender

* Remember, you can grow most of the plants listed for zones *colder* than yours.

Leptodermis oblonga	3'	5	Pu	Su–F	—	—	Chinese Leptodermis
Lespedeza species	6–9'	4–5	P–Pu	S	—	—	Bush-clovers
E Leucothoe fontanesiana	6'	4	W	Sp	—	—	Drooping Leucothoe
DE Ligustrum species	4–15'	3–7	W	Sp	B	F–Wi	Privets
DE Lonicera species	3–15'	2–7	W–R	Sp	Y, R	S	Honeysuckles
E Mahonia species	3–12'	5–6	Y	Sp	Bl	F	Mahonias
E Michelia fuscata	15'	7–8	W	Sp	—	—	Banana-shrub
Myrica species	9–36'	2–7	—	—	G	F–Wi	Bayberry
E Myrtus communis	5–10'	8–9	W	Su	B	F	Myrtle
Nandina domestica	8'	7	W	Su	R	F–Wi	Nandina
E Nerium oleander	20'	7–8	W–R	Sp–Su	—	—	Oleander

SHRUBS WITH ORNAMENTAL FLOWERS AND/OR FRUITS (continued)

SCIENTIFIC NAME	HEIGHT	HARDI-NESS ZONE *	FLOWER COLOR	FLOWER TIME	FRUIT COLOR	FRUIT TIME	COMMON NAME
E *Osmanthus* species	12–30′	6–8	Y	Su	B	F	Osmanthus
E *Pernettya mucronata*	1½′	6–7	—	—	W–Pu	F–Wi	Chilean Pernettya
Philadelphus species	4–9′	3–5	W	S	—	—	Mock-orange
Physocarpus species	2–9′	2–5	W	Sp	R–Br	F	Ninebark
E *Pieris* species	6–12′	4–7	W	Sp	—	—	Andromeda
E *Pittosporum tobira*	10′	8	W	Sp	—	—	Japanese Pittosporum

* Remember, you can grow most of the plants listed for zones *colder* than yours.

Botanical name	Height	Zone	Flower	Bloom	Fruit	Fruit season	Common name
Potentilla species	2″–4′	2	W–Y	Sp–F	—	—	Cinquefoil
DE *Prunus* species	4–18′	2–7	W–P	Sp	R–B	S	Cherries, Almonds
E *Punica granatum*	15′	7–8	R	Sp	Y–R	F	Pomegranate
E *Raphiolepis umbellata*	6′	7	W	Sp	B	F–Wi	Yeddo-hawthorne
Rhamnus frangula	18′	2	—	—	R–B	Su–F	Alder Buckthorn
Rhododendron species	1½–12′	3–7	W–P	Sp	—	—	Azaleas
Rhodotypos scandens	6′	5	W	Sp	B	F–Wi	Jetbead
Rhus aromatica	3′	3	Y	Sp	R	Su	Fragrant Sumac
Rosa species	1–12′	2–6	W, Y, R	Sp–S	R	F–Wi	Roses
E *Rosmarinus officinalis*	3′	8	Bl	Wi–Sp	—	—	Low Rosemary
E *Skimmia* species	1½–4′	7	W	Sp	R	F	Skimmia
Sophora davidii	7′	5	Bl	Sp	—	—	Vetch Sophora
Spiraea species	1½–9′	3–6	W–R	Sp–Su	—	—	Spireas
Symphoricarpos species	2–6′	2–4	W	Su	R	F	Coralberry

SHRUBS WITH ORNAMENTAL FLOWERS AND/OR FRUITS (continued)

| | | HARDI-NESS | FLOWER | | FRUIT | | |
SCIENTIFIC NAME	HEIGHT	ZONE *	COLOR	TIME	COLOR	TIME	COMMON NAME
E *Taxus* species	1–60'	4–6	—	—	R	F	Yews
Viburnum species	1–12'	2–7	W	Sp	Y, Bl, R	F–Wi	Virburnum
Weigela florida	9'	4–5	W–P	Sp	—	—	Weigela

* Remember, you can grow most of the plants listed for zones *colder* than yours.

TREES WITH ORNAMENTAL FLOWERS AND/OR FRUITS

E = Evergreen. Those not marked are deciduous.

Sp—Spring	B—black	P—pink
Su—Summer	Bl—blue	Pu—purple
F—Fall	Br—brown	R—red
Wi—Winter	G—gray	W—white
	O—orange	Y—yellow

		HARDI-NESS	FLOWER		FRUIT			
SCIENTIFIC NAME	HEIGHT	ZONE *	COLOR	TIME	COLOR	TIME	COMMON NAME	
E *Arbutus unedo*	10-30'	8	W	F	R	Wi	Strawberry-tree
E *Camellia japonica*	45'	7	W–R	F–Sp	—	—	Common Camellia
Cercis canadensis	36'	4	W–P	Sp	—	—	Eastern Redbud
Cladrastis lutea	50'	3	W	Su	—	—	American Yellow-wood

* Remember, you can grow most of the plants listed for zones *colder* than yours.

TREES WITH ORNAMENTAL FLOWERS AND/OR FRUITS (continued)

SCIENTIFIC NAME	HEIGHT	HARDI-NESS ZONE *	FLOWER COLOR	FLOWER TIME	FRUIT COLOR	FRUIT TIME	COMMON NAME
Clethra barbi-nervis	30'	5	W	Su	—	—	Japanese Clethra
Cornus florida	40'	4	W–R	Sp	R	F	Flowering Dog-wood
Cornus kousa	21'	5	W	Sp	R	Su	Japanese Dog-wood
Cornus nuttallii	75'	7	W	Sp	R	F	Pacific Dogwood
Davidia involu-crata	60'	6	W	Sp	—	—	Dovetree
Franklinia ala-tamaha	30'	5	W	F	—	—	Franklinia
Halesia species	30–90'	5	W	Sp	—	—	Silverbells
E Ilex cassine	36'	7	—	—	R	F–Wi	Dahoon

* Remember, you can grow most of the plants listed for zones *colder* than yours.

	Height	Zone					
E *Ilex pedunculosa*	30'	5	—	—	R	F–Wi	Long-stalk Holly
E *Juniperus chinensis*	60'	4	—	—	G	F–Wi	Chinese Juniper
E *Juniperus scopulorum*	36'	5	—	—	G	F–Wi	Western Red-cedar
E *Juniperus virginiana*	90'	2	—	—	G	F–Wi	Eastern Red-cedar
Kalopanax pictus	90'	4	W	Su	B	F	Castor-aralia
Koelreuteria paniculata	30'	5	Y	Su	Y	F	Golden-rain-tree
Lagerstroemia indica	21'	7	P–R	Su	—	—	Crape-myrtle
E *Ligustrum lucidum*	30'	7	W	Su	B	F–Wi	Glossy Privet
Liriodendron tulipifera	150'	4	Y–O	Sp	—	—	Tulip-tree
D E *Magnolia species*	15–90'	4–7	W–R	Sp	R	F	Magnolias

SCIENTIFIC NAME	HEIGHT	HARDI-NESS ZONE *	FLOWER COLOR	FLOWER TIME	FRUIT COLOR	FRUIT TIME	COMMON NAME
Malus species	8–50′	2–5	W–R	Sp	Y–R	F–Wi	Crab Apple
Myrica cerifera	36′	6	—	—	G	F–Wi	Wax-myrtle
Oxydendrum arboreum	75′	5	W	Su	Br	F–Wi	Sorrel-tree or Sourwood
Phellodendron amurense	30′	3	—	—	B	F	Amur Corktree
E Photinia serrulata	36′	7	W	Sp	R	F–Wi	Chinese Photinia
E Podocarpus macrophyllus	60′	7	—	—	Pu	F	Yew Podocarpus
Poncirus trifoliata	35′	5–6	W	Sp	Y	F	Hardy-orange

* Remember, you can grow most of the plants listed for zones *colder* than yours.

Sophora japonica	75'	4	W	Su	—	—	Japanese Pagoda Tree
Sorbus alnifolia	60'	5	W	Sp	O	F	Korean Mountain-ash
Stewartia species	15–60'	5	W	Su	—	—	Stewartias
Styrax species	30'	5–6	W	Sp	—	—	Snowbells
Tilia species	60–120'	3–5	W	Su	—	—	Lindens
Viburnum lentago	30'	2	W	Sp	B	F–Wi	Nannyberry
Viburnum prunifolium	15'	3	W	Sp	B	F	Black Haw
Viburnum rufidulum	30'	5–6	W	Sp	Bl	F	Southern Black Haw
Viburnum sieboldii	30'	4	W	Sp	R–B	Su	Siebold Viburnum

TREES AND SHRUBS OF SPECIAL INTEREST FOR COLORED FOLIAGE

E = Evergreen. Those not marked are deciduous.

Bl—bluish
G—gray
Pu—purplish
R—red to reddish
Y—yellow to yellowish

SCIENTIFIC NAME	COLOR	HEIGHT	HARDI-NESS ZONE *	COMMON NAME
Acer japonicum 'Aureum'	Y	25'	5	Goldenmoon Maple
Acer palmatum 'Atro-purpureum'	R	20'	5	Red Leaved Japanese Maple

* Remember, you can grow most of the plants listed for zones *colder* than yours.

Acer palmatum 'Burgundy Lace'	R	20'	5	Burgundy Lace Maple
Acer palmatum 'Elegans'	R variegated	20'	5	Elegant Japanese Maple
Acer palmatum 'Ohsakazuki'	Y–R	20'	5	Ohsakazuki Maple
Acer palmatum 'Ornatum'	R	20'	5	Ornate Maple
Acer palmatum 'Sanguineum'	R	20'	5	Blood Red Maple
Acer platanoides 'Crimson King'	R	90'	3	Crimson King Maple
Acer pseudo-platanus 'Purpureum'	Pu	90'	5	Purple Sycamore Maple
Amorpha canescens	G	4'	2	Lead-plant
Artemisia species	G	1½–9'	2–5	Wormwood, Sagebrush
Arundinaria viridi-striata	Y striped	1½–2½'	6	Dwarf Japanese Bamboo
Arundinaria variegata	white striped	2–3'	6	Dwarf Whitestripe Bamboo
Berberis thunbergii atro-purpurea	R	7'	4	Red Japanese Barberry

TREES AND SHRUBS OF SPECIAL INTEREST FOR COLORED FOLIAGE (continued)

SCIENTIFIC NAME	COLOR	HEIGHT	HARDI-NESS ZONE *	COMMON NAME
Berberis thunbergii 'Crimson Pygmy'	R	3'	5	Crimson Pygmy Barberry
E *Cedrus atlantica* 'Argentea'	G	120'	6	Silver Atlas Cedar
E *Cedrus atlantica* 'Glauca'	Bl	120'	6	Blue Atlas Cedar
E *Chamaecyparis obtusa* 'Cripsii'	Y	30'	3	Cripps Hinoki False Cypress
E *Chamaecyparis pisifera* 'Plumosa Gold Dust'	Y	2'	3	Gold Dust Sawara False Cypress

* Remember, you can grow most of the plants listed for zones *colder* than yours.

E *Chamaecyparis pisifera* 'Squarrosa'	Bl	100'	3	Moss Sawara False Cypress
Cornus alba 'Argenteo-marginata'	White variegated	9'	2	Creamedge Tatarian Dogwood
Cornus alba 'Gouchaultii'	Y to pinkish	9'	2	Mottled Tatarian Dogwood
Cornus alba 'Spaethii'	Y variegated	9'	2	Spaeth's Tatarian Dogwood
Corylus maxima 'Purpurea'	Pu	15–30'	4	Purple Giant Hazel
Elaeagnus species	G	4–20'	2–4	Elaeagnus
Fagus sylvatica 'Atropunicea'	Pu	90'	4	Purple Beech
Fagus sylvatica 'Purpureo-pendula'	Pu	90'	4	Weeping Purple Beech
E *Juniperus chinensis* 'Blaauw'	B	60'	4	Blaauw Chinese Juniper

TREES AND SHRUBS OF SPECIAL INTEREST FOR COLORED FOLIAGE (continued)

SCIENTIFIC NAME	COLOR	HEIGHT	HARDI-NESS ZONE *	COMMON NAME
E *Juniperus chinensis* 'Mountbatten'	G	60'	4	Mountbatten Chinese Juniper
E *Juniperus communis* 'Suecica'	Bl	15'	2	Swedish Juniper
E *Juniperus excelsa stricta*	Bl	20'	7	Spiny Greek Juniper
E *Juniperus horizontalis* 'Douglasii'	Bl	12–18"	2	Waukegan Juniper
E *Juniperus horizontalis* 'Plumosa'	Pu (in fall)	12–18"	2	Andorra Juniper
E *Juniperus scopulorum* 'Chandler Blue'	Bl	36'	5	Chandler Blue Rocky Mountain Juniper

* Remember, you can grow most of the plants listed for zones *colder* than yours.

E *Juniperus scopulorum* 'Hill's Silver'	Bl	36'	5	Hill's Silver Rocky Mountain Juniper
E *Juniperus scopulorum* 'Moonlight'	Bl	36'	5	Moonlight Rocky Mountain Juniper
E *Juniperus scopulorum* 'Pathfinder'	Bl	36'	5	Pathfinder Rocky Mountain Juniper
E *Juniperus virginiana* 'Burkii'	G	90'	2	Burk's Red-cedar
E *Juniperus virginiana glauca*	Bl	90'	2	Silver Red-cedar
D E *Lavardula officinalis*	G	3'	5	True Lavender
E *Leucothoe fontanesiana* 'Girard's Rainbow'	Y variegated	6'	4	Girard's Rainbow Drooping Leucothoe
Ligustrum ovalifolium 'Aureum'	Y	15'	5	Golden California Privet

TREES AND SHRUBS OF SPECIAL INTEREST FOR COLORED FOLIAGE (continued)

SCIENTIFIC NAME	COLOR	HEIGHT	HARDI-NESS ZONE *	COMMON NAME
Ligustrum vicaryi	Y	12'	5	Vicary Golden Privet
Malus purpurea 'Lemoinei'	R	25'	4	Lemoine Purple Crab Apple
Malus 'Baskatong'	R	30'	4	Baskatong Crab Apple
Malus 'Evelyn'	R	20'	3	Evelyn Crab Apple
Malus 'Makamik'	R	40'	4	Makamik Crab Apple
Malus 'Okonomierat Echtermeyer'	R	15'	4	Okonomierat Echtermeyer Crab Apple
Malus 'Rosseau'	R	40'	4	Rosseau Crab Apple
Malus 'Sissipuk'	R	40'	4	Sissipuk Crab Apple

* Remember, you can grow most of the plants listed for zones *colder* than yours.

Scientific name	Color	Height	No.	Common name
Philadelphus coronarius 'Aureus'	Y	9'	4	Yellow Sweet Mock-orange
Physocarpus opulifolius 'Luteus'	Y	9'	2	Yellow Eastern Ninebark
Rosa rubrifolia	R	6'	2	Redleaf Rose
E *Rosmarinus officinalis* 'Prostratus'	G	3'	8	Low Rosemary
E *Taxus baccata* 'Elegantissima'	Y	60'	6	Elegant English Yew
E *Taxus baccata* 'Fastigiata Aurea'	Y	60'	6	Golden Irish Yew
E *Taxus cuspidata* 'Aurescens'	Y	1'	4	Goldtip Japanese Yew
Weigela florida 'Foliis Purpuriis'	P	9'	5	
Weigela florida 'Variegata'	Y variegated	9'	5	

A FEW PLANTS CREATING WORK

It's a good idea to know plants that can create work. Some may be troubled with serious pests, so much so that it is just asking for extra work to attempt to grow them properly. Others may be afflicted with one or two pests that might be controlled with one spraying at the proper time. The broad-leaved evergreen rhododendrons, for example, are troubled with several pests of which the most persistent is the lace bug. This small insect feeds on the undersurface of the leaves, and, as a result, often goes unnoticed until the infestation is serious and considerable damage has been done. Spraying can control it, if done with the proper materials at the proper time. Often a second brood hatches that may also have to be controlled. There may be areas where rhododendrons can be grown and not be subjected to attacks by this pest, but usually if a planting of rhododendrons is left alone, unsprayed, for a number of years they will suffer serious injury. Hence these evergreens require maintenance work to keep them in a healthy condition.

Lilacs are another example. Many an old lilac has not been sprayed or pruned for years. It does not actually die, but the sucker growth is usually so thick that comparatively few flowers develop. Lilacs require considerable care in order to look well and bloom profusely. It is not advisable to plant them in any garden unless extra maintenance work can be provided for them.

Then there are plants that require special soils or conditions to make possible even normal growth. The beautiful clematis hybrids are examples of this, for without precisely the right conditions they fail miserably. In addition there are many plants, like the deutzias, that are always in need of renewal pruning each year.

And so it is with many of the other plants in the following list. Some are greatly admired by gardeners, like the hybrid roses and evergreen azaleas, and such plants will always be planted in great numbers because gardeners are willing to take the extra time to care for them properly. They are listed here merely to emphasize the fact that they do require extra maintenance if they are to be prime ornamental specimens.

PLANTS CREATING WORK

> 1—Insect or disease prone
> 2—Vigorous—requires too much pruning
> 3—Exacting as to soil requirements
> 4—Dropping bark or branches or objectionable fruits
> —i.e. requiring work to keep in neat condition

Aesculus species 1,4	Horse-chestnuts
Ailanthus altissima 1	Tree-of-heaven
Albizia julibrissin 1	Silktree
Alnus species 1	Alders
Amelanchier 1	Service-berries
Arbutus menziesii 4	Pacific Madrone
Azaleas—evergreen types 1,3	Evergreen Azaleas
Betula species 1	Birches
Carya species 1	Hickories, Butternut
Castanea species 1	Chestnuts
Ceanothus species 1	Ceanothus
Celastrus species 2	Bittersweets
Celtis occidentalis 1	Common Hackberry
Chaenomeles speciosa 1,2	Flowering Quince
Chamaecyparis—tree types 2	False Cypress
Chionanthus species 1	Fringetrees
Choisya 2	Mexican-orange
Clematis species 3	Clematis
Cotoneaster—several species 1	Cotoneaster
Crataegus species 1	Hawthorns
Daphne—several species 3	Daphne

Deutzia species 2	Deutzias
Eucalyptus 4	Gum trees
Euonymus species 1	Euonymus
Fraxinus species 1	Ashes
Heteromeles arbutifolia 1	Christmas-berry
Ilex aquifolium 1	English Holly
Ilex opaca 1	American Holly
Jasminum species 1	Jasmines
Juglans species 1	Walnuts and Butternuts
Larix species 1	Larches
Melia azedarach 4	Chinaberry
Paeonia suffruticosa 1,3	Tree Peony
Picea engelmannii 1	Englemann Spruce
Picea pungens 1	Colorado Spruce
Picea orientalis 1	Oriental Spruce
Pinus mugo 1	Mugo Pine
Pinus resinosa 1	Red Pine
Platanus occidentalis 1	Buttonwood
Populus species 2,4	Poplars
Prunus—tree types 1	Cherries, Plums, Apricots
Pyracantha species 1,2	Firethorns
Pyrus—most species 1	Pears
Rhododendron—ever- green types 1,3	Evergreen Rhododendrons
Ribes species 1	Currants and Gooseberries
Robinia species 1,2,4	Locusts
Rosa hybrids 1,2	Hybrid Tea Roses
Rosa multiflora 2	Japanese Rose
Salix species 1,2,4	Willows
Sorbaria species 2	False Spireas
Sorbus—most species, except *S. alnifolia* 1	Mountain-ashes
Symphoricarpos albus laevigatus 1	Snowberry
Syringa species 1,2	Lilacs
Ulmus species 1	Elms

4

A-Z Listing of Low Maintenance Plants

The following section lists, in alphabetical order, all the bulbs, perennials, ground covers, vines, shrubs, and trees covered in the previous specialized lists. Each plant is listed by its Latin and English names; by Height; Season of Bloom (if any); Hardiness Zone; and Country of Origin. A brief description is also included.

The letters given at the left-hand side of the scientific name of the plant are provided for quick identification:

E—Woody plant with evergreen foliage

E D or D E—Woody plant which is either deciduous or evergreen, depending on location

H—Herbaceous plant; the foliage dies to the ground in winter

B—Bulbs or bulblike plants

No letter given—the plant is a deciduous woody plant

x—Means the plant is of hybrid origin (no country of origin, obviously, will be given)

'—Single quotes—as 'Barbara Ann'—indicate that the plant is a clone or cultivar which will not breed true from seed, but must be asexually propagated by cutting, budding, or grafting.

This use of single quotes to designate a clone or cultivar has been adopted internationally in the 1969 edition of the *International Code of Nomenclature for Cultivated Plants.*

Time of Bloom (shown between Height and Hardiness Zone)—For the approximate time the plant blooms in the vicinity of Boston, Massachusetts. (See page 100 for approximate time of bloom in other areas.)

Hardiness Zone—Remember that most plants that can be grown in climates *colder* than yours, will also grow in your area. To locate your own Hardiness Zone, consult the map on the inside covers of this book.

Hyphen in English Name of Plant—this indicates that this plant is not a member of the true genera. For example, the White Fir is a true fir, compared to the Douglas-fir which is not a true fir or member of the genus *Abies.*

E **Abelia floribunda**　6′　Summer　Zone 8
　　Mexican Abelia
　　　　With large, rosy, pendulous flowers.　Mexico

E D x **Abelia grandiflora**　5′　June–October
　　Zone 5　Glossy Abelia
　　　　Handsome, half evergreen, with lustrous leaves and pink, tubular flowers. Widely popular from Florida to New York, frequently used as a hedge. **'Sherwood'** is only half the size of the species.

E D x **Abelia 'Edward Goucher'**　5′　August　Zone 5
　　　　A hybrid of *Abelia grandiflora x A. schumannii,*

this resembles **A. grandiflora** except that the flowers are long and purplish.

E **Abies cephalonica**   90′   Zone 5   Greek Fir
 A stiff, upright fir, not so widely grown as some of the others but a fine ornamental nevertheless.

Greece

E **Abies concolor**   120′   Zone 4   White Fir
 The best of the firs for ornamental use, of special merit for its ability to withstand city conditions. The needles vary from green to a definite bluish color.

Western United States

 Variety:
 conica—pyramidal, slow growing, having a "sheared" appearance.

E **Abies firma**   150′   Zone 6   Momi Fir
 A stiffly sturdy evergreen.   Japan

E **Abies homolepis**   90′   Zone 4   Nikko Fir
 A popular tree for its luxuriant, dark green needles.   Japan

---

E **Abies koreana**   54′   Zone 5   Korean Fir
 One of the smaller firs, this might be considered for the small garden.   Korea

---

E **Abies nordmanniana**   150′   Zone 4   Nordmann Fir
 Widely planted, but not so colorful an ornamental as some of the other firs.   Asia Minor

---

E **Abies veitchii**   75′   Zone 3   Veitch Fir
 One of the hardier firs, it does not require the moist, cool climate so necessary for the good growth

of **Abies balsamea.** Of special merit is the extremely white undersurface of the needles. Japan

---

Acanthopanax sieboldianus 9′ Zone 4 Five-leaf Aralia

A foliage plant especially for the shady or city garden where it does better than most other shrubs. Flowers and fruits are mostly inconspicuous. Japan

---

Acer argutum 24′ Zone 5

With gracefully erect branches, one of the many maples that might be considered for planting on the small property. Japan

---

Acer buergerianum 20′ Zone 6 Trident Maple

This is beginning to be planted in the central United States as a small shade tree. Japan

---

Acer campestre 25′ Zone 4 Hedge Maple

Although this does not have the prominent autumn color of the native American species, it is a densely growing, sometimes almost shrubby tree. Excellent for a screen planting.

Europe, Western Asia

Acer capillipes 30′ Zone 5 Japanese Striped Maple

The Japanese counterpart of our striped maple, this has red autumn color and the twigs are striped with white. Japan

---

Acer carpinifolium 30′ Zone 5 Hornbeam Maple

Leaves are similar to those of a hornbeam. It might be considered for planting on a small place, since it makes a neat and compact tree. Japan

---

Acer circinatum 25′ April Zone 5 Vine Maple

One of the most ornamental in flower of all the

maples, this also has red and yellow autumn foliage in the fall.   British Columbia to California

---

Acer davidii   45′   Zone 6   David Maple
Leaves turn yellow and purple in the fall, and the branches are striped white throughout the winter.
China

Acer diabolicum purpurascens   30′   Zone 5   Red Devil Maple
The young leaves are purplish when they unfold in the spring, and the fruit is also purplish when young. Hence, a colorful tree in the spring.   Japan

---

Acer ginnala   20′   April   Zone 2   Amur Maple
Very hardy, now becoming widely used in the northern United States, this sturdy little maple turns a brilliant scarlet autumn color. One of the very few maples with fragrant flowers. The fruits are red, starting to color by the end of the summer, when they are shown off to excellent advantage against the small green leaves.   China, Manchuria, Japan

---

Acer glabrum   25′   Zone 5   Rocky Mountain Maple
A small maple for the West Coast with upright, almost fastigiate branches.   Rocky Mountain Area

---

Acer griseum   25′   Zone 5   Paperbark Maple
The beautiful, brown, paperlike bark is outstanding. Since it is difficult to propagate from seed, not many commercial growers in America offer it but it is worth trying to find.   China

---

Acer japonicum   25′   Zone 5   Fullmoon Maple
A handsome, low maple with 7- to 11-lobed green leaves turning a rich red in the autumn.   Japan

Varieties:

'Aconitifolium'—extremely finely divided leaves
Fernleaf Maple

'Aureum'—leaves yellow   Goldenmoon Maple

Acer macrophyllum   90′   Zone 6   Bigleaf Maple
The rather coarse leaves are 6 to 12 inches long, but this is a popular tree in the Pacific Northwest, where it is native. Especially noted for its bright orange autumn color, it does not seem to do well in the East.   Pacific Coast of North America

Acer mandshuricum   30′   Zone 4   Manchurian Maple
Rather open in habit with wide spreading branches, its leaves are compound, like those of the Box Elder, and turn red in the fall.

Manchuria, Korea

Acer monspessulanum   24–30′   Zone 5
Montpelier Maple
A round-headed tree proving popular as a street tree in Washington and Oregon, somewhat resembling *A. campestre*.   Southern Europe

Acer nikoense   25′   Zone 5   Nikko Maple
A vase-shaped maple with trifoliate leaves. Few maples have this good form while they are young.

Japan and China

Acer opalus   45′   April   Zone 5
One of the most ornamental of the early flowering maples but not commercially available in the United States at present.   Southern Europe

Acer palmatum   20′   Zone 5   Japanese Maple
There are at least 80 varieties of this species

being grown in the United States today. The identification of some is most difficult and they are unquestionably mixed in many nurseries. It is impossible to give a detailed selection of all of them. They vary in form, height, foliage, and color, and all should be propagated asexually and not from seed. The leaves have 5 to 9 lobes, and the color ranges from green to dark red; those with variegated leaves are more difficult to grow.

Of the hardiest, some of the best varieties might be:

'Atropurpureum'—leaves red
Red Leaved Japanese Maple

'Burgundy Lace'—interesting cut-leaved form
Burgandy Lace Maple

dissectum—leaves divided to the base in 5 to 9 lobes
Cut Leaved Japanese Maple

'Elegans'—leaves 5 inches long, green
Elegant Japanese Maple

'Oksakazuki'—one of the best for fall color
Oksakazuki Maple

'Ornatum'—a cut-leaved form with red leaves
Ornate Maple

'Sanguineum'—one of the most hardy, leaves light purplish red most of the season
Blood Red Maple

Acer pensylvanicum   36′   Zone 3   Striped Maple

This coarse-leaved tree should only be used in wooded areas. The leaves color a bright yellow in the fall and the bark is white striped.

Eastern North America

Acer platanoides   90′   April   Zone 3   Norway Maple

The Norway Maple has become one of the standard trees both in gardens and along streets in the eastern United States. For the small home garden it may be too tall, but there are some compact forms that are well suited for general planting. It grows rapidly and because the feeding roots are fairly close to the surface it often is difficult if not impossible to grow prized plants underneath it. Its yellowish flowers in the spring are conspicuous, as well as its yellow fall color.   Europe

    Among the best varieties are:

    'Cleveland'—oval and upright in habit.

    'Columnare'—the 30-year-old plant in the Arnold Arboretum is 40 feet tall, 24 feet wide.

    'Crimson King'—one of three varieties (the others are 'Fassen's Black' and **'Goldsworth Purple'**) with red leaves throughout the entire growing season.

    'Erectum' (*ascendens*)—this is supposed to be conical, but a 20-year-old tree in the Arnold Arboretum is 30 feet tall with a total width of only 6 feet.

Erect Norway Maple

    'Globosum'—an excellent, low-growing, round-headed tree for placing under electric wires. It should be grafted high (about 6 feet) on *A*. *platanoides* understock, otherwise it grows into a mere shrub.

Globe Norway Maple

Acer pseudoplatanus   90′   Zone 5   Sycamore Maple

    A large, popular street tree in Europe, this species is especially adaptable for planting near the seacoast. Usually this species, like so many other European natives, has no autumn color.

Europe, Western Asia

    Varieties:

    'Erectum'—narrow and upright

Erect Sycamore Maple

    'Purpureum'—leaves have dark purple undersides   Purple Sycamore Maple

---

Acer rubrum   120′   April   Zone 3   Red Maple
Popular because of its fast growth, early, red, spring flowers, and red autumn color. It should not be used promiscuously because its wood is weak and it will break or split in heavy snow and ice, thus causing considerable work for the busy gardener. For the swampy place there is nothing that will grow so well.   Eastern and Central North America
Variety:
'Columnare'—the 60-year-old plant in the Arnold Arboretum is 75 feet tall and 36 feet wide
Column Red Maple

Acer saccharum   120′   Zone 3   Sugar Maple
Well known to everyone as a standard shade tree. Though it does grow slowly when compared with the Red and Norway Maples, it is more sturdy than either and is noted for its fiery red and yellow autumn color.   Eastern North America
Varieties:
'Globosum'—with excellent, dense, low, rounded form and dense habit   Globe Sugar Maple
'Newton Sentry' (formerly var. *columnare*)—the 40-year-old plant in the Arnold Arboretum is 50 feet tall and 12 feet wide. This tree has a main central leader.
'Temple's Upright' (formerly *monumentale*)—the 75-year-old tree in the Arnold Arboretum is 50 feet tall and 12 feet wide. This tree does not have a main central leader.

Acer spicatum   25′   Zone 2   Mountain Maple
A small native tree recommended for planting in the woods only.
Eastern and Central North America

Acer tataricum   30′   Zone 4   Tatarian Maple
   Grows as wide as it does tall. The leaves are slightly glossy, red to yellow in the fall. It is upright, elliptical, and dense, with fruits turning red in the late summer, and very colorful against the green foliage.
Europe, Western Asia

Acer tschonoskii   20′   Zone 5   Tschonoski Maple
   A graceful shrubby tree, beginning to be used as a shade tree in the central United States.   Japan

H **Achillea millefolium 'Rosea'**   6″–2′   July–September   Zone 2   Pink Yarrow
   Small pink flowers in flat clusters, blooming 6 weeks. Almost evergreen foliage, can be mowed, aromatic. Can grow in full sun in poor, dry soil.
Europe

H **Achillea ptarmica**   2′   July–August   Zone 2–3   Sneezewort
   Small white flowers are usually double. Blooms about 8 weeks.   Europe, Asia, North America

Actinidia arguta   Twining Vine   Zone 4   Bower Actinidia
   Vigorous twining vine with dense foliage making it one of the better vines for screening purposes. Sexes separate but neither flowers nor fruit is ornamental.
Japan, Korea, Manchuria

Actinidia chinensis   Twining Vine   Zone 7   Chinese Actinidia
   Vigorous twining vine. Sexes separate. Fruit has flavor similar to gooseberries, and occasionally available on the market. Young growth covered with prom-

inent red hairs. Handsomest and most vigorous of the Actinidias. China

Actinidia kolomikta   Twining Vine   Zone 4
  Kolomikta Actinidia
   Twining vine with leaves variegated with white to pink blotches, especially the male plants.
Asia, Japan

H **Ajuga genevensis**   6–9″   May–June   Zone 2–3
  Geneva Bugle
   Bright blue flowers in small spikes. Tends to grow in clumps, hence is good for the rock garden.
Europe

H **Ajuga reptans**   4–12″   May–June   Zones 2–3
  Carpet Bugle
   A flat, fast-growing ground cover, even grows in grass, with small blue, white, or purple flowers. Grows equally well in sun or in shade. Europe

H **Ajuga reptans** 'Variegata'   4–12″   May–June
  Zone 2–3   White Carpet Bugle
   White flowers and white variegated leaves.
Europe

Akebia quinata   Twining Vine   May   Zone 4
  Fiveleaf Akebia
   A dainty but vigorous twining vine, with five leaflets to each leaf and small, purplish, pendulous flowers followed by fleshy purple fruit pods. Can become a pest unless roots are restrained but this is easy. One of the neatest and best of the foliage vines.
China, Korea, Japan

B **Allium albopilosum**   3′   June   Zone 4
  Stars-of-Persia
    Lilac-colored flowers in globelike clusters, 8–12
inches across. Excellent as cut flowers or in dried arrangements. Plant 6 inches deep.   Asia Minor

---

B **Allium flavum**   2′   August   Zones 2–3   Yellow
  Onion
    Flowers yellow, bell-shaped.   ·   Europe

B **Allium giganteum**   5′   June   Zone 5   Giant Onion
    Huge balls, 4–5 inches across of bright blue
flowers on 5 foot stalks. Excellent as cut flowers or in
dried arrangements.   China

B **Allium moly**   1½′   June   Zone 2–3   Golden
  Garlic
    Yellow starlike flowers. Leaves gray green. Good
in dried arrangements.   Europe

B **Allium senescens glaucum**   4–8″   July   Zone 3
    Blue gray, curved leaves. Good for rock garden.
                    Germany to Siberia

Amorpha canescens   4′   July   Zone 2   Lead-plant
    A gray-leaved shrub used in many old-fashioned
gardens for its colored foliage. Conspicuous spikes
of blue flowers, for poor, dry soils.

                    Eastern North America

Amorpha nana   2′   July   Zone 2   Dwarf Indigo Bush
    It is surprising that this delicate native is not
found in gardens. The foliage is extremely fine, the
compound leaves being under 4 inches long and the
individual leaflets less than ¼ of an inch long. It

has small purple flowers in racemes. The whole plant gives one the impression of extremely fine texture.

Central North America

Ampelopsis arborea   Vine   Zone 7   Pepper-vine
Semievergreen, grown throughout the southeastern United States. Climbs by means of attaching tendrils to a means of support.

Southeastern United States

H **Anchusa azurea**   3–5′   June–July   Zone 3
Italian Alkanet or Italian Bugloss
Bright blue flowers, ½ inch in diameter, profuse, borne in one-sided clusters. Should be in full sun.

Southern Europe

Anisostichus capreolatus (*Bignonia capreolata*)
Clinging Vine   May   Zone 6   Crossvine
Popular throughout the South because of its orange red flowers, 1½ to 2 inches long. The evergreen foliage turns a reddish green in the fall.

Southern United States

H **Anthemis tinctoria**   3′   July–August   Zone 3
Golden Marguerite
Profuse, yellow, daisylike flowers 2 inches in diameter. Finely cut, aromatic foliage, does best in sunny situations. An old-time favorite.

Europe and Asia

H **Aquilegia canadensis**   3′   July–August   Zones 2–3
American Columbine
Nodding red to yellow flowers with red spurs. Sunny to semishaded situations in rather dry, sandy soil.

Eastern North America

H **Arabis albida 'Flore-pleno'**   6–10″   April–May
   Zone 3   Double Wall Rock-cress
   White-pink flowers, ½ inch wide; fragrant and in loose clusters.   Europe

---

H **Arabis caucasica**   4–10″   April–May   Zone 6
   Caucasian Rock-cress
   White flowers, gray foliage.   Southern Europe

E **Araucaria araucana**   90′   Zone 7   Monkey-puzzle-tree
   With unique whorled branches, producing poor shade and an ungainly mass of foliage and twisted stems. It is not a desirable ornamental, but some people admire it because its shape is so unique.   Chile

---

E **Arbutus unedo**   10–30′   October–December
   Zone 8   Strawberry-tree
   A shrub or small tree with white flowers which develop strawberrylike fruits in the fall. These may remain on the tree for months. An additional characteristic is that the normal bark cracks open and exposes a brilliant red underbark. This plant requires acid soil, and young plants are far easier to transplant than larger and older specimens.   Southern Europe

---

E **Arctostaphylos uva-ursi**   6–12″   May   Zone 2
   Bearberry
   An excellent evergreen ground cover for sunny (or shady) sandy soils. The red fruits are ¼ inch wide and appear in the summer. It requires poor soil to grow well. Autumn color is bronze.
                          Europe, Asia, North America

H **Arisaema triphyllum**   12–18″   June   Zone 4
   Jack-in-the-pulpit

Interesting flower followed by red berries. Bulbs poisonous. Does best in rich, moist soil.

Eastern United States

Aristolochia durior   Twining Vine   Zone 4
  Dutchman's-pipe
    An old-fashioned favorite with large, rounded leaves about a foot in diameter, and peculiar flowers like the shape of a small Meerschaum pipe. Excellent for screening. A vigorous grower.

Central United States

Aronia arbutifolia   9′   May   Zone 4   Red
  Chokeberry
    Small white flowers, red fruits in the fall (slightly smaller than marbles), and red autumn color.

Eastern United States

Aronia melanocarpa   1½–3′   May   Zone 4   Black
  Chokeberry
    This black-fruiting shrub is sometimes used on the edges of woodlands.   Eastern United States

---

Artemisia absinthium   4′   Summer   Zones 2–3
  Wormwood
    A common garden favorite for its silky, whitish foliage.   Europe

---

Artemisia frigida   1½′   August   Zone 2   Fringed
  Sagebrush
    The foliage is finely divided, silvery and aromatic, giving this plant possibilities for use as a gray accent in an otherwise green border.

Western North America and Siberia

H **Artemisia lactiflora**   4–5′   August–October
Zone 3   White Mugwort

White to grayish flowers, fragrant leaves whitish underneath.   China

---

H **Artemisia schmidtiana** 'Nana'   4″   August–October
Zones 2–3   Silvermound Artemisia

An excellent, mounded, rock-garden plant, with silvery foliage. Plant in the sun.   Japan

---

H **Artemisia stelleriana**   2½′   Summer   Zones 2–3
Beach-wormwood (Dusty Miller)

A common gray-leaved plant for seashore gardens, sometimes used as a perennial with the tops dying to the ground in winter; in warmer areas used as a subshrub.

Northeastern North America, Northeastern Asia

Artemisia tridentata   9′   August–September   Zone 5
Sagebrush

For dry alkaline soils only, this should not be used where better ornamentals will survive.

Western North America

H **Arundinaria variegata**   2–3′   Zone 6   Dwarf
Whitestripe Bamboo

Leaves are striped with white. It can spread rapidly and must be restrained in good soils.   Japan

---

H **Arundinaria viridi-striata**   1½–2½′   Zone 6
Dwarf Japanese Bamboo

With leaves 2 to 5 inches long, striped yellowish in spring and early summer. Best grown in partial shade. Can spread rapidly and must be restrained in good soils.   Japan

---

Asarum caudatum   7″   Zone 4   British Columbia
Wild Ginger

An herbaceous ground cover for shady places with leaves 2 to 6 inches across.

British Columbia to California

E **Asarum europaeum**   5″   Zone 4   European Wild Ginger

One of the best evergreen ground covers for a shady place, with glossy leaves 2–3 inches across.

Europe

H **Asclepias tuberosa**   3′   August–September   Zone 3 Butterfly Milkweed

Showy orange flowers each only ½ inch wide, borne in flat clusters, grows well in full sun in hot, dry, sandy soils.   Eastern United States

---

H **Asperula odorata**   8″   May–June   Zone 4   Sweet Woodruff

Delicate 4-petaled white flowers ¼ inch across. Foliage sweet scented. An excellent ground cover in moist soils.   Europe and Asia

---

H x **Aster frikartii** 'Wonder of Staffa'   1½–2′ July–November   Zone 4

Violet blue, daisylike flowers 3 inches across. Fragrant.

H x **Aster novae-angliae**   3–5′   August   Zones 2–3 New England Aster

Flowers an inch wide, pink, daisylike. A showy plant, for moist sites.   Eastern North America

---

H x **Aster novi-belgii**   3–5′   September–October Zones 2–3   New York Aster

Flowers about an inch across, daisylike, blue violet, white, pink, purple—many varieties.

North America

213

H **Astilbe japonica** varieties 2′ June Zone 5
Japanese Astilbe
Several varieties with white to deep red, small flowers in large feathery pyramidal clusters. Needs moist, rich soil.
Japan

E **Aucuba japonica** 15′ March Zone 7 Japanese
Aucuba
The thick, glossy, evergreen leaves of this shrub are up to 7 inches long. The fruits are brilliant red berries, but because the sexes are separate, several of the dozen varieties being grown should be planted in a group to ensure fruiting.
Japan

H **Aurinia saxatilis** (*Alyssum saxatile*) 6″
April–May Zone 3 Golden-tuft
Easily grown, popular, rock-garden plant with small yellow flowers in many clusters and silvery gray foliage. Requires full sun. Does well in moist soil. Several varieties.
Europe

Baccharis halimifolia 12′ Fall Zone 4 Groundsel-bush
Seashore gardens and areas with saline soil conditions are where this plant is best used. In better soils, better plants should be selected.
Eastern United States

H **Baptisia australis** 3–4′ May–June Zones 2–3
Blue Wild Indigo
Blue, pealike flowers, 1 inch long with 6-inch terminal spikes. Prefers soils in shade or sun. Attractive, bluish green foliage. Eastern United States

Berberis
Barberry
All species and varieties mentioned here are comparatively immune to the black stem rust of

214

wheat, a serious disease that lives on many barberry species as alternate hosts. This is the reason the majority of the barberries are prohibited from being grown (by the U.S. Department of Agriculture) in the wheat-producing areas of the United States.

E **Berberis buxifolia nana**   18″   Zone 5   Dwarf
　　Magellan Barberry
　　　　From South America, excellent for low hedges.
　　　　　　　　　　　　　　　　Straits of Magellan

E **Berberis candidula**   2′   May   Zone 5   Paleleaf
　　Barberry
　　　　Bright yellow flowers, purplish berries, and evergreen leaves 1½ inches long make this barberry of interest.　　　　　　　　　　　　　　　　China

---

E x **Berberis chenaultii**   4′   May   Zone 5   Chenault
　　Barberry
　　　　A comparatively recent addition to the barberry group, this is a cross between *B. gagnepainii* and *B. verruculosa*. Hybrid vigor is apparent and its profuse flowers, excellent and dense foliage will make it shortly one of the best evergreen barberries for the North.

Berberis concinna   3′   May   Zone 6   Dainty
　　Barberry
　　　　More delicate in appearance than the other barberries, the undersurface of the leaves is white. It is only half evergreen, having red autumn color and red fruits.　　　　　　　　　　　　　　　Himalayas

---

E **Berberis darwinii**   10′   May   Zone 7   Darwin
　　Barberry
　　　　In the South this plant is deservedly popular for its pendant racemes of yellow flowers in the spring

215

and its evergreen foliage. It is named after Charles Darwin who found it while on a voyage in his famous ship *Beagle* in 1835. Usually it is seen in gardens only about 3 feet high.

Chile

Berberis gilgiana 6′ May   Zone 5   Wildfire
  Barberry

Both the autumn color and the fruits of this vigorous bush are a fiery red. It is an excellent substitute for the Common Barberry (*B. vulgaris*), which of course is an alternate host for the black stem rust of wheat and so should not be grown in wheat-producing areas.

China

E **Berberis julianae** 6′ May   Zone 5   Wintergreen
  Barberry

A vigorous evergreen with leaves up to 3 inches long, similar to but hardier than the Sargent Barberry. The fruits are bluish black.

China

Berberis koreana 6′ May   Zone 5   Korean
  Barberry

Another excellent substitute for the old-fashioned Common Barberry. The clustered, globular fruits are a brilliant red, as is the autumn color. A fine barrier plant.

Korea

E D x **Berberis mentorensis** 7′ May   Zone 5
  Mentor Barberry

Semievergreen, and a hybrid between *B. julianae* and *B. thunbergii,* this was introduced in 1924 and has since proved its ability to withstand the hot and dry summers of the Midwest better than most of the other barberries mentioned here.

E x **Berberis stenophylla**　9′　May　Zone 5
   Rosemary Barberry
   This develops into a beautiful, graceful, ever-green specimen.

Berberis thunbergii　7′　May　Zone 5　Japanese
   Barberry
   An all-purpose deciduous shrub used in barrier hedges or as an ornamental specimen of value in good or poor soils, sun or shade. This thorny plant bears small yellow flowers in mid-spring, has good foliage turning a brilliant scarlet in the fall, and bright red fruits that frequently remain on the plant all winter. There are some excellent ornamental varieties:

Japan

   Varieties:
   atropurpurea—the leaves are a dull red most of the growing season.
      'Aurea'—leaves yellowish, especially in full sun.
      'Crimson Pygmy'—a dwarf form of var. *atropurpurea*. Unfortunately this is also in the trade as 'Little Gem' and 'Little Pygmy.' Three feet high.
      'Erecta'—an erect form, 7 feet high.
      'Minor'—only about 4 feet tall at maturity, the whole plant—leaves, flowers, and fruits—is slightly smaller than those of the species. An excellent shrub to use in many situations. In a hedge it will require very little, if any, pruning.
      'Globe'—even smaller than *B. thunbergii* 'minor.' A 15-year-old plant is 2½ feet tall and 4 feet wide—another excellent type to use.

E **Berberis triacanthophora**　4′　May　Zone 5
   Threespine Barberry
      Has black fruits and leaves up to 2 inches long.
China

E **Berberis verruculosa** 4′ May Zone 5 Warty Barberry

Chenault's Barberry and this species are perhaps the two best evergreen barberries for the North. Lacking the hybrid vigor of *B. chenaultii*, this species makes a dense, rounded mass of glossy foliage.

China

Betula papyrifera 90′ Zone 2 Canoe Birch

Many of the birch trees have their troubles, but of the white-barked species this is the best to use. It is not so susceptible to the bronze-birch borer as is the European Birch. In many situations, gardeners are willing to spray its foliage annually for leaf-eating insects for the privilege of enjoying its white-trunked beauty throughout the year. It does require this annual spraying in most situations and should not be planted unless this special care will be provided.

North Central and Northeastern North America

E **Bougainvillea spectabilis** Twining Vine Summer Zone 10 Brazil Bougainvillea

Conspicuous because of the red flower bracts or leaflike appendages around the rather inconspicuous flowers. Does best in normal soil but full sun. Brazil

---

Buddleia alternifolia 12′ May Zone 5 Fountain Buddleia

The only truly hardy buddleia, justly deserving its common name when its lilac-purple flowers are in full bloom. For the remainder of the year there is little about it that would warrant its being given valued space in the smaller garden. China

---

B **Bulbocodium vernuum** 6″ April Zone 5 Spring Meadow Saffron

Similar to crocuses with large, rose violet, funnel-shaped flowers, 1 to 3 per stalk. Good for rock gardens. Europe

---

E Buxus Box, Boxwood

Because several pests infest the boxwoods, the taller growing species and varieties are not in this "care-free" listing. However, there are a few of the lower types that might be tried, either because they may be more pest resistant or because, being small plants, pest control should be a relatively simple, easily performed operation.

E Buxus microphylla 'Compacta' 1′ Zone 5
Compact Littleleaf Box

A 26-year-old plant of this variety was only 11 inches high, so it does grow slowly—possibly too slowly for the average gardener.

E Buxus microphylla 'Curly Locks' 2′ Zone 5

Small, dark green leaves; its branches have a slight curling or twisting habit. At 6 years of age one plant was 18 inches tall and 2 feet wide.

E Buxus sempervirens 'Handsworthiensis' 1½′
Zone 5 Handsworth Box

One of the lower forms of the Common Box, a 28-year-old plant of this species is only 18 inches high but 4 feet across.

E Buxus sempervirens 'Suffruticosa' 3′ Zone 5
True Dwarf Box

Difficult to eliminate from ornamental plantings. Admittedly this variety has its troubles, especially foliage-burn in the winter, but it makes a splendid edging plant.

E **Buxus sempervirens** 'Vardar Valley'   4′   Zone 5

A hardy variety of the Common Box. A plant of this variety is only 2 feet high but 4 feet across at the age of 23 years. It is a wide-spreading, flat-topped variety of exceptional hardiness.

E **Calocedrus decurrens** (*Libocedrus decurrens*)   135′
   Zone 5   California Incense-cedar

Excellent, formal, evergreen tree; aromatic foliage when crushed. Requires a moist, rich soil.

Oregon and Northern California

H **Caltha palustria**   1–3′   April   Zone 3   Marsh
   Marigold

A bright yellow flowered plant for moist to wet situations. Flowers resemble those of a large buttercup.

North America

B **Camassia cusickii**   3′   April   Zone 5   Cusick
   Camas

Has 50 to 300 pale blue flowers in a cluster. Plant in semishade, 4 inches deep. *C. leichtinii* similar but only 2 feet tall.

West Coast of America

E **Camellia japonica**   45′   October–April   Zone 7
   Common Camellia

A beautiful, glossy-leaved evergreen tree or shrub, even without flowers. There are hundreds of varieties being grown in America today, especially for their white to red flowers. It makes an excellent garden specimen, serviceable throughout the entire year.

China, Japan

H **Campanula carpatica**   1′   July   Zone 3
   Carpathian Bellflower

220

Bright blue, bell-like flowers, 1½ inches in diameter. Several varieties with white and pink-tinted flowers.
Europe

H **Campanula latifolia**   3′   July   Zone 3   Great Bellflower
Purplish blue flowers 1¼ inches wide, borne singly or several to a stalk.
Europe and Asia

H **Campanula percisifolia**   3′   July–August   Zone 3
Peach-leaved Bellflower
A very popular blue to white flowered perennial growing in leafy clumps with a few 1½-inch wide flowers on each stalk. Several varieties. A good garden plant.
Europe

Campsis grandiflora   Clinging Vine   August   Zone 7
Chinese Trumpetcreeper
Showiest of *Campsis* species with funnel-shaped, scarlet flowers 3 inches wide. Foliage is coarse in texture. Although it clings to a support, it may need assistance.
China

Campsis radicans   Clinging Vine   July   Zone 4
Trumpetcreeper
Orange to scarlet trumpet-shaped flowers 2 inches wide. Foliage is coarse in texture. May need additional support.
Southeastern United States

---

x **Campsis tagliabuana** 'Madame Galen'   Clinging Vine   July   Zone 4
Orange and scarlet funnel-shaped flowers 2½ inches wide. Foliage is coarse in texture. May need additional support.

Caragana arborescens 18′ May Zone 2 Siberian
Pea-tree
An extremely hardy shrub, but of little interest except when its yellow pealike flowers are open.

Siberia, Manchuria

Variety:

'Pendula'—with pendulous branches

Weeping Siberian Pea-tree

Carpinus betulus 60′ Zone 5 European Hornbeam
With its several varieties, this is a favorite tree in European gardens. If shade is desired, the wider spreading species should be planted, since the varieties are more for accent in formal planting.

Europe and Asia Minor

Varieties:

'Incisa'—leaves narrow, deeply lobed

Cutleaf European Hornbeam

'Fastigiata'—upright habit with one or several branches from the base, an excellent form

Pyramid European Hornbeam

'Globosa'—densely rounded in form, almost as if it were sheared, with many leaders from the base; slower in growth than 'Fastigiata.'

Globe European Hornbeam

Carpinus caroliniana 36′ Zone 2 American
Hornbeam
A difficult-to-transplant species, yet valued for its gray bark and orange to red autumn color. This species has more open branching than does *C. betulus*.

Eastern North America

Variety:

'Pyramidalis'—actually fan shaped in habit, one specimen being 40 feet high with a 30-foot spread, with ample room underneath for tables and chairs; it is an excellent shade producer.

Castanea mollissima 60′ July Zone 4 Chinese Chestnut

Apparently resistant to the virile chestnut blight that has killed most of the mature American chestnuts in the United States. Because Chinese Chestnut trees are self-sterile, several cultivars or seedlings should be grown in close proximity in order to ensure proper fertilization. The tree has large, glossy, green leaves, is usually seen in this country under 40 feet high. The long, tassellike flower clusters have ornamental value and the autumn color is yellow to bronze. This is the species to select if chestnuts are to be planted.   China, Korea

---

E **Castanopsis chrysophylla** 105′ Zone 7 Giant Evergreen Chinquapin

A broad-leaved evergreen with lustrous leaves 2 to 5 inches long, growing well on poor, dry soils.

Oregon to California

E **Cedrus atlantica** 120′ Zone 6 Atlas Cedar

A distinctly colorful and stately evergreen tree, used widely.   Northern Africa

Varieties:
'Argentea'—needles grayish Silver Atlas Cedar
'Glauca'—needles blue Blue Atlas Cedar
'Pendula'—with pendulous branches
Weeping Atlas Cedar

E **Cedrus deodara** 150′ Zone 7 Deodar Cedar

There are few conifers with pendulous branchlets as graceful as those of this species.   Himalayas

Variety:
'Pendula'—very pendulous branches
                              Weeping Deodar Cedar

E **Cedrus libani stenocoma**   120′   Zone 5   Cedar of
   Lebanon
   The hardiest variety of the Cedar of Lebanon.
Dark green foliage, stiff habit and picturesque. It
gives little shade but has proved popular in areas
where the other two more graceful species are not
hardy.   Asia Minor

Celtis laevigata   90′   Zone 5   Sugar Hackberry
   This species is taking the place of *C. occidentalis*
in many plantings throughout the South, because it is
mostly resistant to the disfiguring witches'-broom
disease.   Southeastern United States

H **Centaurea dealbata**   2′   June–September   ˉZone 3
   Persian Centaurea
   Flower heads are solitary, inner flowers are red
and marginal ones rosy pink to white.

                                         Asia Minor, Iran

H **Centaurea montana**   2′   May–July   Zones 2–3
   Mountain Bluet
   Flower heads sometimes 3 inches wide, deep
blue. Young leaves silvery white.   Europe

H **Cerastium tomentosum**   3–6″   June   Zone 2–3
   Snow-in-summer
   The grayish woolly foliage makes this conspicuous all summer. Small white flowers ½ inch in diameter. One plant can cover 9 square feet in a short
time. Can be grown in dry, sandy soil. Excellent plant.
                                                Europe

Cercidiphyllum japonicum   60–100′   Zone 5
    Katsura-tree

    A splendid ornamental tree of upright habit, if grown with one central trunk; it needs good soil with plenty of moisture. As a specimen shade or street tree it has much merit; and in our experience, given enough soil moisture, it never needs attention once it has become properly established.   Japan

---

Cercis canadensis   36′   May   Zone 4   Eastern
    Redbud

    A beautiful native tree with purplish pink, pea-like flowers in bloom at the same time as the dogwoods. It is usually flat-topped, and has a yellow autumn color.   Eastern United States

    Varieties:

    'Alba'—white flowers, less hardy than the regular species

    'Flame'—large, semidouble, purplish pink flowers

    'Wither's Pink Charm'—flowers a good soft rose pink; superior in flower to the regular species.

Chaenomeles japonica alpina   1′   May   Zone 4
    Alpine Japanese Quince

    The lowest member of this genus, with bright orange flowers. The many varieties of *C. speciosa* are all 6 feet or higher, and often create serious pruning problems.   Japan

---

E **Chamaecyparis lawsoniana**   120′   Zone 5   Lawson
    False Cypress

    Tall and graceful with flat, scalelike, evergreen leaves; this should not be grown except near its native habitat or where there is always moisture in the atmosphere. Over twenty varieties are supposedly available, varying in form and color of foliage.

Oregon and California

E **Chamaecyparis nootkatensis**   120′   Zone 4
Nootka False Cypress

This evergreen also requires a moist atmosphere in which to grow, and bears less flat, scalelike, evergreen leaves.

Alaska to Oregon

Chamaecyparis obtusa   120′   Zone 3   Hinoki False Cypress

A variable species with some excellent dwarf varieties, all with flat, scalelike evergreen leaves.

Japan

Varieties:
'Compacta'—a dwarf conical bush—7 feet

Compact Hinoki False Cypress
'Crippsii'—with rich, yellow leaves—20 feet

Cripps Hinoki False Cypress
'Erecta'—fastigiate form with ascending branchlets—40 feet   Column Hinoki False Cypress
'Filicioides'—tall with twisted branchlets—40 feet   Fernspray False Cypress
'Gracilis'—compact pyramidal form—15 feet

Slender Hinoki False Cypress
'Pygmaea'—slow in growth, very old plants being only 18 to 24 inches tall

Pygmy Hinoki False Cypress

E **Chamaecyparis pisifera**   150′   Zone 3   Sawara False Cypress

A tall evergreen tree, this is a variable species with varieties of many forms and colors. There are some that are truly dwarf, but others are definitely tree types even though they appear to be ideal shrubs for foundation plantings when young. One should be careful to select the right varieties for the right situations. Leaves are scalelike and often sharp pointed.

Japan

Varieties:

'Filifera'—branchlets threadlike—100 feet
Thread Sawara False Cypress

'Filifera Nana'—a small bushy type that is only about 2 feet tall at 25 years of age
Dwarf Thread False Cypress

'Plumosa'—foliage frondlike but slightly feathery—100 feet
Plume Sawara False Cypress

'Plumosa Nana'—a slow-growing, rounded plant, one about 25 years old measures 3 feet tall and 7 feet across
Dwarf Plume False Cypress

'Plumosa Roger's'—a yellow-leaved evergreen, growing into a small upright conical bush of excellent foliage

'Squarrosa'—foliage very feathery, soft and bluish in color, not flat and frondlike—100 feet
Moss Sawara False Cypress

H **Chelone lyonii**   3′   July–August   Zone 3   Pink
Turtle-head

Has pink purple flowers an inch long, somewhat like those of a snapdragon. Does best in moist soils with some shade.   Southeastern United States

---

Chimonanthus praecox   9′   April   Zone 7
Wintersweet

With very fragrant yellow flowers, it does best in light shade.   China

Variety:

'Grandiflorus'—flowers larger, deeper yellow but less fragrant than those of the species

B Chionodoxa luciliae   3″   April   Zone 4
Glory-of-the-snow
With starry blue, white or pink flowers, good for naturalizing in full sun. Plant 3 inches deep.

Asia Minor

H Cimicifuga racemosa   6–8′   June–September
Zones 2–3   Cohosh Bugbane, Snakeroot
Effective tall spikes of small white flowers may be 3 to 4 feet long. Only for the rear of the flower border.   Eastern United States

---

Cladrastis lutea   50′   June   Zone 3   American
Yellow-wood
This tree produces long, wisterialike clusters of white flowers. The smooth gray bark and orange to yellow autumn color are definite assets.

North Carolina, Kentucky,Tennessee

Clematis paniculata   Vine   August   Zone 5   Sweet
Autumn Clematis
White, profuse, very fragrant flowers and plumey seed heads. One of the best ornamental clematis because of its great vigor, lustrous leaves, and good flowers. It climbs by winding its leaf petioles around the means of support.   Japan

---

Clematis virginiana   Vine   August   Zone 4
Virgin's Bower
White and very small, but its plumey seed heads are very ornamental in the fall. Good for the wild garden or in a wooded planting.

Eastern North America

Clethra acuminata   18′   July   Zone 5   Cinnamon
Clethra

Producing smooth, polished, cinnamon-brown bark and white nodding racemes of small flowers.

Southeastern United States

Clethra alnifolia   9′   July   Zone 3   Summersweet
With white, fragrant flowers, produced on 4 to 6 inch narrow spikes, this too is one of the few summer flowering shrubs. It needs normal soil moisture and withstands seashore growing conditions.

Eastern United States

Variety:
rosea—flower buds pinkish   Pink Summersweet

Clethra barbinervis   30′   July   Zone 5   Japanese Clethra
The tallest of these clethras, this one has the unique habit of bearing its racemes of small, white flowers in a horizontal position.   Japan

Cobaea scandens   Vine (tendrils)   Spring and Summer Zone 9   Cup-and-saucer Vine
Tenacious tendrils attach to the means of support. Pendulous, lavender, bell-shaped flowers are 2 inches across and produced on graceful, foot-long stems.   Mexico

B **Colchicum autumnale**   6″   October   Zone 4
Common Autumn-crocus
Rosy purple, crocuslike flowers, 4 inches in diameter. There is a double-flowered variety, 'Waterlily.' Plant in August as soon as available, 3 to 4 inches deep.   Europe, Northern Africa

Colutea arborescens 'Bullata'   2′   May   Zone 5
Dwarf Bladder-senna
A dense-growing, deciduous dwarf with small,

compound leaves, this is not necessarily an outstanding ornamental; but in a small space where such a low plant is desired chiefly for its foliage, it has merit.

Southern Europe

H **Convallaria majalis**   8″   May   Zones 2–3
Lily-of-the-valley
White, extremely fragrant flowers, followed by orange berries. Grows in semishade, making a good ground cover. Will increase rapidly. Plant just below soil surface.   Europe, Asia, North America

---

H **Coreopsis auriculata** 'Nana'   6″   June–August
Zone 4   Dwarf Eared Coreopsis
Deep yellow, daisylike flowers 2 inches in diameter. Good plant for the rockery or as a ground cover. Length of bloom—8 weeks.

Southeastern United States

H **Coreopsis lanceolata**   2′   July–August   Zone 3
Lance Coreopsis
Yellow, daisylike flowers 2½ inches in diameter. Double-flowered variety 'Flore-pleno' is worth finding.

Eastern North America

H **Coreopsis verticillata**   2½′   July–August   Zone 6
Threadleaf Coreopsis
Almost fernlike leaves, yellow daisylike flowers 2 inches in diameter, borne over a 2-month period.

Central United States

Cornus alba 'Sibirica'   9′   May   Zone 2   Siberian
Dogwood
Because of its brilliant red twigs, especially if they are kept young and vigorous, this is one of the best of the shrubby dogwoods. The flowers are small, yellowish white, and are borne in flat clusters followed

by white to slightly blue berries. The foliage turns red in the fall. Siberia to Manchuria

Varieties of *Cornus alba* with variegated foliage are:

'Argenteo-marginata'—leaves bordered with white Creamedge Tatarian Dogwood

'Gouchaultii'—leaves variegated yellowish and pink Mottled Tatarian Dogwood

'Spaethii'—leaves bordered with yellow Spaeth's Tatarian Dogwood

---

Cornus florida 40' May Zone 4 Flowering Dogwood

One of the best of the small trees for the small property, native over a wide area of the eastern United States, and planted by the thousands from Massachusetts to Florida. Because of conspicuously ornamental flowers, good foliage, red fruits, horizontal branching habit, the native Flowering Dogwood should always be among those deciduous trees given consideration for ornamental planting anywhere within its hardiness range. Eastern United States

Varieties:

'Rubra'—red flower bracts Red Flowering Dogwood

'Pendula'—pendulous branches Weeping Flowering Dogwood

'Pluribracteata'—flower bracts double Double Flowering Dogwood

'Xanthocarpa'—fruits yellow Yellowberry Flowering Dogwood

Cornus kousa 21' June Zone 5 Japanese Dogwood

There is little difference between this species and its Chinese variety (listed below) except that the latter is a little less hardy and may have slightly larger flower bracts. The flowers of both have the bracts pointed, not rounded and notched as they are in *C. florida* and bright colored red fruits like large raspberries. Small trees display a most interesting mottled bark on their trunks, which adds to winter interest.

Japan, Korea

Variety:
chinensis—flower bracts sometimes only slightly larger   Chinese Dogwood

---

Cornus mas   24′   April   Zone 4   Cornelian-cherry
A serviceable, all-round shrub or small tree of merit in any garden where it has the space to grow. Early yellow spring flowers, red fruits (summer), good foliage, and red autumn color combine to make this plant one of the best shrubs. It can be sheared into hedges; its flower buds force easily indoors in winter.   Southern Europe, Western Asia
Variety:
'Flava'—yellow fruit

Cornus nuttallii   75′   April   Zone 7   Pacific Dogwood
The western counterpart of *C. florida,* this is considered one of the most beautiful flowering trees native to North America. Unfortunately, it does not grow well on the East Coast, but in its native area it is excellent.   British Columbia to California

---

Cornus sericea (*C. stolonifera*)   7′   May   Zone 2 Red Osier Dogwood
Creeping by stolons, especially in wet soils, this native and its varieties are chiefly of interest for their colorful winter twigs—red in this species. This color is augmented by keeping the twigs young and vigor-

ous. They are ideal shrubs for planting along stream banks to keep the soil in place, but are rather coarse and open for the compact, neat garden.

Eastern United States

Varieties:
'Flaviramea'—twigs brilliant yellow
Yellowtwig Dogwood
'Nitida'—twigs green   Greentwig Dogwood

H **Coronilla varia** 'Penngift'   2′   June–October
Zone 3   Penngift Crown Vetch
With white to pink pealike flowers, a vigorous-growing ground cover especially adapted for covering banks. Tolerates shade, thrives in full sun. Spreads too rapidly to plant in the garden where it can become a viscous pest, but is best on waste land and banks.

Europe

Corylopsis glabrescens   18′   April   Zone 5
Fragrant Winter-hazel
A dense, neat, flat-topped shrub with fragrant, yellow flowers before the leaves appear. Probably too large for the small garden, this species is the hardiest of several.

Japan

Corylopsis griffithii   10′   April   Zone 7   Griffith
Winter-hazel
The most ornamental of the species in this genus, its only value is its early yellow spring flowers.

Himalayas

Corylopsis spicata   6′   April   Zone 5–6   Spike
Winter-hazel
A relative of the Witch-hazel, of chief interest for its very early racemes of small, yellow flowers before the leaves appear in early spring.

Japan

233

Corylus avellana 'Contorta'   15'   Zone 3   Curly
  European Hazel
    A unique shrub with peculiarly contorted and
twisted branches. For those who are interested in unusual plants or want twisted stems for arrangements
indoors.   Europe

Corylus colurna   75'   Zone 4   Turkish Hazel
    A pyramidal ornamental tree of interest for its
good form and good foliage.
             Southern Europe, Western Asia

Corylus maxima 'Purpurea'   15–30'   Zone 4   Purple
  Giant Hazel
    A coarse-growing shrub, its only garden value
is its purplish leaves, about 5 inches long. Grows too
tall for most gardens.
             Southern Europe, Western Asia

Cotinus coggygria   15'   Zone 5   Smoketree
    Old-fashioned favorite, and its red-leaved form
is now being offered by several nurseries under specific cultivar names. Note that some plants are male
and the desired fruiting panicles giving the fluffy or
"smoky" appearance are only on the female plant.
                    Europe, China
    Variety:
    'Purpureus'—leaves purplish red. One should be
certain to obtain a female plant that will produce
these fruits; otherwise much of the ornamental value
of the plant is lost.   Purple Smoketree

Cotoneaster
    Many species and varieties of these shrubs are
grown chiefly for their red or black fruits, only one

234

or two being known for their flower. Since all are susceptible to fire blight and attacks of lace bug and red spider, none are recommended as work-saving shrubs. However, the following species are widely grown, not only because of their colorful red fruits and good foliage but also because of their form. There may be areas in America where they are not seriously affected by pests. These species are selected as the only representatives of this large genus to be listed here, because they grow no higher than three feet, ideal for the small garden.

Cotoneaster adpressa   2′   Zone 4   Creeping
Cotoneaster
Prostrate shrub with rounded leaves about ½ an inch long and bright red berries in the early fall. It is not so vigorous as *C. horizontalis,* and can be used where space is more limited.   China
Varieties:
'Little Gem'—6 inches to 1 foot high but seldom bearing flowers and fruits. A good ground cover.
'Park Carpet'—1 foot high; an excellent ground cover bearing masses of bright red fruits.
praecox—3 feet high; actually growing in a dense, round mound of twiggy branches, and not as flat on the ground as the species. This can make an interesting mound in the foreground of the foundation planting.

Early Creeping Cotoneaster

Cotoneaster apiculata   1–1½′   Zone 4   Cranberry
Cotoneaster
This and the more common *C. horizontalis* are somewhat similar except that this has larger fruits, about the size of small cranberries.   China

---

E **Cotoneaster dammeri** 'Skogsholmen' 10″ June
Zone 5 Skogsholmen Cotoneaster
An excellent, flat, ground cover with profuse small white flowers but not too many fruits. A 2-year-old plant may be 3 feet in diameter and spread several feet each year.

Cotoneaster horizontalis 3′ Zone 4 Rock Spray
Commonly grown because of its wide-spreading branches that lie flat on the ground and can easily cover small rock outcrops with which they come in contact. The small, bright red fruits last long into the fall, and the horizontal low-branching habit of this shrub lends much interest. A good plant, it should be allowed considerably more space for growing than either of the other two species. China

---

E **Crassula radicans** 6″ Zone 9
The succulent perennial leaves turn bright red in the full sunshine. Each leaf is only ½ inch long, but they are densely clustered. Small flower clusters are borne on foot-long spikes. South Africa

---

E **Crassula schmidtii** 3″ Zone 9 Schmidt Crassula
Small, mat-forming succulent with gray green leaves sending up many clusters of small, carmine red flowers. Sometimes used as a ground cover in California. South Africa

---

B **Crocus sativus** 3–6″ Fall Zone 6 Saffron Crocus
Lilac colored or white flowers, 4 inches in diameter. Asia Minor

---

B **Crocus speciosus** 3–6″ September Zone 5
Autumn Flowering Crocus
Light blue flowers. Europe, Asia Minor

B **Crocus susianus**   3–6″   March   Zone 4
    Cloth-of-gold Crocus
        Bright orange-yellow flowers 3 inches in diameter.
ameter.   Crimea

B **Crocus vernus**   3–6″   March   Zone 4   Common
    Crocus
        Lilac colored or white flowers, often striped purple, 3 inches in diameter. This is the most common species grown in the United States.   Europe

B **Crocus zonatus**   3–6″   Fall   Zone 5
        Rose lilac flowers spotted with orange, 4 inches in diameter.   Asia Minor

E **Cryptomeria japonica**   150′   Zone 5   Cryptomeria
        Several varieties of this dense, upright, often pyramidal narrow-leaved evergreen tree are available, and are widely planted.   Japan

E **Cunninghamia lanceolata**   75′   Zone 7   Common
    China-fir
        The evergreen needles of this are 1 to 2½ inches long, and it has the unusual ability (for a coniferous evergreen) of sprouting readily from the stump after the tree is cut down.   China

E **Cupressus macrocarpa**   75′   Zone 7   Monterey
    Cypress
        The best cypress for seaside planting, and used for this purpose especially in California. It grows more rapidly than most other narrow-leaved evergreens.   California

E **Cupressus sempervirens**   75′   Zone 7   Italian
    Cypress
        This evergreen species, and especially its col-

umnar form (which incidentally is the most narrow of all columnar trees, often being only a few feet in branch spread, yet 20 feet or more in height), is typical of southern European gardens. The columnar variety 'Stricta' is of course used only in strictly formal gardens where narrow vertical lines are desired to emphasize the design.

Southern Europe and Western Asia

Cytisus   Brooms

All brooms are difficult to transplant, but they should not create work if pot-grown or "canned" plants are used and placed in their final growing spot immediately. Moving them around in the garden can result in many of them dying and thus creating considerable work if the practice is maintained. Leaves are minute and most species have green stems.

Cytisus albus   1′   June   Zone 5   Portuguese Broom

The only low, white-flowering broom.   Europe

---

x **Cytisus beanii**   14″   May   Zone 5   Bean's Broom

A fine, low, dense, yellow-blooming (early May) plant, sometimes two or three times as broad as it is high.

Cytisus decumbens   8″   May, June   Zone 5

Prostrate Broom

Makes a good ground cover with its dark yellow flowers in May and June. Moundlike in growth habit.

Europe

---

x **Cytisus kewensis**   10″   May   Zone 6   Kew Broom

With pale yellow flowers, a single plant of this hybrid species may grow to be 6 feet across.

Cytisus nigricans 3–5′ July Zone 5 Spike Broom
      The yellow, upright, flower spikes of this spe-
cies are dependable summer displays every year, regardless of the weather during the preceding season.
                                                        Europe

---

x **Cytisus praecox** 6′ May Zone 5 Warminster
      Broom
      More hardy in Boston's winters than the Scotch
Broom—certainly the lemon-yellow-colored-flowers
of the species are unique among most woody plants
when the wealth of pealike blossoms opens and literally hides the green stems. The more compact growing variety *Luteus* has deeper yellow flowers than
the species, but both are excellent in flower. Their
green twigs give them an evergreen appearance.
      Variety:
      luteus—dwarf, more compact habit

Cytisus procumbens 2½′ May Zone 5 Ground
      Broom
      An excellent ground cover with bright yellow
flowers. One plant can produce a mat of growth several feet in diameter.   Europe

---

Cytisus purgans 3′ May Zone 5 Provence Broom
      Another broom with deep golden yellow flowers,
a dense habit of growth, and rigid upright branches.
                                            Southwestern Europe

---

Cytisus purpureus 18″ May Zone 5 Purple
      Broom
      More open in habit than some of the other
brooms, and without as much winter interest, this species produces purple flowers.   Europe

---

Cytisus scoparius 6′ May Zone 5 Scotch Broom
    The deep yellow flowers of the Scotch Broom are familiar sights on Cape Cod, Virginia, and certain areas of the Pacific Northwest where this introduced plant has become naturalized. There are some beautiful red and yellow flowering hybrids that have originated over the years, and where hardy, they add color to any garden. This species also has green twigs that are effective in the landscape all winter.   Europe

---

E **Daphne cneorum** 6″ May Zone 4 Rose Daphne
    Although no particular insect or disease pests mar its growth, this Rose Daphne can be difficult to grow in some situations that have very acid soils. The bright, rosy pink, fragrant flowers are conspicuous. It is worthy of trial, carefully planted with a ball of soil about the roots or from pots, not bare root. If it should fail, even with good care in the particular situation where it was tried, the soil may not be just right, and it may be discarded from this list and classified as a "work-producing" plant.
                                    Central and Southern Europe

---

Davidia involucrata 60′ May Zone 6 Dovetree
    Sometimes called the "Handkerchief Tree" because of its graceful, white flower bracts as much as 7 inches long, this tree is beautiful in flower but has little else to recommend it. Broadly pyramidal with dense, rather coarse foliage, it does not produce a good flower display in all situations.   China

---

Deutzia gracilis 3–6′ May Zone 4 Slender Deutzia
    The only one of the deutzias suggested here, this plant is normally about 3 feet tall, very dense, and covered with white flowers in spikes. Taller deutzias

require considerable pruning, but this one, being small, can be cut to the ground in one quick operation if dead branches appear.   Japan

---

E **Dianthus gratianopolitanus**   4″   Summer   Zone 3
   Cheddar Pink
      An evergreen plant, moundlike in habit, mat-forming, with very narrow leaves and single, rose pink, fragrant flowers less than an inch across. Excellent for in front of the flower border or rock garden.   Southern Europe

---

H **Dicentra eximia**   1–2′   May–September
   Zones 2–3   Fringed Bleeding-heart
      Pink, heart-shaped flowers on 12-inch spikes. Excellent ground cover if planted 8 inches apart or at front of flower border. Does not spread, grows in clumps. Makes a colorful display for 6 to 12 weeks or more.   Eastern United States

---

H **Dicentra formosa**   1′   May–September   Zones 2–3
   Pacific Bleeding-heart
      Deep pink flowers, otherwise similar to *D. eximia*.   Western North America

---

H **Dicentra spectabilis**   2′   May–June   Zones 2–3
   Common Bleeding-heart
      Common garden plant with pink, heart-shaped flowers on drooping spikes. Needs good drainage and partial shade.   Japan

---

E **Dichondra repens**   3″   Zone 10   Dichondra
      A grass substitute for lawns widely used in the southwestern United States and wherever winter temperatures do not drop below 25°F. A creeping, broad-leaved perennial with rounded leaves ½ inch in

diameter. Can be planted either as seed or plugs (set at soil level 6 to 12 inches apart).   West Indies

---

H **Dictamnus albus**   3′   July   Zones 2–3   Gasplant
     White, purple, or brownish flowers or stalks 2 to 3 feet tall. Long lived once established. Foliage is a good, glossy, dark green and does best in full sun. Seed pods are poisonous. Makes a fine specimen in the flower border.   Europe, China

---

Diervilla lonicera   3′   Zone 3   Dwarf Bush-honeysuckle
     Not much as an ornamental, but it does grow well on banks and poor soil, probably its best use. Flowers and fruits not conspicuous.
          Eastern North America .

H **Doronicum caucasicum**   2′   May–June   Zone 4
     Caucasian Leopardsbane
     Yellow, daisylike flowers, 2 inches in diameter on long stems, good for cutting. The variety 'Madam Mason' is superior to the species, good for any garden.
          Sicily, Asia Minor

E **Doxantha unguis-cati**   Clinging Vine   Spring
     Zone 8   Cat-claw Vine
     With tenacious tendrils clinging to the means of support; yellow, funnel-shaped flowers 3 inches long and 2½ inches across. Evergreen leaflets are 2 inches long.   West Indies

---

E **Echeveria** species   3″–1′   Zone 9   Echeveria
     Tender succulent perennials, usually with rosettes of fleshy, blue gray leaves and red, pink, or yellow flowers on slender stalks, used as house plants in the

242

North and for massing out-of-doors in southern California.
                                                    Mexico

H Echinacea purpurea 3½′ July–August Zone 3
   Purple Echinacea
       Has red purple, daisylike flowers. It can be
grown in dry soils in full sun. Somewhat weedy in appearance.   Southeastern United States

---

H Echinops exaltatus 3–12′ July–September
   Zone 3 Russian Globe-thistle
       Globular heads of spiny blue flowers. The leaves
are also spiny, but the plants are excellent in the
flower border.   Siberia

H Echinops ritro 1–2′ July–September Zone 3
   Small Globe-thistle
       This is the lowest-growing of the Globe-thistles,
has blue flowers, and as yet is difficult to find in American nurseries. The foliage is whitish on the underside
and can be dried easily for flower arrangements.
                                          Europe to Siberia

Elaeagnus angustifolius 20′ June Zone 2 Russian-
   olive
       Valued especially for its gray foliage, it is rather
ungainly in general habit and may best be considered
for its foliage color only.   Europe, Asia

Elaeagnus multiflorus 9′ May Zone 4 Cherry
   Elaeagnus
       This species is of little ornamental value except
for its red fruits, shaped something like elongated
cherries, in midsummer.   China, Japan

E Elaeagnus pungens   12′   October   Zone 7
Thorny Elaeagnus

A popular shrub in southern gardens. At least eight varieties are offered, some with variegated foliage. The leaves are evergreen, 1½ inches to 4 inches long, and the very small flowers are decidedly fragrant.

Japan

Elaeagnus umbellatus   12′   May   Zone 3   Autumn
Elaeagnus

Planted chiefly for its silvery young foliage and for its silvery berries in the fall.   China, Korea, Japan

---

Enkianthus campanulatus   30′   May   Zone 4
Redvein Enkianthus

A shrub for acid soils where azaleas and rhododendrons thrive, this deciduous plant bears beautiful pendulous clusters of bell-like flowers. They appear just before the leaves. Autumn color is a brilliant scarlet.

Japan

Enkianthus deflexus   21′   May   Zone 5   Chinese
Enkianthus

Similar to *E. campanulatus* but with larger flowers.

Himalayas, China

Enkianthus perulatus   6′   May   Zone 5   Japanese
Enkianthus

Smaller in every way than *E. campanulatus,* it also has brilliant scarlet autumn color.   Japan

---

H Epimedium species

Excellent long-lived perennials, for partial shade with foliage remaining well into the winter. Good as ground covers for they spread readily. The flowers, about ½ inch wide, resemble a Bishop's hat.

H **Epimedium alpinum rubrum**   6–9″   May, June
   Zone 3   Red Alpine Epimedium
      Red and yellow flowers. Young foliage is reddish.
                                    Southern Europe

H **Epimedium grandiflorum**   9″   May–June   Zone 3
   Long-spur Epimedium or Bishop's-hat
      Red to white to violet flowers. The foliage has a
   bronze autumn color.   Manchuria, Korea, Japan

H **Epimedium pinnatum**   9–12″   April–July   Zone 5
   Persian Epimedium
      Bright yellow flowers.   Asia Minor

B **Eranthis hyemalis**   3″   April   Zone 4   Winter
   Aconite
      Bright yellow flowers 1½ inches in diameter.
   Plant the tubers in semishade, in fall, about 2 inches
   deep in moist soil. Good for naturalizing, massing in
   large numbers.   Europe

B **Erythronium** species
      These species have small flowers, 1 inch across,
   like miniature lilies. Good for naturalizing. Plant in
   shade 3 inches deep. Sometimes called Dogtooth Violets.

B **Erythronium americanum**   1′   March   Zone 3
   Common Fawn-lily
      Yellow flowers.   Eastern North America

B **Erythronium denscanis**   6″   March   Zone 2–3
   Dogtooth Fawn-lily
      Rose colored flowers.   Europe and Asia

B **Erythronium grandiflorum**   2′   March   Zone 5
   Lamb's Tongue Fawn-lily
      Yellow flowers.   Northwest Pacific Coast

Euonymus alatus   9′   Zone 3   Winged Euonymus

Most euonymus species are susceptible to the euonymus scale, but this species and its compact-growing variety seem to be least affected. The "Cork Bush," as it is often called, has horizontal branches and corky ridges along the stem. The variety 'Compactus' is dense and compact, and has been used in hedges that require clipping only once in two or three years. Because of the ease of growing these two plants, and their apparent resistance (not immunity) to serious infestations of the euonymus scale, they are included in this list of shrubs and trees. Both have fiery scarlet autumn color.   Northeastern Asia

---

Euonymus fortunei vegetus   4′   Zone 5   Bigleaf Wintercreeper

A shrubby evergreen, if planted against a wall it develops into a clinging vine, sometimes dropping its leaves in midwinter in the North. Valued for its good foliage—the rounded leaves are 1 to 1½ inches long—and its orange fruits. It is susceptible to bad attacks of Euonymus scale, the reason it is not recommended for massed plantings. It is a good dual-purpose plant.   Japan

---

H **Eupatorium maculatum**   6–10′   August Zones 2–3   Joe-pye-weed

Purple, tubular flowers in terminal clusters. Grows best in low, marshy land. With coarse leaves 10 to 12 inches long and rank growth. Good only for the wild garden.   Eastern North America

---

H **Euphorbia cyparissias**   1′   April–August   Zone 3 Cypress Spurge

A vicious-spreading perennial, with underground stolons. Leaves are small and linear, about 1½ inches long. Flowers are small and yellowish. Should only

be used as a ground cover but even then should be confined.
Europe

H **Euphorbia epithymoides**   1′   Summer   Zone 4
Cushion Euphorbia

A globe-shaped plant, growing in clumps. Floral leaves are yellow and attractive; flowers are actually minute, having no petals, but the floral leaves make the plant most colorful.   Eastern Europe

---

Exochorda giraldii wilsonii   15′   May   Zone 5
Wilson Pearlbush

The best of the Pearlbushes, this grows vigorously upright and produces white flowers on upright racemes. Of little ornamental value otherwise.   China

---

Fagus grandifolia   90′   Zone 3   American Beech

Beautiful at every season of the year because of its light gray trunk, as well as its good branching habit and bronze autumn color. When its branches are near the ground it is practically impossible to get any other plants to grow beneath them.   Eastern North America

---

Fagus sylvatica   90′   Zone 4   European Beech

This species and its varieties make some of the best of the specimen trees for shade and general beauty, but they must be given plenty of room in which to grow. Without any question the beech is for the large, open garden.
Europe

Varieties:

'Asplenifolia'—finely cut leaf ·   Fernleaf Beech

'Atropunicea'—foliage purplish to bronze-red
Purple Beech

'Fastigiata'—narrow and columnar in habit
Dawyck Beech

'Laciniata'—slightly cut leaves
Cutleaf European Beech

'Pendula'—with pendulous branchlets
>Weeping Beech

'Purpureo-pendula'—pendulous branches, purple leaves
>Weeping Purple Beech

'Rotundifolia'—leaves rounded, only ½ to 1¼ inches in diameter. Horizontal branches turn upward at end. A beautifully branched pyramidal tree.
>Roundleaf Beech

Ficus carica 12–30′ Zone 6 Common Fig

Giving a dense shade, the evergreen (or sometimes deciduous) foliage of the common fig is coarse but interesting.
>Asia

E **Ficus pumila** Clinging Vine Zone 9 Creeping Fig

Excellent evergreen vine for covering walls. Leaves are heart shaped, 1 to 4 inches long, and are held closely to the stem so that a mature vine displays a solid wall of green.
>China, Japan, Australia

H **Filipendula ulmaria variegata** 6′ Zones 2–3

Variegated Queen-of-the-meadow

Yellow variegated foliage, whitish underneath, and small white flowers in loose clusters. Best used at the rear of the flower border.
>Europe

H **Filipendula vulgaris** 'Flore-pleno' 3′ June–July
Zone 3 Dropwort

A plant with delicate foliage, small white to pink double flowers, about ¾ of an inch across, for the front of the flower border. Does best in full sun.
>Europe to Siberia

---

x **Forsythia intermedia** 'Spectabilis' 9′ April Zone 4
Showy Border Forsythia

One of the most popular and heavily flowered of the forsythias. Dark yellow flowers which are about the largest of all, with upright, vigorous, slightly arching branches, this seldom needs attention unless it grows too vigorously.

Forsythia suspensa 'Sieboldii'   9′   April   Zone 5
   Siebold Forsythia
   This long, graceful, often procumbent branched variety is sometimes planted at the edge of a wall where the long stems have the opportunity to hang down vertically for several feet. The stems root easily wherever they touch moist soil. The flowers are a brilliant yellow, not so deep as those of *F. intermedia* 'Spectabilis.'   Japan

x **Forsythia** 'Arnold Dwarf'   4′   April   Zone 5
   The flowers of 'Arnold Dwarf' are few and a poor light yellow. It makes up for this defect by growing in low, mounded clumps with the ever-increasing stems rooting wherever they touch moist soil. Because of this habit of growth, it makes an ideal woody ground cover, especially for rocky terrain or banks.

x **Forsythia** 'Beatrix Farrand'   9′   April   Zone 4
   The flowers of this upright shrub may be as much as 2½ inches in diameter and in some situations may be a slightly deeper yellow than those of *F. intermedia* 'Spectabilis.' The variety 'Karl Sax' is similar but slightly more hardy.

x **Forsythia** 'Lynwood Gold'   9′   April   Zone 4
   Considered an improvement over *F. intermedia* 'Spectabilis' because its flowers are more open, seem to be better distributed along the stem, and they are a slightly lighter yellow. The habit is upright, although possibly a little stiff, but it is still a beautiful plant in flower.

Forsythia 'Spring Glory' 9′ April Zone 4

Has flowers a lighter yellow color than the other forsythias.

Fothergilla major 9′ May Zone 5 Large
  Fothergilla

This and *F. monticola* are top-notch ornamentals, closely allied to the witch-hazels. The flowers are thimblelike and white, produced before the leaves and always in great profusion. The leaves turn a brilliant yellow, orange, and red in the fall, making this among the best of all shrubs for fall display. Georgia

---

Fothergilla monticola 6′ May Zone 5 Alabama
  Fothergilla

More spreading in habit than *F. major,* otherwise similar in every way. Both make excellent ornamentals. North Carolina to Alabama

---

Franklinia alatamaha 30′ September–October
  Zone 5 Franklinia

John Bartram of Philadelphia is credited with first finding this plant in Georgia in colonial days and saving it for posterity. The large (3 inch), white flowers have a yellow center full of stamens. The autumn color is a brilliant red and orange. Grown as a small tree or large shrub, it is one of the very few late-summer-flowering woody plants, and as such merits consideration for garden planting. Georgia

---

Fraxinus holotricha 'Moraine' 35′ Zone 5

A small, dense tree producing very few seeds, grown from seed collected in Rumania and distributed by the U.S. Department of Agriculture in 1937. This may well prove to be a valued addition to the group of small shade trees now becoming so popular.

East Balkan Peninsula

Fraxinus pennsylvanica lanceolata   60′   Zone 2
   Green Ash
      Variety:
      'Marshall Seedless Ash'—This is a male form of the Green Ash and is one of two varieties to be listed here because it does not seed and hence does not become a serious pest in the garden. A good shade tree.

B **Fritillaria meleagris**   1′   April   Zone 3   Guinea-
      hen Flower
         Nodding, bell-shaped, reddish brown to purple flowers, often 3 inches across. Plant in semishade, 3 inches deep.   Europe, Asia

---

H **Gaillardia aristata**   2–3′   July–August   Zones 2–3
      Common Blanket-flower
         An excellent garden plant with 4-inch wide, daisylike yellow and red flowers, providing color as long as 14 weeks. Excellent for cut flowers in arrangements.   Western North America

---

B **Galanthus elwesii**   1′   March   Zone 4   Giant
      Snowdrop
         White flowers 1¼ inches in diameter.
                                         Asia Minor

B **Galanthus nivalis**   8″   March   Zone 3   Snowdrop
         Diminutive white flowers 1 inch in diameter. This is the most commonly used species in America.

Europe

         These two species have small solitary flowers, the first to appear in spring. Often completely covered by snow and ice, but not injured. They grow best in partial shade. Plant 4 inches deep.

E **Galax aphylla** 6–12″ May–July Zone 3 Galax
An evergreen with shiny, rounded leaves 2 to 3 inches in diameter, this is an ideal ground cover in moist, rich soils in shaded situations. The small white flowers are borne on unbranched stalks a foot high. The leaves are excellent for use in corsages and flower arrangements. Virginia to Georgia

---

B **Galtonia candicans** 3–4′ August Zone 5
Summer-hyacinth
Fragrant, bell-shaped, white flowers, 1½ inches long, borne in upright pyramidal spikes. Plant bulbs 3 inches deep in rich soil. Mulch heavily to bring them through winters in the North. South Africa

---

E **Gaultheria miqueliana** 1′ May Zone 5 Miquel
Wintergreen
Bearing white flowers in nodding racemes 1 to 2½ inches high, and often showy white to pink berries in the fall. Japan

---

E **Gaultheria shallon** 1½′ June Zone 5 Salal,
Shallon
Evergreen, dark, leathery leaves to 5 inches long, with white to pink flowers about ½ inch long. Can be used along the borders of evergreen plantings, in either full sun or shade. Alaska to California

---

E **Gaylussacia brachycera** 18″ May Zone 5
Box-huckleberry
With evergreen leaves an inch long and small white or pink bell-shaped flowers, this is a rare but excellent ornamental somewhat resembling the Moun-

tain Cranberry. Especially suitable for the rock garden. Pennsylvania to Kentucky

---

E D Gelsemium sempervirens   Twining Vine
March–May   Zone 7   Carolina Jessamine
The shiny leaves and yellow, inch-long, funnel-
shaped fragrant flowers make this popular from North
Carolina southward.   Southeastern United States

Genista cinerea   2½′   June   Zone 7   Ashy
Woadwaxen
Flowers are pealike and yellow, in racemes 8
inches long. It is notable that this species, like so
many *Cytisus* species, actually requires poor, dry soil,
in which it will do best.   Europe

Genista hispanica   1′   June   Zone 6   Spanish Gorse
For poor, dry soils, this spiny species has an
evergreen appearance in the winter because of green
stems. The yellow, pealike flowers practically cover
the bush when they are fully open.   Spain

Genista pilosa   1′   May   Zone 5   Silky-leaf
Woadwaxen
With yellow, pealike flowers, sometimes used as
a ground cover on poor soils.   Europe

Genista tinctoria   3′   June   Zone 2   Dyer's
Greenweed
The hardiest of the *Genista* species, but, like the
other members of the genus, it requires full sun and
poor soil. The variety 'Plena' produces a wealth of
double yellow flowers, and as a flowering specimen is
better than some of the other species.
Europe to Western Asia

Geranium sangiuneum   12″   May–August   Zone 3
  Blood-red Geranium
    Purple red to magenta, with single flowers. Stems
may trail along ground for 2 feet or more.
                                                    Europe and Asia

---

Geranium sangiuneum 'Prostratum'   6″   May–August
  Zone 3   Dwarf Blood-red Geranium
    A compact dwarf variety of the preceding spe-
cies with bright pink blossoms, freely produced.
                                                    Europe and Asia

---

Ginkgo biloba   120′   Zone 4   Ginkgo or Maidenhair
  Tree
    One of the best of trees for use in the city; of
picturesque, open-branching habit. The autumn color
of the foliage is a brilliant clear yellow. Male or staminate trees only should be purchased, since the fruit
has a most objectionable odor.   Eastern China
  Variety:
  fastigiata—upright, narrow habit
                                                    Sentry Ginkgo

---

Gleditsia triacanthos 'Inermis'   135′   Zone 4
  Thornless Honey-locust
    The species *G. triacanthos* is a tree that should
not be planted because it has truly vicious thorns and
long fruiting pods that fall to the ground and must be
raked up and removed. The variety 'Inermis' is thornless, and several staminate or nonfruiting forms have
been selected, named, and even patented, and it is
these which should be grown. 'Moraine' does not bear
fruits. 'Inermis' is a large tree with compound leaves
composed of small leaflets giving a light shade. It has
no autumn color, and withstands city conditions re-
markably well.   Central United States

Gymnocladus dioicus   90′   Zone 4   Kentucky
Coffee-tree
    The compound leaves of this tree give it a very coarse appearance, but it does have very wide-spreading branches and produces good shade over a large area. Other, better ornamental trees may be selected for the small place.   Central United States

---

H **Gypsophila paniculata** 'Bristol Fairy'   3′   July
Zones 2–3   Double Baby's-breath
    The very small, double white flowers and finely divided feathery foliage combine to give this plant a texture missing in most others. A common garden plant.   Europe to Northern Asia

---

H **Gypsophila repens** 'Rosea'   18″   June–August
Zone 3   Rosy Creeping Gypsophila
    With small, buttonlike, pink flowers, making a good ground cover.   Pyrenee and Alp Mountains

---

Halesia carolina   30′   May   Zone 5   Carolina
Silverbell
    A small, rounded, flowering tree bearing white bell-like flowers.   Southeastern United States

---

Halesia monticola   90′   May   Zone 5   Mountain
Silverbell
    The tallest of the two species with larger, bell-shaped flowers up to 1 inch long. The foliage is rather coarse, and it is not outstanding when not in bloom.
    Tennessee, North Carolina, Georgia

Variety:
rosea—flowers pinkish
    Pink Mountain Silverbell

---

x **Hamamelis intermedia** 'Arnold Promise'   15'
   February–March   Zone 5

   The profuse, yellow, ribbonlike flowers are certainly more numerous than those of its parents and the plant has far more vigor. It is one of the best of this group. Yellow and red autumn color.

Hamamelis mollis   30'   March   Zones 5–6
   Chinese Witch-hazel

   The ribbonlike flowers of this tree are the largest flowers of all the witch-hazels, up to 1½ inches wide, and they are fragrant. Yellow autumn color.   China

---

Hamamelis vernalis   10'   February   Zone 4   Vernal Witch-hazel

   Perfectly hardy in Boston, and has the most fragrant, although the smallest, flowers of this group. They are the first to appear, sometimes even in January, and are yellow to reddish. The autumn color is a brilliant clear yellow.   Central United States

---

Hamamelis virginiana   15'   October   Zone 4
   Common Witch-hazel

   Of interest because it will grow almost equally well in full sun or shade, the yellow ribbonlike flowers of this species are the last of all the shrubs to bloom in the North. Like most of the other witch-hazels, the autumn color is a clear yellow, one of the best for fall display.

   Eastern and Central United States

E **Hebe traversii**   6'   July   Zone 7   Travers Hebe
   An evergreen with dull green leaves up to an inch long. It blooms profusely with white flower spikes 2 inches long.   New Zealand

---

E **Hedera canariensis**   Clinging Vine   Zone 7
   Algerian Ivy
      With very glossy leaves, 2 to 6 inches long and
burgundy red twigs and leaf petioles.   Canary Islands

E **Hedera helix**   Clinging Vine   Zone 5   English Ivy
      Commonly grown evergreen vine with over 50
varieties in the trade. Good as a ground cover, for
climbing on stone walls, and for use as a house plant.
Withstands shade. Roots readily.   Europe

H **Helenium autumnale**   6′   July–October   Zone 3
   Common Sneezeweed
      Yellow to red, daisylike flowers, grows in marshy
areas, can be used in the background of the wild garden or perennial border.   United States and Canada

---

B **Helianthus tuberosa**   12′   August–September
   Zone 4   Jerusalem Artichoke
      Too tall for the small garden, this is often con-
sidered a perennial weed growing in moist, peaty
soils. The yellow sunflowerlike flowers are up to 3½
inches wide and the leaves are 8 inches long.
                Eastern United States and Pacific Coast

E **Helleborus niger**   1′   Winter   Zone 3   Christmas-
   rose
      A stemless, herbaceous, evergreen perennial with
solitary white flowers, flushed pink, nearly 2½ inches
across. If it is sheltered, as near the foundation of a
building, it will bear its fleshy flowers at Christmas.
Often a conversation piece because of its late bloom.
                                                 Europe

B **Hemerocallis flava**   3′   June   Zone 3   Lemon Daylily

Yellow, lilylike, fragrant flowers 4 inches long. Many modern hybrids are now being used instead of this species. All grow in poor soil and need no attention whatsoever.   Asia

---

B **Hemerocallis fulva**   2½–3′   July–August Zones 2–3   Tawny Daylily

Orange to red lilylike flowers 5 inches long and 3½ inches wide, but not fragrant. A common garden plant needing no care once established.

Europe and Asia

H **Heuchera sanguinea**   1–2′   May–September Zone 3   Coral-bells

Another extremely popular garden plant with basal rounded leaves and 20 inch spikes of small pink to red flowers only ¼ inch in diameter. They will tolerate some shade. Several varieties available.

Arizona to Mexico

Hibiscus syriacus   15′   August   Zone 5   Shrub Althea

Popularly called the "Rose of Sharon," this shrub has been grown in America in one form or another since colonial times. It makes a sturdy shrub and can be heavily pruned to force larger flowers, the white to blue and red single or double flowers being 2 to 4 inches in diameter. It has no other particularly ornamental features.   China, India

Many varieties are being offered by American nurserymen. For general effect the following varieties might be considered:

White

Single—'Snowdrift,' 'Totus Albus,' 'Monstrosus' (white with purplish red center)

Semidouble—'Jeanne d'Arc'

Double—'Admiral Dewey,' 'Banner,' 'Pulcherrimus,' 'Anemonaeflorus' (white with dark red center)

White to Pink

Single—'W.R. Smith'

Semidouble—'Bicolor,' 'Elegantissimus,' 'Lady Stanley,' 'Leopoldii,' 'Comte de Hainault'

Deep Pink

Semidouble—'Speciosus Plenus'

Double—'Duc de Brabant'

Pink to Red

Single—'Hamabo'

Red

Single—'Woodbridge'

Double—'Amplissimus,' 'Boule de Feu,' 'Pompon Rouge,' 'Ruber Semiplenus'

Purple

Semidouble—'Ardens,' 'Souvenir de Charles Breton'

Blue

Single—'Coelestis'

Semidouble—'Coeruleus'

H **Hosta** species   Plantain-lily

A fine group of serviceable Japanese plants for the garden, growing in clumps. Given a good soil, they will thrive for many years. Light shade is best. They bear white or blue-to-purple, small, lilylike flowers in spikes during the summer. Leaves of most are large. Very old plants, in clumps, can be 5 feet across.

H **Hosta decorata**   1–2′   July   Zone 3   Blunt
Plantain-lily

Blunt leaves 3 to 8 inches long and dark blue flowers 2 inches long. Excellent for edging.   Japan

---

H **Hosta fortunei**   2′   July   Zone 3   Fortune's
  Plantain-lily
  Lavender to whitish flowers on tall spikes, sometimes 3 feet tall. Glaucous pale green leaves 5 inches
long and 3 inches wide.   Japan

H **Hosta lancifolia** 'Albo-marginata' 1½–2′ August
  Zone 3   Variegated Narrow-leaved Plantain-lily
  Lavender flowers, leaves 6 inches long and 1½
to 2 inches wide with a white margin.   Japan

H **Hosta plantaginea**   10″   August   Zone 3
  Fragrant Plantain-lily
  An old-fashioned favorite because of its pure
white, fragrant flowers, the only Hosta with scented
flowers.   Japan and China

H **Hosta sieboldiana**   18″   July   Zone 3   Siebold
  Plantain-lily
  Lilac colored lilylike flowers and glaucous bluish
leaves as much as 10 to 15 inches long and 6 to 10
inches wide. Valuable for its colored foliage.   Japan

H **Hosta undulata**   2–3′   July   Zone 3   Wavy-leaved
  Plantain-lily
  The wavy margined leaves of this species are
variegated white, 6 to 8 inches long and about 5 inches
wide, but this is only pronounced in shade. Lavender
colored, lilylike flowers are 2 inches long, with many
on each spike.   Japan

B **Hyacinthus orientalis**   15″   April   Zone 6
  Common Hyacinth
  White, red, and blue flowers in upright pyramidal clusters. This is the most common species,
needing a good winter mulch in the North in order to

live through the winter. Plant bulbs 5 to 6 inches
deep.   Greece and Asia Minor

Hydrangea anomala petiolaris Clinging Vine   June
    Zone 4   Climbing Hydrangea
    One of the best woody clinging vines, this is ex-
cellent for stone walls, rambling over boulders or even
climbing up tree trunks, for it does not twine and
girdle the tree branches. White flowers are borne in
flat flower clusters 6 to 8 inches across, and the lateral branches sometimes extend from the wall about
3 feet.   China and Japan

Hydrangea arborescens 'Grandiflora'   3′   July
    Zone 4   Hills-of-snow
    An old-fashioned favorite found originally in
Ohio before 1900, this has completely sterile flowers
in round snowball-like masses from 4 inches in diameter. It will flower well, even though cut to the
ground in early spring. Its general effect is to create
a feeling of coolness in the summer.
    Variety:
    radiata—with white flower clusters 2 to 5 inches
across. The undersurface of the leaves is white.
                          Silverleaf Hydrangea
                          North and South Carolina

Hydrangea macrophylla   12′   August   Zones 5–6
    House Hydrangea
    This popular big-leaf hydrangea has been grown
in gardens in Europe for centuries and in gardens of
the Orient for centuries before that. There are literally
hundreds of cultivars being grown in Europe, Japan,
and Australia. The flowers are 5 to 10 inches in diameter, completely sterile, and pink, red, and blue
flowering cultivars are available. All are supposed to

change the color of their flowers from blue or bluish to pink or pinkish, depending on the amount of iron or aluminum in the soil, for the blueness of the flowers depends on the soil acidity; the more acid the soil, the bluer are the flowers.   Japan

---

Hydrangea paniculata 'Grandiflora'   30′   August
   Zone 4   Peegee Hydrangea
     Unfortunately far too common in American gardens, this is a coarse-leaved, coarse-flowering shrub (sometimes even a small tree) that is most difficult to work in the proper garden design. The large pyramidal flower clusters may be 18 inches long and remain on the plant in dried condition well into the fall, giving it a grotesque appearance.   Japan

---

Hydrangea quercifolia   6′   July   Zone 5   Oak-
   leaved Hydrangea
     The flower clusters are erect panicles 4 to 10 inches high and the leaves are about the same general size and shape as those of the red oak. It is stoloniferous, has a dull reddish autumn color, and can be grown in situations that are drier than for most other hydrangeas.   Georgia, Florida, Mississippi

---

Hypericum buckleyi   1′   June   Zone 5   Blue Ridge
   St. Johnswort
     Procumbent creeping shrub with yellow flowers an inch in diameter. Used as a mass in the rockery or as a ground cover.   North Carolina to Georgia

---

E D **Hypericum calycinum**   1–1½′   July   Zone 6
   Aaron's Beard St. Johnswort
     An excellent ground cover, evergreen or half evergreen with solitary bright yellow flowers 3 inches

in diameter and a purplish autumn color. Especially good in sandy soils, thriving in semishade.

Europe, Asia Minor

Hypericum frondosum   3′   July   Zone 5   Golden St. Johnswort

An upright shrub with yellow flowers 2 inches in diameter.

South Carolina to Texas

Hypericum kalmianum   3′   July   Zones 2–3   Kalm St. Johnswort

Bright yellow flowers about 1 inch in diameter. One of the hardiest in this genus.

Northeastern North America

Hypericum patulum henryi   3′   July   Zone 6   Henry St. Johnswort

This variety is superior to the species with yellow flowers 2½ inches in diameter. It is very good for garden use.

China

Varieties:

'Hidcote'—18 inches high with fragrant golden yellow flowers 2 inches in diameter.

'Sungold'—flowers about the same as those of 'Hidcote.'

Hypericum prolificum   4′   July   Zone 4   Shrubby St. Johnswort

With flowers about the smallest (¾ of an inch) of this group but borne profusely. The small narrow leaves are on compact twiggy branches, giving a generally mounded effect.

New Jersey to Louisiana and Georgia

E **Iberis sempervirens**   12″   May   Zone 5
   Evergreen Candytuft

A common garden plant of which several low varieties are available, such as 'Little Gem,' 'Purity,' and 'Snowflake.' All have narrow evergreen or semi-evergreen leaves about 1½ inches long and small white flowers in umbels. The varieties mentioned are usually superior to the species merely because they make a more uniform and lower mat on the ground.

Europe and Asia

E **Iberis tenoreana**   8″   May   Zone 5   Tenore
   Candytuft

Similar in most respects to *I. sempervirens* except that it blooms a week earlier, and at the same time as *Aurinia saxatilis,* the Golden-tuft, with which it might be planted for contrast.   Italy

---

E **Ilex cassine**   36′   Zone 7   Dahoon

Native in swampy areas, where this evergreen holly is widely popular. The profuse, small, red berries, ¼ inch in diameter, which are massed along the stems of the pistillate plants, are its chief ornament in fall and winter.   Southeastern United States

---

E **Ilex cornuta**   9′   Zone 7   Chinese Holly

About the only member of the genus in which the fruits of the female or pistillate plant can develop to red berry size without pollenization. Usually it is necessary to have both sexes present in the same garden to ensure fruiting. The broad, glossy evergreen leaves have few spines. 'Burford' is an unusually good variety, mostly with only one terminal spine on the leaf, more globular and with darker foliage, proving an excellent plant from Texas north to Connecticut.

In fact, in some of the hot areas of the South, this has proved to be one of the best of the evergreens.   China

---

E Ilex crenata   20′   Zone 6   Japanese Holly

In Japan this is a very popular native species which has many forms. It has proved most serviceable in America also for its dark evergreen foliage, compact habit of growth, and ability to withstand city growing conditions. The fruits are small, inconspicuous black berries.   Japan

Varieties:

'Convexa'   10′   Zone 4   Convexleaf Japanese Holly

One of the hardiest forms of the Japanese Holly, this plant has slightly convex leaves about the same size as those of Box. It is vase-shaped, densely branched, and of value as either a clipped hedge plant or as an unclipped specimen.

'Glass'   4′   Zone 4

An open-branched shrub.

'Green Island'   4′   Zone 5

Dense, flat-topped shrub, an 11-year-old plant being 3 feet high and 9 feet wide. The leaves are approximately similar in shape to those of var. *latifolia*.

'Helleri'   4′   Zone 5

One of the first dwarf forms of *Ilex crenata* to be widely distributed in America, appearing in 1936, it is still one of the best. The small leaves are about ½ inch long. It is rounded on top, and differs from 'Stokes,' which is more or less flat.

'Hetzi'—a dwarf clone of *I. crenata* 'Convexa,' hardy in Zone 5.

'Kingsville'   4′   Zone 5

The parent now 46 years old, is 4 feet high and 7 feet wide. The leaves are the same size as those of variety 'Microphylla.'

latifolia 5′ Zone 6 Bigleaf Japanese Holly

Sometimes listed in nursery catalogues as var. *rotundifolia,* this is a shrubby form with leaves definitely elliptic or obovate and about an inch long.

'Microphylla' 20′ Zone 5 Littleleaf Japanese Holly

The leaves of this variety are slightly smaller than those of the species, being about ½ inch or less in length; it seems to be more hardy than the species.

'Stokes' 4′ Zone 5

Densely dwarf plant, 3 feet high and 5 feet wide at ten years of age. Rather flat on top and in this way differing from variety 'Helleri.'

E **Ilex glabra** 9–21′ Zone 3 Inkberry

A fine evergreen with glossy leaves 1 to 2 inches long, found especially in swampy areas. It can be easily restrained by pruning to below eye-level heights, and its variety 'Compacta' is even better for this purpose, probably growing no higher than 9 feet. The fruits are black, hence not conspicuous, but its evergreen foliage and upright willow branches are its chief ornamental characteristics. Eastern North America

---

E **Ilex pedunculosa** 30′ Zone 5 Long-stalk Holly

A large evergreen shrub or small tree, this has lustrous leaves somewhat like those of Mountain-laurel, 1 to 3 inches long. It should be better known, not only for its bright red fruits borne on inch-long stalks on pistillate plants but also for its excellent foliage, which we have not seen infested with the holly leaf miner so troublesome on *Ilex opaca.* Japan

---

E **Ilex rugosa** Spreading Zone 3 Rugose Holly

A low-spreading shrub with lustrous, rugose evergreen leaves about ½ to 2 inches long, bearing red fruits in the fall. Low evergreens such as this have considerable value if they produce bright red fruits.

Japan

Ilex verticillata   9′   Zone 3   Black Alder, Winterberry
Found especially in swampy land, the red fruits often remain on the plant until Christmas. It will do well in normally good loam (acid), but of course both staminate and pistillate plants must be present to ensure fruiting.   Eastern North America

Varieties:
'Chrysocarpa'—yellow fruit
Yellow Winterberry
'Nana'—3½ feet tall, with bright red fruits
Dwarf Winterberry

E **Illicium floridanum**   9′   July   Zone 7   Florida
Anisetree
This unusual evergreen has red flowers 2 inches in diameter and its leaves are 6 inches long. It grows best in slightly shaded, acid soils.

Florida and Louisiana

Indigofera amblyantha   6′   June   Zone 5   Pink
Indigo
The flowers last for many weeks throughout the summer. They are small, pale lilac-purple on 3–4 inch spikes.   China

---

Indigofera kirilowii   3′   June   Zone 4   Kirilow
Indigo
With rose-colored flowers in 5 inch spikes, this makes a dense, low mass of suckering stems, well suited to keeping the soil from eroding. Because the flowers appear on the current year's growth, it can be

267

cut to the ground in very early spring, if necessary, and still be expected to flower the same year.

China and Korea

Indigofera potaninii   3′   June   Zone 5   Potanin Indigo

Flowers appear on 2 to 5 inch spikes, of a lilac pink color, and last for many weeks during the early summer.

China

H **Iris kaempferi**   2′   June–July   Zone 4   Japanese Iris

White, red to blue flowers with much reddish purple, up to 10 inches wide in some varieties.

China and Japan

H **Iris sibirica**   2′   June   Zone 3   Siberian Iris

Has 2 to 5 flowers in one terminal head, bluish purple, lavender, and occasionally white. Many varieties.

Europe and Russia

E **Juniperus** species

Juniper

There are far too many junipers being grown in America to discuss them all here. The evergreen leaves are small, sharp, pointed, scalelike or needle-like and sometimes vary in shape on the same plant. They vary from the lowest kind of ground cover or dwarf to the Red-cedar that can grow 90 feet tall. Listed here are some of the most outstanding ornamental types. They come chiefly from Asia and North America. As a rule, they do best in alkaline soils, but many grow well in acid soils also. Some native to certain parts of North America where they thrive may not do nearly so well elsewhere. To select the proper types the gardener would do well to note which ones are thriving in his locality before he attempts some that are untried.

There is one disease that should be mentioned. The junipers (chiefly *J. virginiana*) serve as alternate hosts for the "Juniper Rust," a disease living on shadbush, hawthorn, native crab apples, and so on. To control the disease effectively, one or the other of the hosts could be removed. Sometimes this is not always feasible; then the disease can be controlled by spraying with Ferbam or Thiram.

For those who value specimens of shadbush, hawthorns, native crab apples, and so on, and do not wish to take the trouble of spraying, it might not be advisable to plant junipers on the small property.

The sexes of the species are separate, so that if fruiting trees are desired both sexes should be in the near vicinity to ensure fruiting.

The foliage of all junipers varies considerably, sometimes on the same plant. A truly variable group, but containing many excellent garden plants.

E **Juniperus chinensis**   60′   Zone 4   Chinese Juniper
This is a variable tree form with many varieties and cultivars now available. Usually they are upright in habit, with a single trunk. There are some excellent shrubs in the group too.   China and Japan
Varieties:
'Blaauw'—vase-shaped shrub, deep blue foliage
'Keteleeri'—with broadly pyramidal ascending branches
'Mas'—narrow, dense, conical
'Mountbatten'—compact, very dense and pyramidal, one of the best forms with silvery green foliage
'Pfitzeriana'—10 feet, broad, often flat-topped shrub, one of the best evergreens for trying city conditions; growth is unique   Pfitzer's Juniper

'Nick's Compact'—an excellent compact low-growing form of Pfitzer's Juniper

'Pyramidalis'—narrow, bluish green, compact pyramid, about 15 feet tall

sargentii—a ground cover with steel blue, needle-like leaves; sometimes a single plant may be a mat of foliage 8 to 10 feet across, but only 1 foot tall

Sargent Juniper

E **Juniperus communis** 2–36′ Zone 2 Common Juniper

This species varies so widely it might be best to select cultivars in order to be certain of the habit of the plant as it matures. Normally vase-shaped and open in the center, they are mostly low shrubs, but anyone familiar with old New England pastures knows that many forms will appear in the same field. All have light green foliage of a somewhat feathery texture.   Northern North America, Europe, Asia

Varieties:

'Compressa'—1 to 2 feet high, slow-growing fastigiate shrub   Dwarf Common Juniper

depressa—seldom over 4 feet high, a low shrub

Oldfield Common Juniper

'Suecica'—15 feet high, upright and columnar, the tips of the branches are slightly pendulous.

Swedish Juniper

E **Juniperus conferta** 1′ Zone 5 Shore Juniper

A low, flat-growing ground cover, especially suited for growing in the sandy soils at the seashore where other junipers might not succeed. In good soils, better junipers might well be selected.   Japan

---

E **Juniperus excelsa stricta** 20′ Zone 7 Spiny Greek Juniper

The true Spiny Greek Juniper is a slow-growing tree, densely compact, and hardy only in the South.

Greece

E **Juniperus horizontalis** 12–18″ Zone 2 Creeping Juniper

Low, flat evergreen creeper with bluish green or steel blue, needlelike leaves. Excellent ground cover in hot, dry, sunny locations.

Northern and North Central North America

Varieties:

‘Douglasii’—A trailing form with steel blue foliage Waukegan Juniper

‘Plumosa’—foliage more feathery, a lighter green, turning purple in the fall. Branches spread uniformly from the center. Andorra Juniper

‘Wiltonii’—growing flat on the ground, foliage of an outstanding blue color.

E **Juniperus procumbens** 2′ Zone 5 Japanese Garden Juniper

A low-spreading evergreen that may be only 5 inch tall, yet 12 feet across. The foliage is steel-blue green. Japan

---

E **Juniperus rigida** 30′ Zone 5 Needle Juniper

A small, open, yet graceful tree, the needles are borne wide apart and the branchlets are pendulous.

China, Korea, Japan

E **Juniperus scopulorum** 36′ Zone 5 Western Red-cedar, Rocky Mountain Juniper

Over 25 varieties of this Midwest native are listed by American growers. The species is variable, usually being narrowly upright in habit and with few branches at the base as the tree matures. The foliage color varies from green to light blue. The many varieties listed in catalogues vary in color and density of foliage, as well as in the upright pyramidal to columnar habit.   Rocky Mountain Area

Some popular varieties are:

'Chandler Blue,' 'Hill's Silver,' 'Moonlight,' 'Pathfinder'

E **Juniperus virginiana**   90′   Zone 2   Eastern Red-cedar

The Eastern Red-cedar is commonly recognized by most people. Over 30 varieties have been named. Usually it grows slowly into a pyramidal tree of dark green color.   Eastern and Central United States

Some of the outstanding varieties are:

'Burkii'—narrowly pyramidal, steel-blue foliage, slightly purplish in winter.

'Canaertii'—compact, pyramidal, dark green foliage.

creba—the columnar plant in the northern part of its habitat as differentiated from the wider-growing plants of the South.

'Filifera'—broad, pyramidal, with slender divided branchlets.

glauca—pyramidal, dense, light silvery blue foliage.

'Globosa'—a rounded shrubby form, not over 10 feet high at 50 years of age.

'Pendula'—branch tips pendulous.

'Schottii'—narrowly pyramidal, bright green, scalelike leaves.

'Tripartita'—4 feet high, with dark green foliage.

Fountain Red-cedar

E **Kadsura japonica**   Twining Vine   June–September Zone 7   Scarlet Kadsura

Yellowish white flowers ¾ of an inch in diameter

and scarlet berries 1 inch in diameter in the fall. Evergreen leaves to 4 inches long. All female flowers are on one plant, male flowers on another.   Japan, Korea

---

E **Kalmia latifolia**   30′   June   Zone 4
Mountain-laurel

Pink and white flowers are borne in large clusters. Evergreen leaves are often 5 inches long. Requires acid soil. Foliage is excellent in arrangements indoors. Especially used in foundation planting and in wooded areas.   Eastern North America

---

Kalopanax pictus   90′   July   Zone 4   Castor-aralia

This tall tree with maplelike leaves 6 to 8 inches across has small whitish flowers in clusters of small balls, and the small black fruits are quickly eaten by birds. It should be used chiefly for its tropical-appearing foliage effect. Young seedlings have many short spines, but these should gradually disappear as the tree grows older.   China, Korea, Japan

---

E **Keteleeria fortunei**   90′   Zone 7   Fortune
Keteleeria

A cone-bearing evergreen with small needles like the firs, it is pyramidal while young, but at maturity grows into a tree with a flat top.   China

---

Koelreuteria paniculata   30′   Summer   Zone 5
Golden-rain-tree

A tree with large conspicuous clusters of small yellow flowers, later developing into greenish bladderlike fruits, this is one of the few trees for northern gardens with yellow flowers, but it has weak wood and no autumn color.   China, Korea, Japan

---

Kolkwitzia amabilis   10′   June   Zone 4   Beautybush
A popular shrub with pink flowers resembling

those of weigela, but it has been overrated. It has no autumn color; the fruits are merely bristly brown seeds in rounded clusters, so that actually it is only of value for the two-week period it is in bloom. Because of its large size, it may well be that other, lower-growing shrubs would prove better in the smaller gardens.

China

Lagerstroemia indica   21′   August   Zone 7   Crape-myrtle

A widely used plant in the South, this tall shrub or small tree is valued chiefly for its bright white, pink to red, and bluish flowers that appear for an extended time. There are over twenty varieties currently listed by American nurseries, undoubtedly several of them similar, varying chiefly in color of the flowers. It blooms on the current year's growth, is difficult to transplant in larger sizes, and has a beautiful exfoliating bark somewhat similar to that of the *Stewartias*. The leaves are small like those of the Common Privet.

China

E **Laurus nobilis**   30′   June   Zone 7   Laurel, Sweet Bay

Popular in many places because it withstands shearing so well and can be used as a tubbed plant on terraces, this famous evergreen has aromatic densely produced leaves up to 4 inches long.

Mediterranean region

D E **Lavandula officinalis**   3′   June   Zone 5   True Lavender

Used in America since colonial times because of its gray aromatic foliage and its upright spikes of small lavender flowers. There is a dwarf variety listed as var. 'Nana' in nurseries that is only about a foot high and has a rounded, neat appearance.   Europe

Variety:
Nana—supposed to be only 1 foot tall.

Leptodermis oblonga   3′   July–September   Zone 5
   Chinese Leptodermis
   Not seen in gardens too frequently, this low
shrub has violet purple flowers, and does best in the
full sun.   China

Lespedeza bicolor   9′   July   Zone 4   Shrub Bush-
   clover
   The tallest of the bush-clovers, bearing rosy
purple, pealike flowers. Often all three species will be
killed to the ground in winter but will send vigorous
new shoots from the ground each spring, making a
dense, rounded mass of foliage, blooming profusely
on the new growth. Their only value is their summer
flowers.   China and Japan

Lespedeza japonica   6′   October   Zone 5   Japanese
   Bush-clover
   Smaller than *L. bicolor,* valued only because of
its profuse, white, pealike flowers in October, at a
time when few woody plants are in flower.   Japan

Lespedeza thunbergii   6′   August–September   Zone 5
   Thunberg Bush-clover
   The flowers are rosy purple and pealike.
                                        China and Japan

E **Leucothoe fontanesiana** (*catesbaei*)   6′   June
   Zone 4   Drooping Leucothoe
   This excellent evergreen (sometimes in the
North, only half evergreen) is one of the best garden
plants where the soil is acid. The white, waxy, blue-
berrylike flowers are borne all along the underside of

the arching branches. The foliage turns an excellent bronze in the fall. A splendid garden plant for many purposes.　　　Virginia to Georgia and Tennessee

Varieties:

'Girard's Rainbow'—a variegated form, the variegation is sometimes striking with yellow, red, and white color prominently displayed

'Nana'—2 feet high, a dwarf form

H Liatris spicata　1–6′　September　Zone 3　Spike Gayfeather

Purple flowers in clusters 15 inches long. Will grow in poor soil. Single plants look best—not a plant for massing.　　　Eastern North America

---

E Libocedrus decurrens (See *Calocedrus decurrens*)

Ligustrum species　　　　　　　　　　　Privets

Dense-growing shrubs, opposite leaves, some evergreen, with pyramidal clusters of very small white flowers, followed by small black fruits, not very ornamental but attractive to the birds. They will grow in almost any type of soil under all kinds of conditions, and can be heavily sheared. Some, like Regel Privet and the Common Privet, grow well in dry soils. However, as hedges they grow too fast for the busy gardener. He should look for other kinds of hedge plants (pages 136–140) requiring less shearing.

Ligustrum amurense　15′　June　Zone 3　Amur Privet

Hardiest of the privets, of special value for this reason in northern hedges.　　　　China

---

E Ligustrum japonicum　6–18′　July　Zone 7 Japanese Privet

Evergreen leaves 4 inches long make this privet of invaluable service in hedges in the South. The leaves are more glossy than those of *L. lucidum.*

Korea and Japan

Variety:
'Rotundifolium'—only about 6 feet tall, leaves spaced closer together, branchlets shorter, this obviously makes a better hedge plant than the species.

Roundleaf Japanese Privet

E **Ligustrum lucidum**   30′   August   Zone 7   Glossy Privet
A sturdy evergreen privet with glossy green leaves 6 inches long. There are several varieties with different kinds of foliage.   China, Korea, Japan

Ligustrum obtusifolium regelianum   4′   June   Zone 4 Regel Privet
A low variety with horizontal branches, making a hedge of fine appearance.   Japan

Ligustrum ovalifolium   15′   June   Zone 5 California Privet
Probably the most widely planted of all the privets because of its vigorous upright growth, glossy foliage, and general good appearance when sheared.

Japan

Variety:
'Aureum'—leaves variegated with yellow
Golden California Privet

x **Ligustrum vicaryi**   12′   July   Zone 5   Vicary Golden Privet
A splendid hybrid with golden yellow foliage throughout the summer.

Ligustrum vulgare   15′   June   Zone 4   Common Privet

Sometimes half evergreen, this is the most widely used privet of the group. Dense in habit, it grows so rapidly that when used in hedges it should be sheared several times a year.   Europe

Varieties:

'Densiflorum'—dense-growing, upright form.

'Lodense'—grows only about 3 feet tall and makes an ideal hedge plant except for the fact that it may die occasionally as a result of a serious blight. It should not be depended upon in large numbers for a long stretch of hedgerow.   Lodense Privet

'Pyramidal'—of upright habit, without the wide-spreading branches of the species but not as dense as 'Densiflorum.'   Pyramidal European Privet

---

B **Lilium amabile**   3–4′   June   Zones 2–3   Korean Lily

Red, slightly fragrant flowers, 6 to 8 on a stalk.
                                                    Korea

B **Lilium aurantum**   3–12′   August–September
Zone 4   Goldband Lily

White to red fragrant flowers, sometimes as many as 30 on a stalk.   Japan

---

B **Lilium canadense**   2–5′   June   Zone 3   Canada Lily

Yellow orange, bell-shaped nodding flowers, about 6 per stalk.   North America

---

B **Lilium candidum**   3½′   June   Zone 4   Madonna Lily

Pure white, trumpet-shaped flowers, 13 or more per stalk. Plant only an inch below soil surface.
                                                    Europe

B Lilium pumilum   1½′   June   Zone 3   Coral Lily
   Bright red, fragrant flowers, 1 to 20 per stalk, 2 inches in diameter.   **Asia**

B Lilium regale   4–6′   July   Zone 3   Regal Lily
   White, trumpet-shaped fragrant flowers 5 inches wide and 6 inches long, bearing as many as 20 to 30 flowers per stalk.   **China**

B Lilium speciosum   4–5′   August   Zone 4
   Speciosum Lily
   Red to white colored flowers, often 6 inches wide. A well-grown plant may have 40 blooms on one stalk.   **Japan**

B Lilium superbum   6–10′   July–August   Zone 5
   Turk's Cap Lily
   Orange, nodding flowers. Must be grown in acid, moist soils. A well-grown plant may have 40 blossoms per stalk, each about 4 inches in diameter.
                                    Eastern United States

B Lilium tigrinum   3–4′   July   Zone 3   Tiger Lily
   Red flowers, 4 inches in diameter, spotted with black. Very popular in the United States. Grows well in any good soil, especially in the full sun.   **Orient**
   (Flowering bulbs of most lilies should be planted 4 to 6 inches deep, but small bulbs like those of *L. pumilum* only about 3 to 4 inches deep.)

H Linum perenne   2′   June–August   Zone 4
   Perennial Flax
   A very popular garden perennial with deep blue flowers an inch wide. Very narrow leaves.   **Europe**

Liquidambar styraciflua   125′   Zone 5   Sweet-gum
  A broadly pyramidal, deciduous tree, with a brilliant scarlet autumn color, one of its chief assets.
                                        Eastern United States

---

Liriodendron tulipifera   150′   June   Zone 4
  Tulip-tree (Tulip or Yellow Poplar)
  Broadly pyramidal, often with massive branches. The flowers resemble tulips somewhat, at least in shape, and are a greenish yellow marked with orange. It should be remembered that this is a large tree and needs plenty of space (at least 75 feet) in which to grow properly when mature. Specimens are alive that are over 200 years old.   Eastern United States
  Variety:
    'Fastigiatum'—with upright growth habit
                                        Pyramid Tulip-tree

H **Liriope spicata**   8–12″   July–August   Zone 4
  Creeping Lily-turf
  A grasslike plant, often evergreen, light lilac to almost white flowers ⅛ to ¼ inch in diameter. Sometimes used as a ground cover in small areas.
                                        China and Japan

Lonicera species   Honeysuckle
  There are over fifty members of this genus currently being offered by American nurserymen. Some are vines; the shrubs are all valued for their vigorous dense growth, their profuse and often fragrant flowers every spring, and their bright-colored berries about a ¼ inch in diameter in the late spring or summer. Some have blue berries, but these are not nearly as effective landscape forms as the red or yellow fruiting

280

varieties. In general they have no autumn color. The shrubby types will yield to heavy pruning, will grow in either acid or slightly alkaline soils, and some have been common garden plants for many years. The fruits are most attractive to the birds.

Lonicera alpigena nana   3′   May   Zone 5   Dwarf
Alps Honeysuckle
There are only a very few dwarf honeysuckles, and this one is rare. The flowers are small, red, and not too conspicuous, but the bright red fruits in the early fall are as much as ½ inch in diameter.

Southern Europe

---

x **Lonicera bella** 'Rosea'   6′   May   Zone 4   Belle
Honeysuckle
The Belle Honeysuckle is a cross of the common *L. morrowii* and *L. tatarica*. The flowers are usually pinkish; the habit is more dense than that of *L. tatarica,* and the fruits are bright red in the summer.

D E **Lonicera fragrantissima**   6′   April   Zone 5
Winter Honeysuckle
An old-fashioned favorite, and unquestionably one of the best honeysuckles. It is of special merit for its profuse, early spring flowers, which are very fragrant, appearing before the leaves in the early spring. Its leaves are half evergreen and its red berries are borne so early (May) that they provide the birds with some of the first fruit of the season. As a result, they do not remain long on the plants. This is one of the few honeysuckles bearing flowers on the previous year's growth.

China

D E **Lonicera henryi**   Twining Vine   June   Zone 4
Henry Honeysuckle
Half evergreen, yellowish red to purplish red
flowers, slightly more hardy than Hall's Honeysuckle
and much less vigorous, staying well within bounds.

China

Lonicera japonica 'Aureo-reticulata'   Twining Vine
June   Zone 4   Yellownet Honeysuckle
Leaves veined or netted with yellow but a shy
bloomer.

Eastern Asia

D E **Lonicera japonica** 'Halliana'   Twining Vine   June
Zone 4   Hall's Honeysuckle
White, trumpet-shaped, very fragrant little flowers turning brown with age. A viscious grower and
can quickly escape and become a pest. Often used as
a ground cover where it can be restrained. Bronze
autumn color. A good vine for a trellis. Able to grow
in almost any soil in sun or shade and under many
conditions.

Eastern China

Lonicera maackii   15'   May   Zone 2   Amur
Honeysuckle
One of the hardiest of all the honeysuckles, it is
highly probable that this and its less hardy variety
podocarpa (Zone 4) have been mixed up in the trade.
Also one of the tallest of the honeysuckles, it bears
fragrant white flowers. The bright red fruits from
September to November are the last of all on the
honeysuckles. These sometimes remain on the plants
after the leaves have fallen in November. About the
best of the honeysuckles for fall display, but large for
a small place.

Manchuria and Korea

Lonicera maximowiczii sachalinensis   9'   May
Zone 4   Sakhalin Honeysuckle

Proving popular in the midwestern United States, the flowers of this shrub are a dark purplish red, and the berries are a bright red. The variety is more ornamental than the species. **Korea**

E **Lonicera nitida**   6′   June   Zone 7   Box Honeysuckle

A small-leaved evergreen, the leaves being only about ½ inch long, it is frequently grown in the British Isles as a closely clipped hedge. The growth is very dense; the flowers are white and fragrant, and the blue purple fruits are not conspicuous. As a small-leaved evergreen in the South it has proved valuable. **China**

D E **Lonicera pileata**   4′   May   Zone 5   Privet Honeysuckle

With evergreen or half-evergreen glossy leaves up to 1½ inches long, this shrub has stiffly horizontal branching and often dense growth. Neither its flowers nor its fruits are outstanding. **China**

Lonicera sempervirens   Twining Vine   June–August Zone 3   Trumpet Honeysuckle

Orange to scarlet trumpet-shaped flowers 2 inches long. One of the hardier vines for northern gardens. **Eastern United States**

Lonicera syringantha   6′   May   Zone 4   Lilac Honeysuckle

Densely mounded in habit, with small leaves, pinkish white to rosy lilac fragrant flowers, and red to orange berries in June. The variety *wolfii* seems to be more popular because of its carmine flowers and its partly prostrate habit. **China**

Lonicera tatarica   9′   May   Zone 3   Tatarian Honeysuckle

A popular, hardy, upright shrub, this is always a dependable garden plant, with flowers (pink to white) and red berries throughout the summer. Frequently used as a "filler" behind lower growing shrubs.   Russia

Varieties:

alba—with pure white flowers
                          White Tatarian Honeysuckle
'Arnold Red'—with red fruits ⅜ inch in diameter and very dark red and large flowers, the darkest red of all the honeysuckles
                           Arnold Red Honeysuckle
'Leroyana'—5 feet, valued for its small size
                                 Leroy Honeysuckle
lutea—with yellow fruits
                        Yellow Tatarian Honeysuckle
nana—4 feet, valued for its small size and very dense habit   Dwarf Tatarian Honeysuckle
rosea—flowers rosy pink outside, light pink inside ·   Pink Tatarian Honeysuckle
sibirica—flowers deep pink
                             Siberian Honeysuckle

Lonicera xylosteum 'Clavey's Dwarf'   6′   Zone 4

A dense and rather dwarf honeysuckle, at least while young, this might well be used in a low hedge requiring a minimum amount of shearing.

H **Lupinus perennis**   2′   May–July   Zone 4   Wild Lupine   ·

With spikes of many blue, pink or white pealike flowers, this is a fine garden perennial. Can be grown on poor soil. Seeds poisonous.

                                Eastern North America

H Lupinus polyphyllus 2–5′   June–September
   Zone 3   Washington Lupine
      Deep blue is the most common color of the pea-like flowers; but there are also white and pink flowering forms.   Washington to California

---

H Lychnis chalcedonica 2–3′   June–July   Zone 3
   Maltese Cross
      A fine garden perennial with red or scarlet flowers an inch wide in the form of a cross, borne in dense terminal heads.   Russia

---

H Lycoris squamigera 2′   August–September
   Zone 5   Autumn-amaryllis
      Lilac-rose, fragrant flowers 3 inches long. Plant the bulbs 8 inches deep in shade. Leaves die to ground before flowering.   Japan

---

H Lythrum salicaria 3′   June–September   Zone 3
   Purple Loosestrife
      A perennial weed, naturalized in the United States in wet meadows and in marshes. The red purple flowers appear in spikes as much as 16 inches long, each being ¾ of an inch wide. Has value as a bog plant.   Europe

---

Macleaya cordata 6–8′   July–August   Zone 3
   Plume-poppy
      A vigorously growing perennial with leaves 8 inches wide, shaped like fig leaves. The small, cream-colored to pinkish flowers are on foot-long panicles. Does best in full sun, used at the rear of the perennial border.   China and Japan

---

Magnolia acuminata   90′   June   Zone 4
   Cucumber-tree
   Chiefly planted as a shade tree, its pyramidal habit and large 5 to 10 inch leaves are densely borne. The flowers are greenish-yellow and not outstanding. It grows rapidly, and mature specimens lose the pyramidal habit by eventually producing wide-spreading arching branches touching the ground.

Eastern United States

Magnolia campbellii mollicomata   150′   Early Spring
   Zones 8–9
   A rare tree in America, producing 8 to 10 inch, cup-shaped, fragrant pink flowers. The leaves are 6 to 10 inches long. Young plants bloom in 6 to 7 years.

Himalayas

Magnolia denudata   45′   May   Zone 5   Yulan
   Magnolia
   Closely allied to the Saucer Magnolia, this tree has large, fragrant white flowers before the leaves appear.

China

E **Magnolia grandiflora**   90′   May   Zone 7
   Southern Magnolia
   Many a southern garden would lack luster without this tree to give shade, beauty, and evergreen foliage to its garden the year round. The large, white, waxy flowers appear during late May and part of the summer and are about 8 to 12 inches across. The leathery evergreen leaves are 5 to 8 inches long and drop at the end of the second year. A truly magnificent ornamental specimen, it should never be crowded in with other trees but given plenty of room in which to develop properly.

Southern United States

Magnolia liliflora 'Nigra' 9′ May Zone 6 Purple
Lily Magnolia

Actually a shrub, this plant has the darkest purple flowers of any of the magnolias. It is advisable to
grow this with several main leaders from the base and
not train it to a single trunk.   Japan

---

x **Magnolia loebneri** 'Merrill' 50′ April Zone 4

A vigorous, fast-growing tree. It bears larger
white flowers than those of *M. stellata* (one of its parents), and starts to bloom at about five years of age.
A standard pyramidal tree, it blooms before the leaves
appear and is one of the taller growing magnolias for
the North.

Magnolia macrophylla 50′ July Zone 5 Bigleaf
Magnolia

Considered coarse in texture, the large white
flowers are 10 to 12 inches across and the leaves are
20 to 30 inches long and 10 inches wide. In fact, they
are the largest of any native tree in temperate North
America. The leaves can easily be broken and
shredded by winds if it is planted in an unprotected
place.   Southeastern United States

Magnolia obovata 90′ June Zone 5 Whiteleaf
Japanese Magnolia

The Japanese counterpart of *M. macrophylla,* although its leaves and flowers are not quite so large, it
is still considered a tree of coarse texture. However,
it is better than the native Umbrella Magnolia (*M.
tripetala*), the flowers of which have a disagreeable
odor.   Japan

Magnolia salicifolia 30′ April Zone 5 Anise
Magnolia

A closely pyramidal tree with leaves that are aromatic when crushed; the fragrant white flowers, 5 inches across, appear before the leaves. It is a splendid tree both for flower and for form. Japan

---

Magnolia sargentiana robusta   75′   March   Zone 7
Has very beautiful rosy-pink flowers that are similar in size and shape to those of *M. denudata*.

China

Magnolia sieboldii   30′   June   Zone 6   Oyama Magnolia
Blooming after the leaves are open, the 5-inch white flowers have brilliantly colored red stamens. The tree is of open, rather weak growth, but has value because the flowers are produced over a period of several weeks. Japan, Korea

---

x **Magnolia soulangiana**   15′   May   Zone 5   Saucer Magnolia
A hybrid species with several varieties producing 5 to 10 inch cup-shaped flowers from white to purple before the leaves appear. It is often shrublike, rather ungainly, without a main trunk. In some areas it can be troubled with magnolia scale, and then will have to be sprayed. Since it does not have autumn foliage color, and may be troubled with scale, it might be eliminated from this particular listing of easily maintained plants, if better plants can be found.
Varieties:
'Alexandrina'—one of larger and earlier flowering varieties; flowers white inside, flushed rose purple outside
'Andre LeRoy'—flowers white inside, dark pink to purplish outside
'Brozzoni'—very large flowers, 10 inches in diameter fully open, white inside

'Lennei'—flowers white inside, rich rose purple outside, darkest of these varieties

'Speciosa'—flowers white, last to bloom of these varieties

Magnolia stellata   20′   April   Zone 5   Star Magnolia

One of the best and hardiest of the magnolias for northern planting. Comparatively small, planted as a shrub or a small tree, the double, white, fragrant flowers with 12 to 15 petals are excellent. Also, its dense habit of growth is an asset in any garden during the entire summer. One or two recently introduced varieties seem to have flowers that are pink to almost reddish.   Japan

Variety:

rosea—flower buds pink, flowers fading white at maturity   Pink Star Magnolia

---

E D **Magnolia virginiana** (*glauca*)   6–60′   May   Zone 5   Sweet Bay Magnolia

Although the waxy, white, cup-shaped flowers are only 2 to 3 inches wide, they are intensely fragrant. It is a familiar sight in many a garden along the entire eastern seaboard and in swampy lands where it is native.   Eastern United States

---

x **Magnolia watsonii**   30′   June   Zone 5   Watson Magnolia

Pink and red stamens, surrounded by white petals and pink sepals, and fragrance combine to give this magnolia value. It is more robust in growth than *M. sieboldii*.

Magnolia wilsonii   24′   May   Zone 6   Wilson Magnolia

A rare Chinese magnolia, it is often shrubby and open in habit. The white flowers are 6 inches in di-

ameter, and are fragrant. They also have a conspicuous ring of red stamens. China

E **Mahonia aquifolium** 3–6′ May Zone 5 Oregon
Holly-grape

With broad, compound, spiny evergreen leaves,
bearing large clusters of small yellow flowers, followed by clusters of light blue to black fruits in the
early summer. It is especially effective in foundation
plantings where it receives some winter shade and
can thus be coaxed to retain its leaves in good condition all winter with usually a good bronze color.

British Columbia to Oregon

Varieties:

'Compactum'—3 feet tall

'Mayhan'—2½ feet tall, an excellent variety,
with 90 percent of the plants under 20 inches tall

E **Mahonia bealii** 12′ May Zone 6 Leatherleaf
Mahonia

A coarse, large-leaved evergreen with larger
flowers, fruits, and leaves than *M. aquifolium*. The
leathery compound leaves are sometimes 16 inches
long and are held at right angles to the stem, giving
the whole plant a very stiff appearance. Nevertheless,
it makes a striking appearance when grown properly.

China

E **Mahonia repens** 1′ May Zone 5 Creeping
Mahonia

The foliage of this creeping evergreen species is
not lustrous, but it makes a good ground cover because of its stoloniferous habit.

British Columbia to California

Malus species 20–25′ May Zones 2–5 Crab
Apples

The crab apples from the Orient are far more colorful for ornamental planting than the native American species. In fact, all the natives have green fruits in the fall, while the oriental species and their hybrids are loaded with colorful red or yellow fruits from the size of a small pea to 2 inches in diameter. The smaller fruited ones are the best to plant, since these do not have to be sprayed. The larger fruited types must be sprayed to prevent inroads of insects, which obviously mar the larger fruits. Smaller fruits may have their insect problems, but they are not nearly so obvious, and hence can be left unsprayed.

The commercial nurserymen at the moment are offering 140 species and varieties of crab apples, and there are well over 100 more growing in the arboretums and botanical gardens of the country.

These small trees are valued for their beautiful spring flowers (white, pink, red, purple), for colorful fruits in the fall, sometimes as sources for bird food all winter long, and some are additionally valued for their particular habit of growth. All in all they are excellent small shade trees, and even if they must be sprayed once every two or three years they are well worth the effort. The following species and varieties are among the best available.

---

x **Malus arnoldiana** 20′ May Zone 4 Arnold
  Crab Apple
    Pink and white flowers; yellow to reddish fruits up to ⅝ of an inch in diameter.

---

x **Malus atrosanguinea** 20′ May Zone 4 Carmine
  Crab Apple
    Carmine flowers; dull reddish fruits ⅜ of an inch in diameter, an annual bearer.

Malus baccata   50′   May   Zone 2   Siberian Crab Apple

White flowers; orange to red fruits ⅜ of an inch in diameter.   Asia

Varieties:

'Columnaris'—columnar habit

Column Siberian Crab Apple

'Gracilis'—pendant branches

Dwarf Siberian Crab Apple

'Jackii'—excellent glossy red fruits

Jack Crab Apple

mandshurica—one of the earliest to bloom and one of the hardiest   Manchurian Crab Apple

---

Malus brevipes   15′   May   Zone 5   Nippon Crab Apple

Pink flower buds followed by white flowers; fruit red, ⅜ of an inch in diameter; a small, dense, round-headed tree.   Unknown

---

Malus floribunda   30′   May   Zone 4   Japanese Flowering Crab Apple

Pink to red flower buds with flowers fading to white; fruit yellow to red about ⅜ of an inch in diameter; one of the best and most popular of all the crab apples. Annual bearer.   Japan

---

Malus halliana parkmanii   15′   May   Zone 5   Parkman Crab Apple

Deep pink flower buds and double flowers; fruit dull red, ¼ inch in diameter.   Japan

---

x **Malus purpurea** 'Lemoinei'   25′   May   Zone 4   Lemoine Purple Crab Apple

Single and semidouble reddish flowers; fruits purplish red and ⅝ of an inch in diameter. One of the darkest red flowered crab apples.

x **Malus robusta**   40′   May   Zone 3   Cherry Crab
   Apple
   Flowers white; fruits red or yellow, ¾ to 1½
inches in diameter. There are many varieties, of which
two are suggested here.
   Varieties:
   'Erecta'—erect habit
                        Column Cherry Crab Apple
   'Persicifolia'—excellent red fruits ¾ of an inch
in diameter remaining on tree well into winter.
                        Peachleaf Crab Apple

Malus sargentii   8′   May   Zone 5   Sargent Crab
   Apple
   Lowest growing of all the crab apples, frequently
being twice as wide as it is tall. Flowers white; fruit
dark red, ¼ of an inch in diameter.   Japan

---

x **Malus scheideckeri**   20′   May   Zone 4
   Scheidecker Crab Apple
   Flowers double pink; fruits yellow to orange, ⅝
of an inch in diameter.

Malus spectabilis 'Riversii'   24′   May   Zone 4
   River's Crab Apple
   Flowers double pink; fruit yellowish.

Malus toringoides   25′   May   Zone 5   Cutleaf Crab
   Apple
   Flowers white; fruit pear-shaped, red and yellow,
¾ of an inch in diameter. A pyramidal tree, one of
the last to bloom, with very beautiful fruits.   China

---

x **Malus zumi calocarpa**   25′   May   Zone 5
   Redbud Crab Apple
   Pink flower buds, white flowers; fruits red, ½ an

293

inch in diameter. One of the best of the crab apples for red fruits that usually remain on the tree far into the winter.

---

x **Malus** 'Adams'   24'   May   Zone 4

Red flowers; red fruits ⅝ of an inch in diameter, and an annual bearer.

---

x **Malus** 'Almey'   20'   May   Zone 4

Reddish flowers; orange to bright red fruits 1 inch in diameter, retaining its fruits well into the winter.

---

x **Malus** 'Barbara Ann'   25'   May   Zone 4

One of the best for dark red, double flowers 2 inches in diameter. One of the very best new varieties.

---

x **Malus** 'Baskatong'   30'   May   Zone 4

Reddish flowers; red fruits, retaining reddish-bronze foliage throughout the growing season. One of the most ornamental of the so-called "Rosybloom" crab apples.

---

x **Malus** 'Beauty'   24'   May   Zone 4

White flowers; bright red fruits, 1 inch in diameter; fastigiate in habit; fruit is edible.

---

x **Malus** 'Bob White'   20'   May   Zone 4

Pink flower buds followed by white flowers; yellow to brownish fruits ½ inch in diameter; fruit remains on tree throughout the winter or until it is eaten by the birds.

---

x **Malus** 'Dolgo'   40'   May   Zone 3

Flowers white; fruit bright red, 1½ inches in diameter. One of the first fruits to color in mid-August. They should not be planted to overhang sidewalks or street since the fruits can be so profuse as to be objectionable.

---

x **Malus** 'Dorothea'   25'   May   Zone 4
Double pink and white flowers; bright yellow to orange-yellow fruits, ⅝ of an inch in diameter. An annual bearer and one of the very best.

---

x **Malus** 'Flame'   25'   May   Zone 2
Reddish flowers; bright red fruits, ¾ of an inch in diameter. Very hardy.

---

x **Malus** 'Katherine'   20'   May   Zone 4
Flowers are double, light-pink fading to white; fruits are dull red, ¼ of an inch in diameter.

---

x **Malus** 'Makamik'   40'   May   Zone 4
Purplish flowers; red fruits, 1 inch in diameter. One of the best of the "Rosybloom" crab apples, it has bronze-colored foliage and is an annual bearer.

---

x **Malus** 'Marshall Oyama'   25'   May   Zone 4
Pink buds followed by white flowers; yellow or red fruits, 1 inch in diameter. This is an annual bearer and one of the most narrow upright forms of all the crab apples.

---

x **Malus** 'Oekonomierat Echtermeyer'   15'   May   Zone 4
Flowers are purplish red; fruits are reddish purple, 1 inch in diameter. This variety has a semiweeping habit and has been renamed 'Pink Weeper' by certain nurserymen.

---

x **Malus** 'Radiant'   30'   May   Zone 4
Flowers red; fruit red.

---

x **Malus** 'Red Jade'   20′   May   Zone 4
   Flowers white; fruit bright red, ½ inch in diameter. This has pendulous branches, often touching the ground, and the red fruits remain on the plant late in the season.

---

x **Malus** 'Red Silver'   30′   May   Zone 4
   Flowers purplish; fruits purple, about 1 inch in diameter. The foliage is a very good reddish green throughout the entire season, and the undersurfaces of the leaves are whitish, giving an excellent foliage color combination.

---

x **Malus** 'Rosseau'   40′   May   Zone 4
   Red flowers; bright red fruits, about 1 inch in diameter. One of the best of the "Rosybloom" crab apples and an annual bloomer with the foliage bronze in the spring and red in the fall.

---

x **Malus** 'Sissipuk'   40′   May   Zone 4
   Flowers purplish; fruits purple-red, 1 inch in diameter. The last of the "Rosybloom" crab apples to come into flower, it bears annually.

---

x **Malus** 'Tanner'   20′   May   Zone 4
   Flowers white; fruits red, ⅝ of an inch in diameter. This retains most of its fruits throughout the winter.

---

x **Malus** 'Van Eseltine'   20′   May   Zone 4
   Flowers double and pink; fruits yellow and red, ¾ of an inch in diameter. The habit is decidedly upright or columnar.

---

x **Malus** 'Winter Gold'   24′   May   Zone 4
   Pink flower buds followed by white flowers; fruits

yellow, ½ inch in diameter. The fruits remain on the tree until January.

H **Mentha piperita** 1–2′ Autumn Zone 3
Peppermint
Vigorous herbaceous perennial increasing rapidly by runners. Foliage has a strong pungent peppermint odor. Flowers small, purple, in terminal spikes 1 to 3 feet long. Does best in moist soils. Europe

---

H **Mertensia virginica** 2–3′ June–July Zone 3
Virginia Bluebells
Perennial, drooping, trumpet-shaped flowers, about an inch long, pink to blue. Dies to the ground after flowering. Eastern and Central United States

---

Metasequoia glyptostroboides 100′ Zone 5 Dawn-redwood
An upright, pyramidal, deciduous tree, thought extinct until 1947 when a native stand was discovered in China. The foliage resembles that of the hemlock, but the leaves drop off in the fall. Fast growing, needing the same general growing conditions with the same good, moist soil required by hemlocks, it is proving a most interesting tree. China

---

E **Michelia figo** (*fuscata*) 15′ Spring Zones 7–8
Banana-shrub
A broad-leaved evergreen with leaves up to 3 inches long and yellowish white flowers having a fragrance similar to that of bananas. China

---

H **Monarda didyma** 3′ June–August Zone 4
Bee-balm
Upright perennial with terminal clusters of red

flowers nearly 2 inches in diameter. Popular in gardens, attractive to humming birds.

Eastern North America

H **Monarda fistulosa**   2–3′   August   Zone 3   Wild
Bergamot
Similar to *M. didyma* but with lavender flowers.

Eastern North America

Muehlenbeckia complexa   Twining Vine   Zone 6
Wirevine
Leaves less than an inch long, this can quickly cover rocks and fences. Can withstand seashore conditions.

New Zealand

B **Muscari armeniacum**   1′   May   Zone 4
Armenian Grape-hyacinth
Has 20 to 40 small blue or white flowers clustered in a tight pyramid at the end of the 6 inch stalk. Plant 4 inches deep, in sun or shade, in clumps or large masses. Very popular. *Muscari botryoides,* the Common Grape-hyacinth, is also popular.

Asia Minor

Myrica californica   36′   Zone 7   California Bayberry
A lustrous-leaved shrub, with bronze-colored leaves up to 4 inches long. The purple berries are only borne on the pistillate or female plant, for in all *Myrica* species the sexes are separate.

Washington to California

Myrica cerifera   36′   Zone 6   Wax-myrtle
Closely resembling *M. pensylvanica,* being the southern representative of this genus.

New Jersey to Florida and Texas

298

Myrica pensylvanica   9′   Zone 2   Bayberry

A common native especially noted for its gray waxy berries (from which candles used to be made in colonial times); for its aromatic foliage; and for its ability to grow in poor, dry soil, especially at the seashore in the reach of salt spray. Both staminate and pistillate plants should be planted in order to ensure the fruiting of the female plants.

Northeastern United States

E **Myrtus communis**   5–10′   Summer   Zones 8–9
Myrtle

The true evergreen myrtle, of special value for growing in hot, dry situations in seashore gardens. Creamy white flowers, ¾ of an inch in diameter, and aromatic leaves 2 inches long.

Mediterranean Region

Variety:

'Compacta'—5 feet high; growing much more dense and compact than the species, with slightly smaller leaves.

Nandina domestica   8′   July   Zone 7   Nandina

Of chief garden interest for its large clusters of bright red or purplish berries; a white-fruited form and a yellow-fruited form are both available. The leaflets are evergreen, and when they first appear in the spring are slightly pinkish or bronze. Widely grown in the South and on the Pacific Coast.   China, Japan

B **Narcissus asturiensis**   3–5″   April   Zone 4
Asturian Daffodil

Yellow flowers, only ½ inch long, smallest of all the garden narcissus. Place by walk or doorstep where it can be observed with snowdrops in the early spring.   Spain and Portugal

B **Narcissus bulbocodium** 15″ April Zone 6
Petticoat Daffodil
Light yellow flowers, 1 inch long.
Southern France and Morocco

B **Narcissus cyclamineus** 8″ April Zone 6
Cyclamen Daffodil
Drooping yellow flowers, not a good display type.
Portugal

B **Narcissus incomparabilis** 1′ April Zone 4
Nonesuch Daffodil
Small, yellow, drooping flowers, often 3 to 4 inches wide. Many varieties.   Southwestern Europe

---

B **Narcissus jonquilla** 1½′ April Zone 4 Jonquil
Yellow flowers, 2 to 6 on a stem, about 1 inch long, fragrant. Many varieties.   Southern Europe

---

B **Narcissus odorus** 1′ April Zone 6 Campernelle Jonquil
With 2 to 4 yellow flowers on each stem, each flower ¾ of an inch long.   Southern Europe

---

B **Narcissus poeticus** 1½′ April Zone 4 Poet's Narcissus
White, solitary flowers, very fragrant, often rimmed with red. Many varieties good for naturalizing.   Southern Europe

---

B **Narcissus pseudo-narcissus** 15″ April Zone 4
Daffodil
The true daffodil; flowers yellow or white, single or double, often 2 inches in diameter. Many varieties.
Europe

B **Narcissus tazetta**   1½′   April   Zone 8
Polyanthus Narcissus
Flowers yellow, fragrant, 4 to 8 on each stalk. Popular white Paper Narcissus used so much for forcing belongs here. Many varieties.   Europe, Asia

B **Narcissus triandrus**   1′   April   Zone 4   Angels-tears
White flowers, 1 to 6 per stalk, about ¾ of an inch long.   Southwestern Europe

H **Nepeta hederacea**   3″   Zone 3   Ground-ivy or Jill-over-the-ground
A creeping perennial that is sometimes used as a ground cover because its rounded leaves, only 1½ inches in diameter, remain closely on the ground and it grows equally well in sun or shade. However, it is a viscous spreader and can become a weed in the lawn.
Europe and Asia

E **Nerium oleander**   20′   April–August   Zones 7–8
Oleander
Beautiful shrubs, widely planted in the South for their evergreen bamboolike foliage and their fragrant, single or double, large 3 inch flowers of different colors. Over forty varieties are available from American nurseries.   Mediterranean Region

Nyssa sylvatica   90′   Zone 4   Black Tupelo or Black Gum
The dense, lustrous, dark-green foliage of this native tree is its chief ornamental asset. The tree grows in a densely pyramidal shape with slightly pendulous branches, does well in moist swampy situations, and the foliage turns a gorgeous scarlet in the fall.   Eastern United States

H **Oenothera missouriensis** 1′   June–August   Zone 4
   Ozark Sundrops

   Yellow, showy, fragrant flowers are nearly 5 inches in diameter. Stems trail on the ground. Does well in sandy soil. Not especially outstanding.

Missouri to Texas

H **Ornamental Grasses**
   Varieties:

H **Arrhenatherum elatius tuberosum** 1′   Zone 3
   Oat-grass

   A tuberous, rooted grass with interesting fruits for dried arrangements.   Europe

H **Cortaderia selloana** 8–20′   Zone 8   Pampas
   Grass

   Makes magnificent tall clumps of grass, but the female plants have the large, graceful silvery fruiting heads 1 to 3 feet long. Excellent, but needs space.   Southern South America

H **Erianthus ravennae** 8–12′   Zone 5   Ravenna
   Grass

   A stout, vigorous grass with leaves 3 feet long and ½ an inch wide. Produces silky flowering plumes often 3 feet long, resembling Pampas grass.

Southern Europe to India

H **Miscanthus sinensis** 10′   Zone 4   Chinese Silver
   Grass

   One of the best perennial ornamental grasses, growing in large clumps with gracefully arching stalks and leaves 2 to 3 feet long and an inch wide. Feathery, fan-shaped, highly ornamental fruiting clusters up to a foot long, borne late in the season. There are several varieties.   Southern Asia

B **Ornithogalum umbellatum** 1′   May–June   Zone 4
   Star-of-Bethlehem

Flower stalks crowned with 12 to 20 white, star-like flowers. Supposed to be poisonous in all its parts. Excellent for naturalizing. Multiplies rapidly. Europe

---

E x **Osmanthus fortunei**   12′   June   Zones 7–8
Fortune's Osmanthus
This species has hollylike, lustrous leaves 4 inches long, and bears very fragrant flowers, making an excellent specimen evergreen.

E **Osmanthus fragrans**   30′   May   Zones 8–9
Sweet Osmanthus
The least hardy of these three Osmanthus species, it too has very fragrant flowers, and is widely used in the warmer parts of the South.   Asia

---

E **Osmanthus heterophyllus** (*ilicifolius*)   18′   July
Zone 6   Holly Osmanthus
The hardiest of this group of broad-leaved evergreens, with fragrant flowers and lustrous, spiny, evergreen foliage. The leaves have 2 to 4 spines and are somewhat similar to those of the English Holly, but are opposite, while leaves of the hollies are borne alternately along the stems This species can be grown in either full sun or partial shade.   Japan

---

Oxydendrum arboreum   75′   July–August   Zone 5
Sorrel-tree or Sourwood
An excellent ornamental tree in flower and foliage, best in acid soils. The lustrous, laurel-like leaves are beautiful throughout the growing season and in the fall they turn a brilliant scarlet. The nodding clusters of small flowers make the tree an outstanding ornament.   Eastern and Southeastern United States

H **Pachysandra procumbens**   6″–1′   April   Zone 4
　　Allegheny Pachysandra
　　　　The leaves die to the ground in the winter in the
North, but are evergreen in the South. Often used as a
ground cover. The small, whitish-purplish flowers ap-
pear on 5 inch stalks before the leaves appear. Re-
quires shade. Grows in a rounded clump.
　　　　　　　　　West Virginia to Florida and Louisiana

E **Pachysandra terminalis**   6″   May   Zone 5
　　Japanese Spurge
　　　　Best evergreen ground cover for shade. Dark,
lustrous leaves and small, upright flower spikes make
this plant a fine ornamental. It spreads readily by
underground stolons or runners.　　　　　　　　Japan

H **Paeonia officinalis**   3′   May–June   Zone 3
　　Common Peony
　　　　The old-fashioned peony has been popular in
American gardens since colonial times. Hundreds of
varieties have been grown with single or double, white,
pink or red flowers up to 4 inches across. When planting, place buds (on crown of plant) only an inch or
two below soil surface—no deeper—otherwise they
may not bloom.　　　　　　Europe to Western Asia

H **Papaver orientale**   2–4′   May–June   Zones 2–3
　　Oriental Poppy
　　　　Conspicuous bright colored flowers from white
to red, as much as 6 inches in diameter borne on tall
single stalks. A garden favorite with many varieties.
　　　　　　　　　　　　　Mediterranean Region

Parthenocissus henryana   Clinging Vine   Zone 8
　　Silver Vein Creeper
　　　　For the shade, where its striking white varie-

gated leaves, purplish on the undersurface, develop
more color. China

Parthenocissus quinquefolia   Clinging Vine   Zone 3
   Virginia Creeper
      Common native vine with vivid scarlet autumn
color and leaves made up of five leaflets. Very popular. Eastern United States

---

Parthenocissus tricuspidata   Clinging Vine   Zone 4
   Boston-ivy
      Clinging well to stonework, this is one of the best
vines for this purpose. Leaves are maplelike, turning
vivid scarlet in the fall. Endures urban conditions.
China, Japan

E D **Passiflora caerulea**   Tendrils   June–September
   Zones 7–8   Passion-flower
      Semievergreen, a popular vine for southern gar-
dens. The leaves are 5-lobed. The blue to pure white
flowers are 4 inches across. Brazil

H **Penstemon barbatus**   3–6′   June–August
   Zones 2–3   Beardlip Penstemon
      Herbaceous perennial with red flowers an inch
wide, borne in thin spires. Needs full sun.
Utah to Mexico

E **Pernettya mucronata**   1½′   Zones 6–7   Chilean
   Pernettya
      A shiny-leaved evergreen of special value for its
white to dark purple berries, ½ inch in diameter in
the fall and winter. There are a half-dozen varieties
available, named according to the color of the fruits.
The plant forms a neat shrub in the full sun. At least

305

two varieties should be planted together to ensure fruiting. Chile

---

H Phalaris arundinacea picta 2–4′ Zone 3
   Ribbon-grass
       With green leaves striped with white, looks like a small bamboo. Increases vigorously and might have to be restrained in good soil. Grows in poor dry soils in full sun at the lower height and can easily be kept under 2 feet tall by running over with the lawn mower in early summer. An excellent poor-soil plant for use as a ground cover. Europe and North America

---

Phellondendron amurense 30′ Zone 3 Amur
   Corktree
       A large-branched, open tree with visibly corky bark and compound leaves that turn yellow in the fall. Fruiting trees (the sexes are separate) might be overlooked for planting, since the large, black, grapelike fruits are of little value ornamentally. It is excellent for planting in situations where there are electric wires, since it is so open that few branches will have to be removed. China

---

Philadelphus species Mock-Orange
       Gardeners should remember that the plants in this large group of deciduous shrubs are only of ornamental interest for a short two-week period when they are in bloom during June. Their fruits are merely dried capsules; the autumn color is yellowish, but the leaves do not remain on the plants long once they have started to change color. Some have fragrant flowers; none have serious disease or insect pests. In the North there is often serious need for occasional renewal pruning. All in all, there are usually better shrubs for limited space in the small garden. Nevertheless, for

those who wish to plant them, the following are among the best of a large number available.

Philadelphus coronarius   9′   June   Zone 4   Sweet
  Mock-orange
    An old-fashioned favorite and one of the most fragrant. Especially good for dry-soil situations. The flowers are white, single, 1 to 1½ inches in diameter.
    Europe

    Variety:
    'Aureus'—densely rounded in habit, with yellow foliage. This is not for planting in the shade, but in the full sun.   Yellow Sweet Mock-orange

---

Philadelphus grandiflorus   9′   June   Zone 4   .
  Big Scentless Mock-orange
    Pretty tall for the small garden, and the flowers have no fragrance. Flowers white, single, 1¾ inches in diameter.   Southeastern United States

---

x **Philadelphus splendens**   8′   June   Zone 5
    Flowers white, single, 1½ inches in diameter, without much fragrance. The habit is excellent, for the plant grows with branches touching the ground on all sides.
    Hybrid varieties (All white flowers—mostly hardy in Zone 5, June):
    'Albatre'—5 feet, flowers double, 1¾ inches in diameter.
    'Argentine'—4 feet, flowers double, 2 inches in diameter.
    'Avalanche'—5 feet, flowers single, 1 inch in diameter; arching habit and very fragrant.
    'Belle Etoile'—6 feet, flowers single, 2¼ inches in diameter.
    'Bouquet Blanc'—6 feet, flowers single, 1 inch in diameter.

'Conquête'—6 to 8 feet, flowers 2 inches in diameter and very fragrant.

'Frosty Morn'—3 feet, flowers double, fragrant. Hardy in Zone 3.

'Girandole'—4 feet, flowers double, 1¾ inches in diameter.

'Glacier'—5 feet, flowers double, 1¼ inches in diameter.

'Innocence'—8 feet, flowers single, 1¾ inches in diameter and very fragrant.

'Minnesota Snowflake'—6 feet, flowers double, fragrant. Hardy in Zone 3.

'Mont Blanc'—4 feet, flowers single, 1¾ inches in diameter. Of moundlike habit. Hardy in Zone 4.

'Norma'—6 feet, flowers single, 1½ inches in diameter.

'Virginal'—9 feet, flowers double, 2 inches in diameter. Very fragrant, but because it grows tall, with no branches at the base, it should never be used unless smaller plants are in the foreground to hide the unsightly base.

H **Phlox paniculata**   2–4′   June–September   Zone 4
   Garden Phlox

A perennial garden favorite bearing white, red, or purple flowers in terminal pyramidal clusters, 4 to 6 inches long. Does best in full sun. Many varieties available.   Eastern United States

---

H **Phlox subulata**   6″   March–May   Zones 2–3
   Moss-pink

Low rock garden plant or ground cover covered with white, pink, or red flowers in early spring and soft foliage made up of small linear leaves.

New York to North Carolina

E **Photinia serrulata**   36′   Zone 7   Chinese Photinia
    Vigorous evergreen shrub, may need to be re-strained. The new, lustrous foliage is reddish bronze—the reason some gardeners like it.   China

---

H **Physalis alkekengi**   2′   August   Zones 2–3
    Chinese-lantern or Strawberry Ground-cherry
    A perennial ornamental (sometimes grown as an annual) which can become a bad weed if it escapes. Creeps by underground stems. Small cherrylike fruit is enclosed by a bright red, inflated husk about 2 inches long, resembling a miniature Chinese lantern.   Europe to Japan

---

Physocarpus opulifolius   9′   Zone 2   Eastern
    Ninebark
    Coarse in habit and foliage, this shrub grows well in almost any soil. It should not be considered a speci-men plant for the small place but has its uses as a "filler."   Quebec to Virginia, Tennesee, Michigan
    Varieties:
    'Luteus'—yellow to yellowish foliage turning green by mid-August.
    'Nanus'—2 feet high, dwarf form with smaller leaves.

E **Picea** species   Spruce
    Stiffly branched, coniferous evergreens, with small, needlelike leaves. There are some excellent dwarf types that, although very slow growing, have merit in certain situations. A few of the best species and some dwarf varieties follow.

E **Picea abies-dwarf** varieties   Zone 2   Norway Spruce
    There are many cultivars in this group, ranging

in habit from low, almost flat plants, to the rounded, flat-topped, or pyramidal ones. Some grow extremely slowly, only a half-inch or so a year, others faster.

Varieties:

'Clanbrassiliana'—2½ to 6 feet high, wide-spreading, rounded form.

'Maxwellii'—low, moundlike, twice as broad as high.

'Microsperma'—densely pyramidal, a 40-year-old plant can be 10 feet tall and 10 feet across.

'Nidiformis'—upright with a definitely flat top and light green foliage. A 20-year-old plant is about 3 feet tall and 5 feet across.

'Parsonsii'—rounded form, none too regular in outline; an old plant is 5 feet tall and 8 feet across.

'Procumbens'—one of the lowest forms, seldom over 3 to 4 feet tall, but old plants may be as much as 15 feet across.

'Pumila'—low flat habit, a 100-year-old specimen was reported to be only 4 feet tall but over 20 feet across.

'Repens'—a low bush of irregular growth, one plant is known to have been only 18 inches tall but 4 feet across.

E **Picea glauca** 'Conica'   4–12′   Zone 4   Dwarf White Spruce

A tight, dense pyramid of small needles, this dwarf grows in such fashion that it always looks as if it were sheared. It was found in southwestern Canada. Stiffly formal, there are situations where it can be used to good advantage.   Southwestern Canada

---

E **Picea omorika**   90′   Zone 4   Serbian Spruce

The best of the spruces. A pyramidal, almost columnar tree, often with slightly pendulous branches, narrow in habit. The needles are white on the under-surface, and above they are a glossy dark green.

Europe

E **Pieris floribunda** 6′ April Zone 4 Mountain
Andromeda

One of the best of the broad-leaved evergreens for the North, doing well in either acid or alkaline soils. The small, pure white flowers are in upright pyramidal clusters, 4 inches high.

Virginia to Georgia

E **Pieris formosa** 12′ April Zone 7 Himalayan
Andromeda

With larger leaves (up to 6 inches long) than *P. floribunda,* this has white or pinkish drooping panicles of small white flowers. A good evergreen, it is for use in the warmer parts of the country. Young foliage has a deep red color.

Himalayas

E **Pieris japonica** 9′ April Zone 5 Japanese
Andromeda

Another excellent broad-leaved evergreen for the North, this has glossy leaves, somewhat like those of mountain-laurel, 3½ inches long. The small white flowers are in nodding clusters so that the whole plant has a more delicate as well as a more lustrous appearance than *P. floribunda.* A well-grown, well-flowered specimen of the Japanese Andromeda is about as good a broad-leaved evergreen as one can hope to grow, in the North at least.

Japan

Varieties:

'Compacta'—compact habit, leaves only 1½ inches long

'Crispa'—leaves with wavy margins

'Dorothy Wycoff'—compact habit, dark red flower buds, red to dark pink flowers

'Variegata'—leaves with a very thin margin of white

E **Pieris taiwanensis**　6′　Early Spring　Zone 7
　　Formosa Andromeda
　　　Similar to other *Pieris* species in flower and foliage, and worthy of trial in southern gardens, with flower clusters 6 inches long.　　　　　　Formosa

---

E **Pilostegia viburnoides**　Clinging Vine　August–October　Zone 7
　　　White hydrangealike flowers, freely borne, evergreen leaves 3 to 5 inches long, close clinging. One of the best of the evergreen vines, doing best in the shade.
　　　　　　　　　　　　　　　　　China

E **Pinus aristata**　8–45′　Zone 5　Bristlecone Pine
　　　A standard tree with needlelike foliage in Colorado, Arizona, and California, where it is native. In the East it is extremely slow growing (4 feet high in 10 years), but it makes a picturesque, sparsely branched, small specimen of considerable interest when planted in the proper surroundings.
　　　　　　　　　　　　Colorado, Arizona

E **Pinus bungeana**　75′　Zone 4　Lace-bark Pine
　　　A beautiful tree with dark green, heavy, needlelike leaves, and exfoliating bark on the trunk and larger branches. This makes the trunks white and gray in an uniquely beautiful patchwork pattern. The wood is weak; unless the tree is grown with many branches from the ground, there may be serious danger of the limbs breaking on a single-trunked, mature tree in heavy snowstorms.　　　　　　China

---

E **Pinus cembra**   75'   Zone 2   Swiss Stone Pine
    A dense, pyramidal, slow-growing pine.
Europe and Asia

E **Pinus densiflora**   15'   Zone 4   Japanese Red Pine
    Variety:
    'Umbraculifera'—low, flat-topped tree with several branches from the ground and more or less horizontal branchlets, the entire plant reaching 12 to 15 feet in height. The bark is red. Often called Tanyosho Pine.
Japan

E **Pinus griffithii**   150'   Zone 5   Himalayan Pine
    Of special interest for its long (5 to 7 inch), gracefully drooping needles. Making a splendid pyramidal tree with a width of 40 feet.
Himalayas

E **Pinus nigra**   90'   Zone 4   Austrian Pine
    A fast-growing species with dark green needles. These needles are very stiff so that the whole tree has a stiff but strong appearance.
Europe and Asia Minor

E **Pinus parviflora**   90'   Zone 5   White Japanese Pine
    The bluish green needles of this very widespreading tree make it especially outstanding among all the pines. Needs plenty of room, growing almost as broad as it does high.
Japan

E **Pinus radiata**   60'   Zone 7   Monterey Pine
    A dark green pine, especially adapted for seaside planting, used chiefly in southern California.
California

313

E **Pinus strobus**   Zone 3   Eastern White Pine
Varieties:
'Brevifolia'—dense, pyramidal, bushy form, 35 feet
'Fastigiata'—narrow, pyramidal, 100 feet
'Nana'—dwarf form, rounded in habit, 25 feet
'Pendula'—with pendulous branches, 50 feet
'Umbraculifera'—vase-shaped bush with umbrella-shaped head, 25 feet

---

E **Pinus sylvestris**   75'   Zone 2   Scotch Pine
Another very hardy pine having grayish green foliage, reddish bark on the upper trunk and branches; with an open, picturesque habit of growth.

Europe to Siberia
Varieties:
'Fastigiata'—narrow, upright habit

Pyramidal Scotch Pine
'Watereri'—an open, rounded bush with ascending branches   Waterer Scotch Pine

---

E **Pittosporum tobira**   10'   May   Zone 8   Japanese Pittosporum
A broad-leaved evergreen commonly planted in the South, with leathery leaves up to 4 inches long, it is used extensively in sheared hedges.

China and Japan

H **Platycodon grandiflorum**   2½'   June–September   Zone 3   Balloonflower
One of the best garden perennials with white or blue flowers, 2 to 3 inches in diameter, like open bells, doing best in full sun. The Japanese variety, *mariesii,* is only 18 inches tall. Plants have been known to live in one spot for over 20 years.   Asia

---

E **Podocarpus macrophyllus**   60′   Zone 7   Yew
  Podocarpus
    An evergreen tree with leaves similar to, but over
twice as large as, those of the yews. Similar in most
other general respects except that the fruits are purplish.   Japan

H **Polygonum affine**   6–9″   Autumn   Zone 3
  Himalayan Fleece-flower
    Mat-forming perennial, grows in almost any soil.
Flowers are red, very small, borne in 3 inch spikes.
Only used as a ground cover where better plants will
not grow.   Himalayas

Polygonum aubertii   Twining Vine   August
  Zone 4   Silver Fleece-vine
    Handsome, vigorous growing, with small white
flowers produced in dense conspicuous panicles when
few other vines flower. Excellent for growing on a
chain link fence.   China

H **Polygonum cuspidatum compactum**   3′   Summer
  Zone 4   Low Japanese Fleece-flower
    Can become a viscious pest if not restrained.
Only for growing on poor, dry soils where better
plants will not grow. Does best in full sun. Small
greenish flowers, followed by reddish fruits.   Japan

H **Polygonum reynoutria**   4–6″   Zone 4   Reynoutria
  Fleece-flower
    Similar to *P. cuspidatum compactum* but smaller,
and rare.   Japan

H **Polygonum vaccinifolium**   9″   August   Zone 7
  Rose Carpet Knotweed
    Small red flowers in upright spikes 1½ to 3

inches tall. Dark green leaves ½ inch long. Vigorous over-ground creeper, making a good mat of foliage in the full sun. Himalayas

---

Poncirus trifoliata   35′   April   Zones 5–6   Hardy-
orange

Only of value ornamentally as a fast-growing, very thorny barrier plant that can be sheared. The small white flowers and orangelike fruits are interesting, but it is not a worthy subject for specimen planting. China, Korea

---

Potentilla fruticosa   4′   May–September   Zone 2
Bush Cinquefoil

A low, twiggy, summer-flowering shrub available in several varieties, with white to yellow flowers a ½ inch to 1 inch in diameter that appear throughout the entire summer. Because these plants are small; produce profuse, small flowers for such a long period; and require no pruning or attention for years at a time, several of the better varieties are mentioned. A recent study by a Canadian botanist resulted in his dividing *P. fruticosa* into four separate species, but for the purpose of listing here they will be kept all in the one species. Northern Hemisphere

Varieties:

'Beesii'   4′   Zone 6

Flowers yellow, leaves hairy above and below; thus they have a decidedly silvery tinge.

dahurica   1½′   Zone 2   Dahurian Bush
Cinquefoil

Flowers white. This plant grows lower than some of the other varieties.

'Farreri'   2′   Zone 2   Farrer Bush Cinquefoil

This variety is rated one of the prettiest because of its deep yellow flowers and very small leaves. Our plant at the Arnold Arboretum, 20 years old, is 2 feet high and 3 feet across, making it a truly dwarf form.

'Friedrichsenii' 4' Zone 2 Friedrichsen
        Bush Cinquefoil

Flowers creamy white to pale yellow—one of the more vigorous forms. Our plant, about 53 years old, is 4½ feet tall and 6 feet across.

'Grandiflora' 6' Zone 2 Bigflower Bush
        Cinquefoil

Flowers are 1⅜ inch in diameter, bright yellow, and larger than most others.

'Mandshurica' 3' Zone 2 Manchurian
        Bush Cinquefoil

Flowers white, good for a low, flat bush to cover the ground.

'Purdomii' 4' Zone 2 Purdom Bush
        Cinquefoil

Flowers pale yellow, plant bushy and upright, making a very dense and uniform plant.

'Veitchii' 4' Zone 2 Veitch Bush Cinquefoil

This is the best of all the varieties for white flowers. It grows into a compact, upright shrub.

E **Potentilla tridentata** 2–12" Zone 2 Wineleaf
        Cinquefoil

Herbaceous perennial often used as a ground cover. Grows in dry soil in full sun, sometimes evergreen. Compound, dark-green, lustrous leaves have 3 leaflets. Grows on rocky outcrops of the higher mountains.   Greenland to Georgia

---

Prunella vulgaris 2' June–September Zone 3
        Common Self-heal

Perennial weed, sometimes used as a ground cover. Small purple or violet flowers on cylindrical terminal heads 1–2 inches long.   North America

---

Prunus glandulosa   4′   May   Zone 6   Dwarf
Flowering Almond

A low, deciduous shrub valued only for its pink or white, single or double flowers, about the size of buttons. The double-flowered forms 'Albiplena' (white) and 'Sinensis' (pink) are the more popular.

China and Japan

E **Prunus laurocerasus**   18′   May   Zones 6–7
Cherry-laurel

A broad-leaved evergreen, which can be sheared, but with their shiny leaves 2 to 5 inches long, they also make excellent specimens. It is one of the most popular of broad-leaved evergreens in the South.

Europe

Varieties:

schipkaensis—(Zone 5) the hardiest form; hardy in protected places through most winters as far north as Boston

'Otto Luyken'—old plants are 3 feet tall and 6 to 8 feet across, a good dwarf form

---

E **Prunus lusitanica**   6–60′   May   Zone 7
Portugal-laurel

An excellent, glossy-leaved evergreen for southern gardens, with leaves up to 5 inches long and with 10-inch-long racemes of small white flowers.

Spain and Portugal

Prunus tomentosa   9′   April   Zone 2   Manchu
Cherry

Bright red summer fruits that are actually small edible cherries and small spring flowers that are white and ½ inch in diameter are the chief ornamental characteristics of this shrub. Occasionally it is used as an informal flowering hedge.   China and Japan

Prunus triloba 15′ April Zone 5 Flowering
   Almond
   One of the most conspicuous of all the early-flowering deciduous shrubs, this has double pink flowers, 1 inch in diameter, before the leaves appear. Afterward it has little ornamental value, but at the time forsythias bloom there is a two-week period when it is loaded with pink flowers and is most conspicuous.
   China

Pseudolarix amabilis (*kaempferi*) 120′ Zone 5
   Golden Larch
   A beautiful, cone-bearing, deciduous tree with needlelike leaves similar to but larger than those of other larches. The branching is wide and horizontal, and the foliage turns a clear golden yellow in the fall before it drops.
   China

E **Pseudotsuga menziesii** 200′ Zones 4–6
   Douglas-fir
   The Douglas-fir, formerly *P. taxifolia,* is one of the best of the narrow-leaved evergreen trees and has not been planted in the North as much as it might be. More graceful than any spruce, there are some interesting varieties, like 'Compacta,' 'Fastigiata,' and *glauca.* Seedlings from the Pacific Coast are not all hardy in the East, but plants from seeds collected from high in the mountains of Utah and Montana are. Pyramidal in habit, with graceful foliage, it is attacked by a woolly aphid that in most gardens seems to do little harm if not controlled.
   Rocky Mountains and Pacific Coast

Pueraria lobata (*thunbergiana*) Twining Vine July
   Zone 6 Kudzu-vine
   Fastest growing of woody vines outside the

tropics and may grow 60 feet in one season. Rather inconspicuous, violet purple beanlike flowers and leaves, the flowers mostly hidden by the foliage. Twines in a lazy way.
China, Japan

H **Pulmonaria officinalis**   1′   May   Zones 2–3
   Common Lungwort
   Small white to blue, funnel-form flowers gradually turn purple. A common garden perennial. Leaves irregularly spotted with white.
Europe

H **Pumonaria saccharata**   6–18″   May   Zones 2–3
   Bethlehem-sage
   Flowers whitish to blue or reddish violet. Similar to the above except that the leaves are a uniform green.
Europe

Punica granatum   15′   May–June   Zones 7–8
   Pomegranate
   Popular garden shrub for gardens in the deep South, with scarlet flowers an inch wide.
Europe, Asia

Quercus alba   90′   Zone 4   White Oak
   Broad, round-headed native American tree with purplish red autumn color in the fall, this is one of the oaks that is difficult to transplant. It does not grow as fast as some of the others.   Eastern United States

---

Quercus bicolor   60′   Zone 3   Swamp White Oak
   Does well in moist soils; otherwise it is somewhat similar to the White Oak in general habit.
Eastern and Central North America

Quercus cerris   100′   Zone 6   Turkey Oak
   Without autumn color, this small-leaved oak nev-

ertheless makes a good, broadly pyramidal specimen with fine-textured foliage. Europe, Asia

---

E **Quercus chrysolepis** 60′ Zone 7 Canyon Live Oak
A wide-spreading evergreen planted only in California. California

---

Quercus coccinea 75′ Zone 4 Scarlet Oak
A lustrous-leaved tree with brilliant scarlet autumn color. It is considered difficult to transplant.
Eastern and Central United States

Quercus imbricaria 75′ Zone 5 Shingle Oak
With laurel-like deciduous leaves that turn a golden brown in the fall, this makes a fine screen and windbreak. It is still difficult to find this in nurseries.
Central United States

Quercus kelloggii 90′ Zone 7 California Black Oak
In its native habitat, this tree does well in dry, sandy, or gravelly soils. Oregon to California

---

D E **Quercus laurifolia** 60′ Zone 7 Laurel Oak
Frequently used as an evergreen street tree in the South. Southeastern United States

---

Quercus nigra 75′ Zone 6 Water Oak
With slender branches, small leaves, fine texture, this makes a fine street tree.
Southeastern United States

Quercus palustris 75′ Zone 4 Pin Oak
A fine, densely branched, graceful pyramidal tree with the lower branches drooping, it has finely

cut leaves that turn red in the fall. It seems to do best in good soils that are dependably moist.

Central and Mid-eastern United States

Quercus phellos   50'   Zone 5   Willow Oak

Has exceptionally good foliage of a very fine texture. It is round-topped to conical in general habit. Widely used as a street tree throughout the Eastern Seaboard and in the Gulf States.

Eastern United States

Quercus robur   75–100'   Zone 5   English Oak

Closely resembling the American White Oak but with smaller leaves, this has no autumn color. A popular variety, 'Fastigata,' is narrow and columnar in habit and is perhaps used more than the species in this country.

Europe, Western Asia

Quercus rubra (*borealis*)   75'   Zone 3   Red Oak

One of the best of the oaks. It grows rapidly compared with the others, and withstands city conditions, making a splendid avenue tree, and has a lustrous red autumn color.

Northeastern and Central North America

E **Quercus suber**   60'   Zone 7   Cork Oak

The true Cork Oak; this is actually an evergreen with very small leaves. There are many trees of this species being grown in California and the South.

Europe

Quercus velutina   100–150'   Zone 4   Black Oak

Not so widely planted as the Red Oak, this lustrous-leaved tree, nevertheless, is native to a wide area. It is a very large tree, sometimes rather difficult to transplant properly.

Eastern and Central United States

E **Quercus virginiana**   60′   Zone 7   Live Oak
A widely popular, native evergreen tree, easy to transplant when young.   Southeastern United States

---

H **Ranunculus repens pleniflorus**   6–12″   May–August   Zone 3   Double Creeping Buttercup
Makes a nice ground cover with double yellow flowers ¾ of an inch wide. Fast-growing runners may grow 2 feet each season.   Europe

---

E **Raphiolepis umbellata**   6′   May   Zone 7   Yeddo-hawthorn
A leathery-leaved evergreen (leaves 3 inches long), handsome for growing in either full sun or partial shade, with fragrant white flowers in dense upright panicles.   Japan

---

Rhamnus frangula   18′   Zone 2   Alder Buckthorn
The most ornamental of the buckthorns because of its glossy dark green leaves. Dense and vigorous with small red to purple berries through the summer that are most attractive to birds, there is a possibility that it could become a pest, since seedlings sprout easily. It withstands shearing well. There is a fastigiate form (var. 'Columnaris') or Tallhedge that is extremely valuable for its vigorous, narrow habit of growth.   Europe and Western Asia

---

Rhododendron
Azaleas and rhododendrons are a standard asset in every garden with acid soil. Many a gardener with a limestone soil, however, is willing to take the time and trouble to grow them in specially prepared acid-soil mixtures. Even in such soil, though, they are frequently used as foundation plantings around brick, stone, or stucco buildings where lime from the mortar

is gradually washed off by rain, making the soil more and more alkaline until finally more time and trouble must be taken to correct that condition. Further, the broad-leaved rhododendrons (that is, the true rhododendrons) are always troubled with lace bug, and occasionally other insects, which must be controlled. Usually, mulch must also be properly maintained. For all these reasons, no broad-leaved evergreen rhododendrons are included in this listing, for without question they do require proper care.

The azaleas are divided into evergreen and deciduous groups. The evergreen group is omitted from this listing because they, too, acquire lace bug and red spider, and in the South they are currently troubled with a bad disease that causes the blossoms to drop. Even these will not stop people from using them. Possibly their omission from this listing will point up how much time, care, and money they need spent on them, and the gardener can look for possible substitutes. If none are found, then they will plant their azaleas and take their chances with the extra maintenance.

There are some deciduous azaleas which, if grown in normally acid soil areas, should bring no added maintenance problems, provided there is plenty of humus or organic matter in the soil and they are not subjected to drought conditions for long periods.

Rhododendron arborescens 9′ June Zone 4
    Sweet Azalea
      A very sweet-scented, white-flowering azalea with glossy red autumn foliage, blooming after the leaves have fully developed.
                  Pennsylvania to Georgia

Rhododendron atlanicum   1½′.   May   Zone 6
   Coast Azalea
      Has very fragrant, white flowers, one of the very
few with stoloniferous growth habits.
                                  Delaware to South Carolina

Rhododendron calendulaceum   9–15′   June   Zone 5
   Flame Azalea
      Has glorious flame-colored blossoms (actually
yellow through orange to red). The flowers will last
far better in full sunshine than the flowers of several
European varieties.   Pennsylvania to Georgia

---

x **Rhododendron gandavense**   6–10′   May   Zone 4
   Ghent Azalea
      Many hybrid varieties of many colors, well
worth growing even where winter temperatures go to
as low as −20°F.

Rhododendron japonicum   6′   May   Zone 5
   Japanese Azalea
      The flowers are orange red and have a rather bad
odor.   Japan

---

x **Rhododendron kosterianum**   5′   May   Zone 5
   Mollis Hybrid Azalea
      Another group of hybrids with varieties of many
colors, but not so hardy as the Ghent hybrids.

Rhododendron mucronulatum   6′   April   Zone 4
   Korean Rhododendron
      One of the first to bloom, with rosy purple flow-
ers. The variety 'Cornell Pink' has flowers that are
flush pink, with none of the dissatisfying purple in
the color.   China, Korea, Japan

Rhododendron nudiflorum   6′   May   Zone 3
Pinxterbloom
Often referred to as "wild honeysuckle," the flowers are pink to white.

Massachusetts to North Carolina

Rhododendron obtusum kaempferi   12′   May
Zone 5   Torch Azalea
The hardiest of the *R. obtusum* azaleas, with fiery red flowers.   Japan

---

Rhododendron occidentale   9′   May   Zones 6–7
Western Azalea
Hard to grow in the East but a valued plant on the Pacific Coast, with white to pinkish flowers.

Pacific Coast

Rhododendron prunifolium   8′   July   Zone 7
Plumleaf Azalea
One of the few truly crimson-flowered azaleas.

Georgia to Alabama

Rhododendron roseum   9′   May   Zone 3
Roseshell Azalea
Akin to *R. nudiflora* and native through the same area but with bright pink blossoms.

Northeastern North America

Rhododendron schlippenbachii   15′   May   Zone 4
Royal Azalea
One of the most beautiful of those listed here, with large shell-pink blossoms 3 inches in diameter and often with some reddish autumn color in the fall.

Korea, Manchuria, Japan

Rhododendron vaseyi 6–9′ May Zone 4
Pinkshell Azalea
   This dainty azalea is hardy up into central New
England. The flowers are shell pink, and it can grow
well in moist situations.   North Carolina

Rhododendron viscosum 9–15′ July Zone 3
Swamp Azalea
   Fragrant, white-flowering azalea doing best in
swampy places. One of the last natives to bloom in
the East.   Maine to South Carolina

Rhododendron yedoense 5′ May Zone 5
Yodogawa Azalea
   This is a double-flowered, purple azalea. Its
single-flowered variety, *poukhanense* (Zone 4), is
hardier.   Korea, Japan

Rhodotypos scandens 6′ May Zone 5 Jetbead
   Usually, this old-fashioned plant is not well
enough thought of to be widely planted in modern
gardens, but it is pest-free, producing small white
flowers 2 inches in diameter and shiny black fruits.
It is used as a general, all-purpose "filler" in the shrub
border.   China, Japan

Rhus aromatica 3′ May Zone 3 Fragrant Sumac
   Most of the taller growing sumacs create work
because of weak branching and easy splitting. This
low native is truly excellent for mass planting, especially on rocky banks. If necessary, it can be cut to
the ground in the early spring and be expected to recuperate easily. Its small yellowish flowers, small
berrylike fruits in the summer, and brilliant yellow to
scarlet autumn color combine with its dense, compact

growth to make it useful in the gardens, especially in sunny and dry situations.　　　　Eastern United States

---

Rosa species

Hundreds of roses are available to the American plant-buying public. Many of the hybrids, however, are susceptible to diseases and pests that must be controlled if perfect flowers are to be produced. This takes considerable work and a knowledge of what to do at the right time. Many a gardener is gladly willing to perform these rose-growing chores, feeling that the results are well worth the effort.

For those who are unwilling to spend their time in this way, some of the species roses might well be tried. It is not correct to say that they require *no* care, but they will thrive and produce wonderful results with a minimum amount of care. Sometimes they can be neglected for several years and still be specimen plants. Because they are so important in American gardens, they cannot be ignored entirely, particularly those that follow.

---

x **Rosa alba** 'Incarnata'　6′　June　Zone 4　Cottage Rose

Unique among species, this old-fashioned favorite has double white flowers 2 to 3 inches in diameter.

Rosa canina　9′　June　Zone 3　Dog Rose

A single-flowering rose, pink to white, with excellent scarlet fruits.　　　　Europe

---

Rosa carolina　3′　June　Zone 4　Carolina Rose

With single, pink flowers and effectively ornamental red fruits; the foliage is glossy, and the white-flowered variety *alba* is even lower in growth.

Eastern United States

328

Rosa centifolia 6′ June Zone 5 Cabbage Rose
This old-fashioned favorite is often called the Rose-of-one-hundred-petals—pink, double, and fragrant, 2½ inches in diameter. East Caucasus

Rosa damascena 6′ June Zone 4 Damask Rose
Double, bluish to red, fragrant flowers up to 3½ inches in diameter. There are several varieties; one pink-and-white variety is called the 'York and Lancaster' Rose. Asia Minor

Rosa eleganteria 6′ June Zone 4 Sweet Brier
The brilliant orange to scarlet fruits of this common European native are its chief claim to fame, in America at least, since the flowers are merely single and pink. Europe

x **Rosa harisonii** 6′ June Zone 4 Harison's Yellow Rose
An American favorite with double yellow flowers about 2 inches in diameter. The fruits are not ornamental.

Rosa hugonis 7′ May Zone 5 Father Hugo Rose
With single, deep yellow flowers 2 inches in diameter, one of the first to bloom. China

Rosa moyesii 9′ June Zone 5 Moyes Rose
Deep red, single flowers and deep orange fruit as much as 2½ inches long mark this rose in spring and fall. There are now some good cultivars beginning to be grown in America, such as 'Geranium.' China

Rosa omeiensis 12′ June Zone 6 Omei Rose
Although the flowers are small, white, and single, the beautiful, red, pear-shaped fruits and their yellow

fruit stalks make this stand out in the fall. The foliage is fernlike (leaves compound), and a variety *ptera-cantha* is especially conspicuous during the growing season because of brilliant red thorns.   China

---

Rosa pendulina   3′   May–June   Zone 5   Alpine Rose

Another rose of special value for its inch-long red fruits in the fall. Its pink, single flowers are not unusual.   Europe

---

Rosa primula   8′   May   Zone 5   Primrose Rose

The name comes from the fact that the single flowers are a mimosa-yellow color. An excellent substitute for *R. hugonis* where one is wanted.   China

---

Rosa rubrifolia   6′   June   Zone 2   Redleaf Rose

The reddish foliage of this rose is apparent all summer. In the fall the leaves turn a purplish red and even the winter twigs are purplish. Though the flowers are small (only 1½ inches in diameter) and few, the color of this plant throughout the growing season is certainly unique among roses.   Europe

---

Rosa rugosa   6′   June   Zone 2   Rugosa Rose

Sometimes called the "Sea Tomato" in Japan because of its large orange to red fruits, at least an inch in diameter, and its ability to thrive at the seacoast even within occasional reach of salt spray, this has become naturalized in America in several places. The large single flowers are pink to white, 2½ to 3½ inches in diameter, and there are double-flowered varieties as well. To its other sterling qualities is added the fact that the foliage turns a rich orange in the fall.   China, Korea, Japan

---

330

Rosa setigera   15′   July   Zone 4   Prarie Rose

   Important because it blooms in early July and bears its single, pink flowers in rather loose clusters. To do best it needs considerable space; hence it should not be tried if it will have to be restrained.

Central North America

Rosa spinosissima   3′   June   Zone 4   Scotch Rose

   Probably more widely distributed naturally throughout the North Temperate Zone than any other wild rose. It is low, dense, moundlike, has excellent single or double flowers—white, pink, or yellow—depending on the variety. The black or dark brown fruits are not ornamental, but it is one of the easiest roses to maintain.   Europe, Asia, North America

---

Rosa virginiana   6′   June   Zone 3   Virginia Rose

   This rose creeps, sometimes very vigorously by underground stems, and can become a pest if planted in the wrong place. Otherwise it serves its colorful purpose every season of the year. In the spring it has myriads of large, single, pink flowers; in the summer, good foliage; in the fall, red and yellow autumn color and red fruits; and in the winter its vigorous young shoots remain colorfully red all winter.

Eastern North America

D E **Rosa wichuraiana**   1′   July   Zone 5   Memorial Rose

   A splendid ground cover for banks, this is especially adapted for covering rocky slopes, rooting along its procumbent branches wherever they touch moist soil. Semievergreen, with lustrous leaves, and white flowers 2 inches in diameter with trailing branches flat on the ground. A valuable plant.

Japan, Korea, Formosa, China

Rosmarinus officinalis 'Prostratus'   3'   Winter
  Zone 8   Low Rosemary
      An herb or subshrub valued for the aromatic
  fragrance of the leaves and stems. It has violet blue,
  small flowers borne on spikes and evergreen, lustrous,
  gray green leaves. A garden plant used for centuries.

  Europe, Asia Minor

H **Salvia azurea**   3–4'   August–September   Zone 4
  Blue Sage
      Blue flowers in whorls; leaves slightly bluish.

  South Carolina to Texas

H **Santolina chamaecyparissus**   1½–2'   July–August
  Zones 6–7   Lavender-cotton
      A half shrubby evergreen with aromatic, silvery
  gray, woolly leaves, often used as a ground cover on
  poor, sandy, or gravelly soils. Yellow flowers produced in many heads, ¼–¾ of an inch across.

  Europe

E **Sarcococca ruscifolia**   6'   Fall   Zone 7   Fragrant
  Sarcococca
      This broadleaf evergreen has dark, lustrous
  leaves; small, white, fragrant flowers; and red berries,
  ¼ inch in diameter. It is especially for shaded situations, spreading by means of underground stems.

  China

H **Sasa disticha**   2–3'   Zone 6   Dwarf Fernleaf
  Bamboo
      A good ground cover, increasing by fast-growing
  rhizomes in the soil, but they must be restrained with
  metal strips or concrete or they quickly grow out of
  hand. Leaves are 1–2¼ inches long.   Japan

E Sciadopitys verticillata 120′ Zone 5 Umbrella-
pine

One of the best of the long-needled evergreens
for ornamental planting: this is not a true pine, the
stiff, rubbery needles being in heavy whorls about the
twigs. Dark green foliage and densely pyramidal habit
combine to make a beautiful specimen tree. It is rather
slow-growing in America.   Japan

B Scilla hispanica 20″ April Zone 4 Spanish
Scilla

Blue to rose purple one-inch flowers, 12 per
stalk, giving the impression of an underdeveloped
hyacinth.   Spain and Portugal

Scilla sibirica 6″ March Zones 2–3 Siberian
Squill

An excellent bulb for naturalizing in sunny situations with deep blue, wheel-shaped flowers, ½ an
inch in diameter, each spike about 3 inches long.
Plant 4 inches deep.   Russia

Sedum species 3″–3′ Summer Zones 3–7
Stonecrop

There are many species of this small, succulent
perennial with small, white, yellow or red flowers;
excellent for the rockery and some as ground covers
for small areas. Most grow well in poor soils.

Europe, Asia, Mexico, North America

H Sedum spectabile 18″ August–October Zone 3
Showy Sedum

The showiest of the sedums with large, fleshy,
gray green leaves 3 inches long, and flat flower clusters 3 to 4 inches across, of small pink to red flowers.
Grows in clumps, equally well in sun or light shade.

Japan

H Sedum spurium 6″ July–August Zone 3
    Two-row Stonecrop

A creeping perennial, forming dense mats of stems and foliage, excellent as a ground cover. Small pink to white flowers, ½ inch in diameter, in 2 inch clusters.   Asia Minor

---

E Sempervivum tectorum 1′ Summer Zone 4
    Hen-and-chickens

A low succulent with sturdy rosettes of gray green, fleshy leaves, 3 to 4 inches across; flowers are pink, up to an inch across, on foot-high, hairy stalks. Commonly used in rock gardens.   Europe and Asia

---

E Sequoia sempervirens 365′ Zone 7 Redwood

The redwood of the Pacific Coast with evergreen foliage somewhat like that of the hemlock.

        Oregon to California

E Sequoiadendron giganteum 300′ Zone 6 Giant
    Sequoia

The "big tree" of Sequoia National Park and Mount Whitney, this evergreen tree makes a dense specimen, resembling a juniper when young.

        California

E Skimmia japonica 4′ May Zone 7 Japanese
    Skimmia

Another shade-loving evergreen, popular throughout the South for its yellowish evergreen leaves that are 5 inches long, its yellowish white flowers, and its bright red berries in the fall. The sexes are separate and both male and female plants must be present to ensure fruiting.   Japan

---

E Skimmia reevesiana 1½′ May Zone 7 Reeve's
Skimmia
    Lower than the Japanese species, this one might
be more desirable, especially since the flowers are perfect and fruits are borne on a single plant. This species is not common in American nurseries. China

---

Sophora davidii 7′ June Zone 5 Vetch Sophora
    Available from nurseries under its synonym (*S.
viciifolia*), it is only of value for its bluish violet to
whitish, pealike flowers and for its ability to grow well
in dry situations. China

Sophora japonica 75′ August Zone 4 Japanese
Pagoda Tree
    Large clusters of creamy white, pealike flowers
are borne on this tree in summer. Apparently it withstands city conditions well. The weeping variety 'Pendula,' has seldom been known to flower. When grafted
six or eight feet high on a sturdy understock, it develops into a dense, rounded mass of pendulous
branches. China, Korea

Sorbus alnifolia 60′ May Zone 5 Korean
Mountain-ash
    In general the *Sorbus* species tend to be infested
with borers, which must be controlled or the trees will
gradually die. There are areas in America where this
pest is not troublesome, but for purposes of this particular listing all *Sorbus* have been eliminated (except
S. alnifolia) for this reason. In our experience the
Korean Mountain-ash is the least susceptible to borers. Its excellent, gray, beechlike trunk, good flowers,
and orange fruits, as well as its orange to scarlet autumn color, set this up as a striking ornamental shade
tree. Japan, China, Korea

Spiraea albiflora   1½′   July   Zone 4   Japanese
  White Spirea
    Has white flowers in rounded, flat clusters.

Japan

---

x **Spiraea arguta**   5–6′   May   Zone 4   Garland
  Spirea
    Sometimes referred to as the most free-flowering of the early spireas, the flowers are white in small, flat clusters before the leaves appear. The branching habit is gracefully arching.

---

x **Spiraea billiardii**   6′   June   Zone 4   Billiard
  Spirea
    Bright rose, pyramidal spikes of flowers in late June.

---

x **Spiraea bumalda** 'Anthony Waterer'   2′   June–July
  Zone 5
    A popular plant of long standing because the bright crimson, flat, flower heads are sometimes 6 inches across.
    Varieties:
    alpina—mounded dwarf less than 1 foot high with pink flowers.
    'Crispa'—resembling 'Anthony Waterer' but the leaf margins are beautifully twisted.

Spiraea cantoniensis   3′   May   Zone 6   Reeve's
  Spirea
    Probably the best of the spireas for the South, with gracefully arching branches and pure white, rounded clusters of flowers, 1 to 2 inches in diameter.

China, Japan

Spiraea decumbens   1′   June   Zone 5   Decumbent
Spirea
    One of the lowest of the spireas with small,
white, two-inch clusters of flowers.   Europe

Spiraea japonica 'Atrosanguinea'   4½′   June
Zone 5   Mikado Spirea
    With very deep crimson flowers in flat clusters,
this has color to recommend it, but it is a little bare
at the base to make a nice ornamental.   Japan

Spiraea japonica ovalifolia   18″   June   Zone 5
Oval-leaf Japanese Spirea
    An excellent white-flowering dwarf spirea, it
can and should be used in combination with the *S.
bumalda* forms with red flowers.   Japan

Spiraea nipponica rotundifolia   7′   May   Zone 4
Big Nippon Spirea
    With bluish green foliage and small, white, but
numerous flower clusters, its general habit is upright
and vigorous—rather stiff.   Japan

Spiraea prunifolia   9′   May   Zone 4   Bridalwreath
Spirea
    Unfortunately this has been misnamed generally
—merely because the popular, double-flowered form
is the species. The varietal name *plena* is entirely
synonymous. It is very popular, the small, white, buttonlike flowers appearing before the leaves, and it is
one of the very few spireas to have a good red to orange autumn color.   China, Japan

---

Spiraea thunbergii   5′   May   Zone 4   Thunberg
Spirea
    Very popular, but actually creates work in the
North where numerous small branches die each win-

ter and must be removed. Satisfactory only in the South where its early, single, white flowers appear before the leaves. China, Japan

---

Spiraea tomentosa   4′   June   Zone 3   Hardhack
Spirea
The upright, pyramidal, rosy-colored spiked flowers of this spirea are common sights in eastern North America. Eastern North America

---

x **Spiraea vanhouttei**   6′   May   Zone 4   Vanhoutte
Spirea
Widely popular, almost overplanted, with small clusters of white flowers literally covering the arching branches.

Stephanandra incisa   7′   Zone 4   Cutleaf
Stephanandra
Finely cut small leaves and arching branches with slender stems make this Japanese plant delicate in general appearance. Because of this fine texture the plant has value in some situations where its fern-like foliage is conspicuous.

A new variety, 'Crispa,' has recently been made available. Dwarf (3 feet high), rounded, dense in texture, with small white flowers and brilliant purplish autumn color, this plant grows very well in the shade or sun and makes a good ground cover, rooting readily wherever its branches touch soil.

Japan, Korea

Stewartia species   Zone 5   Stewartias
Big shrubs or small trees, these are especially valued for their large, white flowers in early summer, and their varicolored, flaking bark which is ornamental throughout the year. Unfortunately, small

plants are very difficult to transplant, probably the most important reason why they are not more readily available from nurseries. For early summer display they are excellent.

Stewartia koreana 45′ July Zone 5 Korean
Stewartia
Has white flowers 3 inches in diameter and a conspicuous mass of yellow stamens in the center. The autumn color is a fairly good orange red. Korea

---

Stewartia ovata grandiflora 15′ July Zone 5
Showy Stewartia
With large, white flowers 4 inches in diameter and purple stamens massed in the center. The foliage of this native American shrub usually turns orange to scarlet in the fall. Georgia

---

Stewartia pseudo-camellia 60′ July Zone 5
Japanese Stewartia
With flowers 2½ inches in diameter, about the smallest flowers of the species, but a beautiful tree nevertheless. Japan

---

Styrax japonicum 30′ June Zone 5 Japanese
Snowbell
A small tree noted for its wide-spreading, horizontal branches, underneath which delicate, pendulous, white, bell-like flowers are borne, ¾ of an inch in diameter. A beautiful, wide, flat-topped and densely branched small tree. China, Japan

---

Styrax obassium 30′ June Zone 6 Fragrant
Snowbell
This is coarser in texture than *S. japonicum* and the branching habit is more ascending. Japan

---

x Symphoricarpos chenaultii　3′　Zone 5　Chenault
　　Coralberry

The fruit of this coralberry is larger and more pink than that of the common *S. orbiculatus,* and it is white on the shaded side. A good plant, increasing rapidly, it has merit for use in border plantings.

---

x Symphoricarpos 'Hancock'　2′　Zone 5

A prostrate coralberry, this has value as a ground cover with long, procumbent branches creeping along the surface of the ground. Excellent for covering banks.

Symphoricarpos orbiculatus　3–6′　Zone 2　Indian
　　Currant or Coralberry

A fine low shrub widely used, especially for its currant-sized, purplish red fruits in the fall and its ability to spread rapidly by underground stems, making it useful in bank plantings.

　　　　　　Southeastern and South-central United States

H Tanacetum vulgare　3′　July–August　Zone 3
　　Common Tansy

Perennial weed with strongly scented, aromatic, much-divided leaves and yellow, buttonlike flowers in flat-topped clusters.　　　　　　　　Europe

---

E Taxus species　Zones 4–6　Yews

There are well over 100 species, varieties, and cultivars of *Taxus* species available from American nurseries today. It is impossible to list them all here. The English Yew (*T. baccata*) is the least hardy. The native Canada Yew (*T. canadensis*) is the most hardy, and the Japanese Yew and its many varieties are in between for hardiness.

Planted in the wrong place, any of these are subject to foliage burn in the winter, even in the zone where they are supposed to be hardy. Occasionally there is a *Taxus* black-vine weevil that eats the roots and can seriously injure or even kill the plant, but the yews are such valuable evergreens that they are listed here regardless.

The sexes are separate; both male and female plants should be in the near vicinity to ensure the production of the bright red, fleshy fruits on the pistillate plants.

E **Taxus baccata**   60′   Zone 6   English Yew

It is probable that few plants in America are over half this height, but this narrow-leaved evergreen is still a big shrub.   Europe, Western Asia

Varieties:

'Adpressa'—dense, broad, conical bush, small needles   Shortleaf English Yew

'Elegantissima'—broad, spreading bush with young foliage striped yellow   Elegant English Yew

'Fastigiata'—columnar in habit, one of the most picturesque of all the yews   Irish Yew

'Fastigiata Aurea'—columnar habit with golden yellow foliage   Golden Irish Yew

'Repandens'—4 feet high, rounded in habit with the tips of the branches pendant. This is the hardiest of all *T. baccata* varieties and can be grown in Zone 4.   Spreading English Yew

---

E **Taxus cuspidata**   50′   Zone 4   Japanese Yew

The hardiest of the exotic yews, making excellent specimen or hedge plants at all times. Many varieties of different habits are available, so many, in fact, that they are considerably mixed.   Japan, Korea

Varieties:

'Aurescens'—1 foot high, young foliage is golden yellow   Goldtip Japanese Yew

'Capitata'—actually this is *T. cuspidata,* which is a tree in Japan, but nurserymen carry this fast-growing, pyramidal, often single-trunked form under this name to distinguish it from all other varieties.

'Densa'—4 feet high, rounded, twice as broad as high, with short, stubby growth

Cushion Japanese Yew

'Expansa'—vase-shaped variety

'Nana'—10 feet high, but twice as broad, also with short, stubby shoots   Dwarf Japanese Yew

'Thayerae'—8 to 10 feet high, horizontal, spreading branches, twice as broad as high.

E x **Taxus media**   40′   Zone 4   Anglojap Yew

A cross between the English and Japanese Yews, the hardiness of all varieties is only slightly less than that of the Japanese Yew. In New England winter burning will occur on *T. media* varieties occasionally where it will not occur on the Japanese Yew. Many forms are available.

Varieties:

'Adams'—10 to 25 feet high, upright in habit

'Brownii'—4 to 6 feet high, compact, rounded

'Hatfieldii'—12 feet high, pyramidal, about 18 feet across base at 35 years of age.

'Hicksii'—upright, narrow, 20 feet tall and 10 feet wide at 40 years of age.

'Kelseyi'—often called Kelsey Berry Bush; 12 feet tall and 12 feet across base at 22 years of age. Not to be confused with the 'Kelsey Upright Yew' which is a male plant.

'Stovekenii'—12 feet high, a male plant, but a 20 year old specimen was 12 feet tall and 6 feet in diameter.

Teucrim chamaedrys 10″ Zone 5 Chamaedrys
  Germander
    Dense subshrub, used in rockery, in foreground
of evergreen plantings or as a low hedge.
                                          Europe, Asia

H **Thalictrum rochebrunianum** 4–6′ July–September
  Zone 4 Lavender-mist
    A perennial with large masses of violet blossoms
having no petals but conspicuous yellow stamens. For
the rear of the perennial border in light shade.
                                                    Japan

H **Thalictrum speciosissimum** 3–6′ Summer
  Zone 5 Dusty Meadow-rue
    A perennial with blue gray leaves which are ex-
cellent for use in cut-flower arrangements. Soft yellow
flowers are slightly fragrant. Best for use in light
shade.   Europe

H **Thermopsis montana** 2′ June–July Zone 3
  Mountain Thermopsis
    The racemes of yellow flowers are 8 inches long
on this perennial.   Rocky Mountains

E **Thuja orientalis** 50′ Zone 6 Oriental
  Arborvitae
    A variable evergreen species with flat, scalelike
leaves. There are many dwarf varieties of this available for planting in the South, varying in habit as
well as in color of foliage.   China, Korea

E **Thuja plicata** 180′ Zone 5 Giant Arborvitae
    This is a stately evergreen timber tree of the
Northwest Pacific Coast. Plants grown from seed
collected high in the mountains of Idaho are hardy in

the East and make excellent specimens because of their glossy, flat, scalelike foliage and sturdy, pyramidal habit. The foliage may turn a good bronze in the fall, but does not turn brown in the winter like that of most of the *Thuja occidentalis* varieties.

Alaska to California

H **Thymus lanicaulis** 4″ June Zone 3
  Woolly-stem Thyme
    Tiny, rose pink flowers in rounded heads, leaves ⅓ of an inch long, and white woolly stems. Not as good a ground cover as the other thymes. Balkans

---

E **Thymus serphyllum** 1″ Zone 3 Mother-of-thyme
    Evergreen, small, aromatic leaves ½ inch long, creeping slowly over rocks or between stepping stones. Often used in rock gardens or as a ground cover. Europe, Asia

---

E **Thymus serpyllum lanuginosus** 2–3″ Zone 3
  Woolly Mother-of-thyme
    Similar to the species but with gray pubescent leaves. Europe and Western Asia

---

E **Thymus vulgaris** 6–8″ Zone 5 Common Thyme
    A popular evergreen ground cover for rock gardens or to border stepping stones. Aromatic flowers and foliage. Leaves ½ inch long. Europe

---

H **Tiarella cordifolia** 6–12″ April–July Zone 3
  Allegheny Foam-flower
    An herbaceous plant for the shady wild garden, with leaves from the ground and small white flowers in 1 to 4 inch racemes. A fine ground cover in partial shade. Eastern North America

---

344

B Tigridia pavonia   1½′   Summer   Zone 6
   Mexican Shell-flower
   Yellow to purple multicolored irislike flowers,
3 to 5 inches across. Plant corms about 5 inches deep.
                                                   Mexico

Tilia   July   Zones 3–5   Lindens
   Usually densely pyramidal trees, withstanding
city conditions well and with very fragrant, pendant
flowers. These European lindens are superior in most
respects to American native species. They have little
autumn color, but are primarily valued for their excellent foliage and pyramidal habit.

Tilia cordata   90′   Zone 3   Little-leaf Linden
   Rather slow-growing but an excellent city tree,
and apparently hardy as far north as Dropmore,
Manitoba, Canada. Pyramidal.   Europe
   Variety:
   'Greenspire'—with straight trunk and radially
produced branches, good for street tree planting.

---

x **Tilia euchlora**   60′   Zone 5   Crimean Linden
   With graceful, slightly pendulous branches and
glossy, bright green leaves.

Tilia petiolaris   75′   Zone 5   Pendent Silver Linden
   With slightly pendent branches, one of the most
graceful of the lindens. The leaves are silvery white
underneath.   Europe

Tilia tomentosa   90′   Zone 4   Silver Linden
   Not pendulous like *T. petiolaris* but with a white
tomentum on the undersurfaces of the leaves, giving
a pleasing aspect, especially when the leaves are
blown in the wind.   Europe, Western Asia

E **Torreya nucifera**   75′   Zone 5   Japanese Torreya
    A pyramidal tree with evergreen, needlelike foliage akin to the yews and frequently confused with them.
                                      Japan

E **Trachelospermum asiaticum**   Twining Vine   April–July   Zones 7–8   Yellow Star-jasmine
    Yellowish white, fragrant flowers, evergreen leaves to 3 inches long and the young growth is ruddy bronze.
                               Japan, Korea

H **Tradescantia virginiana**   3′   July–August   Zone 4
Virginia Spiderwort
    An unkempt garden perennial with blue, purple, pink or white flowers of 3 petals, in bloom for only a few hours, still has become a common garden plant. Should not be given a too-conspicuous place in the border.
                 Eastern United States

B **Trillium grandiflorum**   12–14″   April–June
Snow Trillium
    White flowers, 3 inches in diameter with 3 petals. Plant in moist soil in woods, in partial shade. A common wild flower.

           Eastern and Northern United States

E **Tsuga canadensis**   90′   Zone 4   Canada Hemlock
    One of the most beautiful and graceful of evergreen trees. It will withstand close shearing remarkably well and is not only a wonderful evergreen specimen but can be used in all types of sheared hedges and screens. There are many varieties available.
              Northeastern North America
Varieties:
'Bradshaw'—dwarf, compact, pyramidal
globosa—rounded form, about as high as broad

'Pendula'—dwarf, flat-topped, with pendulous branchlets   Scarlet Hemlock

---

E **Tsuga caroliniana**   75′   Zone 4   Carolina Hemlock
Similar in most respects to *T. canadensis* except that the evergreen needles are more distributed about the twig, giving a softer appearance. An excellent specimen tree, pyramidal in outline.   Virginia to Georgia

---

E **Tsuga diversifolia**   90′   Zone 5   Japanese Hemlock
A pyramidal evergreen tree with dense growth, usually smaller and slower in growth than the Canada Hemlock.   Japan

---

E **Umbellularia californica**   75′   Zone 7   California-laurel
A Pacific Coast native evergreen with lustrous, aromatic leaves 2 to 5 inches long. Dense and rounded habit.   California to Oregon

---

Vaccinium angustifolium   8″   Zone 2   Lowbush Blueberry
Used in wooded or open areas as a woody ground cover in acid soils. Autumn color is a vivid scarlet. Berries are edible.   Eastern United States

---

E **Vaccinium arboreum**   27′   Zone 7   Farkleberry
In the South this is occasionally used for its lustrous evergreen leaves 2 inches long.
Southeastern United States

Vaccinium corymbosum   6–12′   Zone 3   Highbush Blueberry
With many clonal selections made for large fruits, this deciduous shrub is also an excellent ornamental in acid soils. It is especially outstanding for its

fiery red autumn foliage when it is grown in the full
sun.   Eastern United States

E **Vaccinium ovatum**   10′   Zone 7   Box Blueberry
A native, broad-leaved evergreen, the foliage of
this plant is cut and shipped for floral decorations.
The lustrous leaves are 1¼ inches long. Not too hardy
in the East.
Pacific Coast of United States and Canada

H **Vancouveria hexandra**   1½′   May–June   Zone 5
American Barrenwort
Delicate herbaceous ground cover for shaded
areas, needing moist soil. Feathery leaves are ½
inch to 1½ inches long. White flowers, ½ inch wide,
are borne in panicles of 6 to 45.
Washington to California

E **Veronica chamaedrys**   1′   May–June   Zone 3
Germander Speedwell
Practically evergreen ground cover of compact
habit because of its creeping rootstock. Leaves ½ to
1½ inches long, flowers blue and ½ inch in diameter.   Europe

---

H **Veronica incana**   2′   June–July   Zone 3   Woolly
Speedwell
Garden perennial with white woolly stems and
porcelain blue flowers, ¼ inch in diameter, in spikes
up to 6 inches long. Popular.   Russia, Asia

H **Veronica longifolia subsessilis**   2½′   July   Zone 4
Clump Veronica
A perennial with striking, royal blue flower
spikes. Grows in a compact clump 2 feet wide.
Europe, Asia

E **Veronica officinalis**   1′   Zone 5   Drug Speedwell

An excellent ground cover with creeping branches and practically evergreen leaves 2 inches long. Pale blue flowers, ¼ inch in diameter, borne in small spikes.   Europe, Asia, North America

---

H **Veronica spicata**   1½′   June–August   Zone 3
Spike Speedwell

Widely popular garden perennial with leaves 2 inches long and blue to pink flowers ¼ inch in diameter borne in racemes. Several varieties available.

Europe, Asia

Viburnum species   Zones 2–9   Viburnums

A group of shrubs, from 2 to 30 feet tall, of many kinds; valued because of their conspicuous white flowers, their profuse red, blue, black, or yellow fruits, their reddish autumn color, and their vigorous shrubby growth. They can be divided into three general groups as far as their flowers are concerned. The largest group is made up of plants bearing completely fertile, small white flowers in small to large flat heads, somewhat similar to those of the Wild Carrot or Queen Anne's Lace. Most viburnums are in this group, all of course bearing fruits.

The next group is the snowballs (*V. macrocephalum, plicatum* and *opulus sterile*), which have all sterile flowers in large, snowball-like clusters, but bear no fruits. Then there are a few species like *V. opulus, sargentii* and *trilobum,* which have many, small, fertile flowers in the center of the cluster, surrounded by large, sterile flowers on the perimeter of the cluster.

Usually all viburnums are conspicuous in flower because the flowers are so profusely borne. The fruits of red and yellow fruiting types are more conspicuous than those of the blue and black fruiting types, but sometimes the latter go through a color change from green to red to black that gives them considerable ornamental value. The fruits are small, single-seeded drupes, about the size of a pea, but are borne in large clusters.

---

x **Viburnum burkwoodii** 6′ May Zone 5
  Burkwood Viburnum

In England and certain parts of California, this has proved semievergreen. The flowers are very fragrant, the foliage is glossy, and it is an improvement over *V. carlesii* even in New England. The fruits are red to black berries.

---

x **Viburnum carlcephalum** 9′ May Zone 5
  Fragrant Snowball

A most interesting hybrid with rounded, fragrant clusters of fertile, white flower heads up to 5 inches in diameter. The foliage has a sheen to it, making it better than the dull foliage of *V. carlesii*. *V. carlcephalum* also makes a greater display in flower than *V. carlesii* and bears red to black fruits.

Viburnum carlesii 5′ May Zone 4 Fragrant
  Viburnum

This old-fashioned favorite is fast being replaced by *V. burkwoodii* and *V. carlcephalum,* for it is often subject to a graft blight disease as it grows older. Because of its current popularity and its fragrance, it will be a hard plant to eliminate from any list. The fruit is blue black, appearing early in the summer. Other species are considered of more enduring ornamental value.
                                      Korea

Viburnum cassinoides 6′ June Zone 3 Withe-rod
  Has red to black fruits with red autumn foliage;

there is always a dependable display of both in the fall. It will grow in either sun or shade. The flat clusters go through an interesting color change from green to yellowish to red to black, sometimes with all those colors on the fruits in the same cluster at the same time. Northeastern United States

---

E **Viburnum davidii** 3′ June Zone 7 David Viburnum

A handsome specimen for the South, with dark, evergreen, leathery leaves 5½ inches long and light blue fruits during September and October. China

---

Viburnum dentatum 15′ June Zone 2 Arrow-wood

Sends up such straight shoots from the base that they were made into arrow shafts by the Indians. With light blue fruits in the fall and a dull reddish autumn color, this is best not used as a specimen but as "filler" in the shrub border, or planted in masses for general effect. Eastern United States

---

Viburnum dilatatum 9′ June Zone 5 Linden Viburnum

Handsome red fruits and russet red autumn foliage combine to make this species one of the best for fall display. Fruiting has been found best when several seedlings are planted together to ensure proper cross-pollination. If a group is planted, grown from cuttings taken from one plant, they will not fruit nearly so well. The flat flower clusters are nearly 5 inches in diameter. Asia

Variety:
'Xanthocarpum'—yellow fruit
Yellow Linden Viburnum

E **Viburnum henryi**   9′   Spring   Zone 7   Henry
   Viburnum
      Evergreen, of special interest because its flowers
and red to black fruits are borne in slightly pyramidal
clusters 4 inches high and about as wide. Leaves are
5 inches long.
                                                   China

E **Viburnum japonicum**   6′   Spring   Zone 7
   Japanese Viburnum
      Lustrous evergreen leaves 6 inches long, with
fragrant flowers in the spring and red fruits in the fall.
                                                   Japan

Viburnum lentago   30′   May   Zone 2   Nannyberry
      This is either a large shrub or, if grown with a
single leader, can develop into a small tree. The large,
flat clusters of small white flowers are most conspicuous, and the fruits go through a colorful change from
green to yellowish to red to blue—sometimes all on
the same cluster. The glossy green foliage turns a
bluish red in the fall. A common shrub, yet dependable for flower and fruit every year.
                                       Eastern United States

Viburnum macrocephalum   12′   May   Zone 6
   Chinese Snowball
      Has the largest flowers of all the snowballs, with
clusters of sterile flowers in a ball up to 6 inches
across. Sometimes this is semievergreen in the South.
                                                   China

E **Viburnum odoratissimum**   10′   May   Zone 9
   Sweet Viburnum
      A magnificent evergreen where it proves hardy,
with pyramidal flower clusters, red to black berries,
and glossy green leaves up to 6 inches long.
                                             India, Japan

Viburnum opulus   12′   May   Zone 3   European
Cranberry-bush

A popular plant in Europe, as well as in America, where it was introduced in colonial times, even though the red fruit does have an unpleasant odor. The marginal flowers in the flat clusters are large and sterile. It is similar to our native *V. trilobum,* but its fruits are too tart to make preserves. It has been popular too long to discard, yet there is no reason why the native *V. trilobum* should not be used in its place. The common European Snowball (Var. 'Roseum') is not recommended here because it always becomes severely infested with plant lice.   Europe, Asia

Varieties:
'Compactum'—5 to 6 feet high, compact growth
Compact European Cranberry-bush
'Nanum'—1 to 3 feet high, dwarf, bears no flowers or fruits.   Dwarf European Cranberry-bush
'Xanthocarpum'—yellow fruits
Yellow European Cranberry-bush

Viburnum plicatum   9′   May   Zone 4   Japanese
Snowball

This old-fashioned, popular, Japanese Snowball is found listed in nursery catalogues either under *V. tomentosum plicatum* or *V. tomentosum sterile.* Although slightly less hardy than the European Snowball, it is not as susceptible to disfiguring infestations of plant lice as the European variety. All forms of *V. plicatum* have a conspicuous habit of bearing their branches horizontally. Because all the flowers in this snowball are sterile, of course it bears no fruits. Flowers in ball-like clusters, 2 to 3 inches in diameter.

China, Japan

Varieties:
'Mariesii'—flower clusters flat. Plant grows twice

as wide as it does tall with fine horizontal branches, all the flower clusters being formed on the upper side of the flat branches. The small, fertile flowers, bearing the bright red to black fruits, are in the center of the cluster, surrounded by conspicuous, white, sterile, ray flowers that do not bear fruit. A splendid ornamental specimen.

'Roseum'—sterile flowers open white, gradually turning pink with age. Some years more deeply colored than others.

tomentosum—called the Doublefile Viburnum, somewhat similar to 'Mariesii' but probably not as good an ornamental, however, it is still widely grown and very popular.

Viburnum prunifolium   15′   May   Zone 3   Black Haw

In the full sun this has a brilliant, shining, scarlet autumn color, making it the best of the viburnums for fall foliage display. Frequently grown as a small tree. It can be used as a substitute for hawthorns because of its twiggy habit of growth and because it is not susceptible to all the pests that trouble hawthorns. The blue fruits (which turn from green to reddish) have been used for making preserves since colonial times, for they are as much as ½ inch long.

Eastern United States

D E **Viburnum rhytidophyllum**   9′   Late Spring Zone 5   Leathery Viburnum

It is not a plant for the open windy place, but the handsome, crinkled leaves of this large viburnum make it an excellent specimen, evergreen in the South, semievergreen and fairly hardy as far north as Boston. The red to black fruits are outstanding.   China

---

Viburnum rufidulum   30′   May   Zones 5–6
  Southern Black Haw
    This is the southern counterpart of *V. prunifolium,* but fairly hardy as far north as Boston.
Northeastern United States

Viburnum sargentii 'Flavum'   12′   May   Zone 4
  Yellow Sargent Cranberry-bush
    The yellow-fruited variety of the Sargent Viburnum might well be considered for planting with other red-fruiting viburnums, merely for the sake of the contrast made by its golden yellow fruits in the fall.
Asia

Viburnum sieboldii   30′   May   Zone 4   Siebold
  Viburnum
    Easily one of the very best of the viburnums because of its long, dark, lustrous, wrinkled leaves; its vigorous, upright, treelike habits; as well as the slightly rounded flower clusters. The fruits are bright red before they turn black and fall; early in the summer they are borne on red fruit stalks that remain on the plant for several weeks after the fruits have fallen, and give the whole plant a reddish color.
Japan

E **Viburnum suspensum**   6′   June   Zone 9
  Sandankwa Viburnum
    Fragrant, white flowers tinged pink; red fruits; and evergreen, glossy leaves 2 to 5 inches long all make this shrub serviceable for planting in shaded southern gardens.
Japan

E **Viburnum tinus**   10–20′   Winter–Spring
  Zones 7–8   Laurestinus Viburnum
    An indispensable shrub in many southern gardens. Several varieties are available; the fruits are

355

metallic blue and the leaves 1½ to 4 inches long are evergreen. It can be used as a clipped hedge and will thrive in the shade, but it flowers better in the sun. The variety 'Lucidum' is probably the best of several, with larger flower clusters than the species, but it is less hardy. Mediterranean Region

---

Viburnum trilobum 12′ May Zone 2 American Cranberry-bush

Similar to *V. opulus,* it may well be that these two viburnums are considerably mixed up in American nurseries. The fruit of the native species (*V. trilobum*) is red, starts to turn color in late July, and remains on the plant a greater part of the winter. The fruits are edible, and several clones have been selected for their good fruits over the years. This species seems to do best only in the North.

Southern Canada, Northeastern United States
Variety:
'Compactum'—3 feet high, dense and compact habit

Dwarf American Cranberry-bush

E **Vinca minor** 6″ April Zone 4 Periwinkle

Very popular evergreen ground cover in America since colonial times, growing well in sun or shade. Leaves are 2 inches long and the blue flowers are ¾ of an inch in diameter. Its vinelike stems creep rapidly over the ground and root readily.

Europe and Western Asia

Viola species 6″ Spring Zones 2–7 Violets

Many species with blue, purple, yellow, or white flowers, chiefly for the wild garden. The Roundleaf

Violet (*V. rotundifolia*) is one of the better ground covers. North America, Europe

---

Vitis coignetiae   Tendrils   Zone 5   Glory-vine
Handsome vine with coarse leaves 10 inches in diameter, vigorous grower. Autumn color is red. Probably grows most rapidly of all the grapes, covering a thousand square feet of trellis in a few years.

Japan

Weigela   9′   May–June   Zone 5   Weigela
This large group of shrubs is actually in the "work-producing" class in the North because there is so much renewal pruning required. Hence they should not be considered in any low maintenance shrub listing. Just in case there are those who do not agree with this attitude, the following are listed as the best of some 60 being grown in the United States today:
Varieties:
'Candida'—pure white flowers
'Conquerant'—early-blooming,   rose-colored flowers
'Dame Blanche'—midseason blooming; flowers white and pink on the same branch
'Floreal'—flowers a moderate purplish pink
'Foliis Purpuris'—purplish green foliage and pink flowers
'Gracieux'—early-blooming, flowers light pink
'Richesse'—early-blooming, flowers uniformly pale pink
'Seduction'—early-blooming, flowers darkest red of any
'Styriaca'—flowers moderate purplish pink
'Vanicek'—flowers red, excellent
'Variegata'—leaves edged pale yellow, a com-

pact shrub to about 4 feet, with flowers a deep rose color.

    'Variegata Nana'—most dwarf of all, only about 3 feet tall

    venusta—with uniformly purple flowers

Wisteria floribunda   Twining Vine   May   Zone 4
    Japanese Wisteria

    With pendulous clusters of pealike flowers, 12 to 36 inches long, often causing much work in pruning but the twisted stems are frequently used in dried flower arrangements. Flowers are white, pink, or violet depending on variety.   Japan

---

Wisteria sinensis   Twining Vine   May   Zone 5
    Chinese Wisteria

    Similar to above, hardier, but flower clusters are only 7 to 12 inches long. Both white- and blue violet-flowering varieties are available.   China

---

Xanthorhiza simplicissima   2′   Zone 4   Yellow-root

    An excellent woody ground cover increasing rapidly by underground stems, of uniform height, growing in sun or light shade. Autumn color yellowish to reddish orange.   Eastern United States

---

E **Yucca filamentosa**   3′   July   Zone 4   Adam's
    Needle

    Thriving in hot, dry situations, their evergreen, rigid, pointed leaves, 10 to 30 inches long and an inch wide, are borne at the base of the plant and can be used in arrangements indoors. This is one of the hardiest sepcies. Creamy white, pendulous flowers, 2 to 3 inches across are borne on 1 to 3 feet spikes.
          Southern United States

Zelkova serrata   90′   Zone 5   Japanese Zelkova

This deciduous tree is becoming increasingly popular because it is resistant (but not immune) to the Dutch elm disease. It has the general appearance of one of the small-leaved elms, with an arching habit, and the autumn foliage is colored an excellent yellow to russet. 'Village Green' is a good variety.   Japan

Index

The Index lists plants alphabetically by their common name with their Latin name in parentheses. For an alphabetical listing of plants by their Latin name see pages 197–359.

By the same author

Ground Cover Plants
Shrubs and Vines for American Gardens
Trees for American Gardens
Wyman's Gardening Encyclopedia

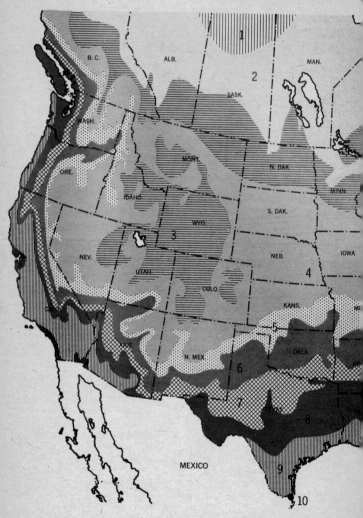

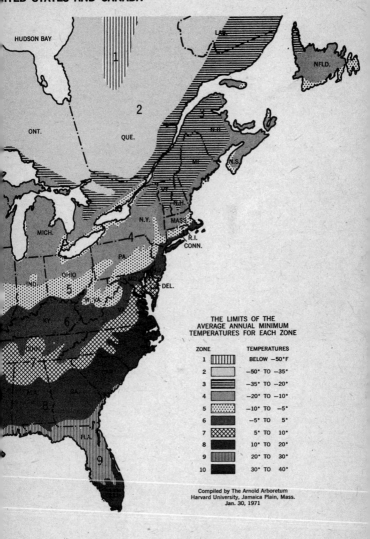

ITED STATES AND CANADA

HUDSON BAY

NFLD.

ONT.

QUE.

MICH.

N.Y.

MASS.

R.I.

CONN.

IND.

OHIO

PA.

DEL.

KY.

ALA.

GA.

FLA.

THE LIMITS OF THE
AVERAGE ANNUAL MINIMUM
TEMPERATURES FOR EACH ZONE

ZONE		TEMPERATURES
1		BELOW −50°F
2		−50° TO −35°
3		−35° TO −20°
4		−20° TO −10°
5		−10° TO −5°
6		−5° TO 5°
7		5° TO 10°
8		10° TO 20°
9		20° TO 30°
10		30° TO 40°

Compiled by The Arnold Arboretum
Harvard University, Jamaica Plain, Mass.
Jan. 30, 1971